Divine Encounters

DIVINE ENCOUNTERS

A new kind of loving for a
New Age of living

Penny Thornton

Aquarian/Thorsons
An Imprint of HarperCollins*Publishers*

The Aquarian Press
An Imprint of HarperCollins*Publishers*
77–85 Fulham Palace Road,
Hammersmith, London W6 8JB

Published by The Aquarian Press 1991
1   3   5   7   9   10   8   6   4   2

A catalogue record for this book
is available from the British Library

ISBN 1 85538 100 1

Typeset by Harper Phototypesetters Limited,
Northampton, England
Printed in Great Britain by
Mackays of Chatham, Kent

For Felix
And he knows why

Table of Contents

Acknowledgements

I WOULD LIKE TO THANK ALL THOSE WHO HAVE CONTRIBUTED TO THIS book: those who have offered me their stories, those who have allowed me to quote from their work, those who have given me their advice and insight and those who have simply 'been there' at a time I have needed them most – Mary Aver, Barbara and Peter Brackley, Walter Broadbent, Bebe Moore Campbell, Eileen Campbell, Antonia Carr, Steven Carter and Julia Sokol, Glennys and Brian Clarke, Tony Coope, Caroline Cossey, Charmian Dopico, Lisa Eldridge, Dr Susan Forward, Robert Johnson, Penny Lawrence, Linda Schierse Leonard, Cordelia Mansall, Susie Mason, Ethel Spector Person, Lynn Picknett, Denise and Charles Price and Whitley Strieber. And finally, my deepest thanks and love to my husband, Simon, who stood by, dropping into the Underworld every so often to make sure that I hadn't disappeared completely.

In the Beginning

*T*HIS BOOK BEGAN LIFE AS 'FATEFUL ENCOUNTERS' BUT BY THE TIME I had reached Chapter 4, Persephone's numinous signature was well and truly on the manuscript and I felt compelled to change the encounters to divine ones. The writing was far from easy. First because of the sheer scope of the material, and second because there was so much of my own heart involved in its creation. As I came to the end of Pluto: *Liebestod*, I felt – somewhat appropriately in light of the Dracula material – as if the last drop of my life's blood had ebbed into that full stop. Every chapter had been, literally and metaphorically, a long day's journey into night: sometimes I would dream about the material and wake with whole sentences imprinted on my mind. And while the writing of the book needed structure and form in the sense of syntax and research, I was also working through a powerful inner process.

Despite its wide-ranging panorama, taking in such diverse and apparently unrelated subjects as Nostradamus and the Holy Grail, the astronomical case for 'Planet X' and the Death Goddess, commitment-phobia and the Ghostly Lover, each theme in the book flows into the next – with encountering the divine, both in the mystical and psychological sense, representing the unifying factor in this stream of consciousness.

The initial spark was ignited on the way to Australia in the January of 1990. I had been given Linda Leonard's book, *On the Way to the Wedding*, to read on the plane. With mounting fascination, I began to see that the inner figures and processes she was depicting were redolent with astrological symbolism. Jungian archetypes are not new to astrology but Leonard's distinctly personal approach to these archetypes brought to the boil some of the ideas about the outer planets that were simmering gently in my unconscious. During the course of my lectures and workshops in Australia, I began to explore some of these ideas so that by the time I returned to England the seeds for *Divine Encounters* had all but germinated.

There were two overriding issues that I wanted to discuss in this book: the first was my suspicion that our experience of and our relationship to the outer planets is changing; no longer, to my mind, are Uranus, Neptune and Pluto merely a collective force, for we are beginning to experience them in a personal way. The reason for this, as I perceive it, is the global raising of consciousness – a change inherent in the concept of a New Age. As consciousness is raised, experiences in our outer world demand that we 'grow' in consciousness to meet them and this necessitates inner work. In this way, we are pummelled and pushed on all levels – a process going on everywhere about us – so that we are fundamentally transformed. A collective change in the nature of humanity depends on individual growth, so that our individual journey to wholeness contributes to the whole sweep of humankind towards a new world. Thus, the second, and most important, issue of the book becomes that individual journey to wholeness.

That journey is depicted here through the outer planets, Uranus, Neptune and Pluto – and one more, Persephone. Given the evidence in the world around us in the form of devastating wars on the one hand and extraordinary alliances on the other, and the catastrophic state of the ecology yet the global unity it is engendering, we appear to be on the threshold of a major leap in planetary consciousness. A leap which is almost certainly to be presaged, or rather synchronized, with the discovery of a new planet – and therefore a 'new' planetary archetype. It is with this in mind that I have begun to explore the potential meaning of Persephone. I took as my 'signposts' current events in the world at large and also those of my own life which seemed to mirror them. As goddess of the Underworld, Pluto's consort, Persephone represents the transformational journey – a journey undertaken to the depths of one's being. It is the heroine's journey and reflects the whole realm of the feminine – especially its darker side.

This theme of the inner journey and its various facets is continued through the chapters on Saturn, Uranus, Neptune and Pluto. Throughout, I have emphasized the importance of considering these planets as great archetypes whose themes can be perceived working through all aspects of life. Like Linda Leonard, I have made full use of fairy-tales to describe the rich inner world of the psyche, but I have drawn these archetypal themes with an astrological pen.

The divine encounter has more than one implication although, in essence, every one is the same. When we fall in love, we experience the divine through merger and union with another. This wonderful encounter essentially puts us in touch with the divine within ourselves. Such a blissful experience is on a par with that of the mystic in his union with God: while for the lover it is the beloved who becomes the catalyst for the divine, for the mystic, it is his God. Yet both, in their separate ways, achieve the same ends – a sense of deep connectedness, of soul contact, of losing separateness and finding absolute completion. In the same way, becoming whole within one's self, whole within one's psyche, is, in essence, a divine encounter; and in becoming a fully related individual we can not only find but sustain an outer union with an Other.

In some ways it may appear that the examples of divine encounters I have chosen to illustrate the book are anything but divine. However, my purpose here is to show the significance of these relationships in fostering the divine process of becoming whole within oneself, of finding the divine within. And while all the case histories involve considerable trauma for the 'heroines', they nevertheless experienced transcendent moments within those relationships and neither Zoë, Caroline nor Amy regret their divine encounters.

It may also seem, in my discussions on misogynism and commitment-phobia, that I have been a little hard on men. As they say, it takes two to tango, but men, on the whole, still have some distance to go before they catch up with women where the work of real relationship is concerned. The feminine is more concerned with relatedness; it is an essential feminine instinct: thus, men need to address and integrate their feminine side in order to work towards wholeness. Until we get the balance right between the masculine and feminine sides of ourselves and between the male and female in outer relationship, the world will continue to be at war with itself.

Persephone is the dark side of the feminine and she is beginning to assert herself in no uncertain terms in the world at large and in the lives and psyches of each and every one of us. She represents union in its most divine sense, yet she is also a creator-destroyer. Most importantly, her route to union is through the gateway of the heart. Thus, before we may find that union of the light, our darkness has to be confronted, and it must be met with our whole heart.

While the seeds of this book were planted in the glorious and sunny land of Australia at a moment when my life was full of light and hope and love, its emergence into being occupied a time when all around me seemed dark and bleak and hopeless. My inner world was one of pain and isolation. But in this forbidding place I found a great storehouse of creativity. Gradually, as I worked my way through the many themes, I felt the darkness that had bound me to myself slip away. And now, as I write these final words, the April sunshine is forcing its way through the windows of my study and I sense that Spring is here. Persephone is returned to Earth. All is well.

Bramshott, April 1991

1

The End of the Millennia

*M*ILLENARIANISM, THE ANCIENT BELIEF THAT THE WORLD WILL END after 7,000 years, has captivated many minds across the centuries. Now, with a mere nine years left until the end of the twentieth century, apocalypse-mania is well and truly on the increase. Are we to believe Nostradamus's prophecy and St John's Revelation of an Antichrist primed to strike terror into men's hearts and bring unmitigated horror into our lives before the Day of Judgement? Are we to assume, like the Hopi Indians of North America and the Hindus, that we are approaching the end of a final World Age which will culminate in a great conflagration? Or is it possible that instead there will be a great flowering of consciousness – the dawning of a New Age – whereby the enlightened shall perceive a new heaven and a new Earth?

While I have to confess a certain morbid fascination for the mostly hair-raising scenarios painted by the Old Testament seers, I have remained stubbornly resistant to the possibility that they might actually contain a grain of truth. Neither have I been at all impressed by other visionaries – both ancient and modern – who predict that in the 'last days' mankind will be nursed through the apocalypse by higher beings and, as such times draw ever nearer, consciousness is expanding globally. But, over recent years, I have done somewhat of a U-turn on a variety of beliefs, and now, with the unassailable evidence of events in the world at large and those of my own smaller microcosm before me, I must admit to a growing feeling that the prophets may well be right – at least in some measure – and, perhaps more significantly, that consciousness is indeed expanding.

I will be enlarging on these contemporary topics later in the book, but first I would like to cover some of the most 'popular' prophesies for the final decade of the twentieth century.

The Bible is our finest repository of prophecies. From Zachiel to Daniel, Joel to St John there are pronouncements on the great and terrible future in store for mankind – much of it allied to the Second Coming. By and large, the Old Testament prophets believed that life on Earth was ordered by a Supreme Being and that far from following an erratic course, the affairs of man were guided by an invisible hand. These ancient seers claimed to have a unique relationship with the Holy Spirit and that God spoke to them directly and allowed them to perceive His divine plan:.

> For the prophecy came not in old time by the will of man: but holy men of God spake as they were moved by the Holy Ghost. [1]

The general themes of the prophesies of the 'last days' centre on relentless terror, bloodshed, war and pestilence, not to mention awesome beasts and other sundry spectres:

> For, behold the day cometh, that shall burn as an oven; and all the proud, yea, and all that do wickedly, shall be stubble; and the day that cometh shall burn them up . . . [2]

> Like the noise of chariots on the tops of mountains . . . like the noise of a flame of fire that devoureth the stubble . . . Before their face the people shall be much pained; all faces shall gather blackness. [3]

> And I will shew wonders in the heavens and in the earth, blood and fire, and pillars of smoke. The sun shall be turned to darkness, and the moon into blood, before the great and the terrible day of the Lord to come. [4]

> The earth shall quake before them; the heavens shall tremble; the sun and the moon shall be dark, and the stars shall withdraw their shining. [5]

> The noise of a multitude in the mountains . . . a tumultuous noise of the kingdoms of nations gathered together . . . the day of the Lord is at hand; it shall come as a destruction from the Almighty . . . therefore shall all hands be faint, and every man's heart shall melt . . . their faces shall be as flames . . . For the stars of heaven and the constellations thereof shall not give their light: the sun shall be darkened in his going forth, and the moon shall not cause her light to shine. [6]

I am not the first person to note that many of the prophets used strikingly similar images to describe the events of the last days. Now, it may be that all of them, as members of a great mystical tradition, deliberately used the same images to convey secret information,[7] but descriptions of pillars of smoke and the sun rendered black are horrifically plausible in light of our present understanding of the effects of nuclear weapons and the nuclear winter and, perhaps, more appositely, redolent of the columns of burning oil rising into the darkening skies above Kuwait in 1991.

Daniel saw the final judgement in much the same combustible terms as other Old Testament prophets, but he alone predicted how long mankind must wait for such things to pass. He also warned of another daunting prospect ahead – four great beasts:

> The first was like a lion and had eagle's wings . . . a second, like to a bear . . . another like to a leopard, a fourth . . . dreadful and terrible . . . it had great iron teeth . . . and ten horns . . .[8]
> Go thy way, Daniel: for the words are closed up and sealed until the time of the end. Many shall be purified, and made white and tried . . . And from the time [of] the abomination that maketh desolate set up, there shall be a thousand two hundred and ninety days.[9]

But nothing in the Old Testament quite matches up to St John's truly awe-ful vision. In Revelations he describes a scroll with seven seals – the first four of which release the ominous quartet of the horsemen of the apocalypse. At the sixth seal we learn:

> There was a great earthquake; and the sun became black as sackcloth of hair, and the moon became as blood. And the stars of heaven fell unto the earth even as a fig tree casteth her untimely figs, when she is shaken of a mighty wind. And the heaven departed as a scroll when it is rolled together; and every mountain and island were moved out of their places.[10]

St John does offer some hope for humanity a chapter later, however, when he tells us that nothing upon Earth shall be harmed 'till we have sealed the servants of our God in their foreheads' – a point I shall take up later.

Clearly echoing Daniel, St John describes four beasts, the first of which has 'seven heads and ten horns . . . like unto a leopard . . . his feet were as to the feet of a bear, and his mouth as to the mouth of a lion . . .' But John expands on Daniel's vision by providing us with a clue to the beast's identity: he has 'the number of man . . . six hundred three score and six'. And while Joel talks of God judging humanity in a place named Jehosophat, St John tells of 'the battle of the great day of God Almighty' at Armageddon.

Aside from the Bible, our greatest source of information about the future of mankind lies with Michel de Nostradame. This great sixteenth-century prophet mixed many of the same biblical ingredients and metaphors in his *Centuries* – a set of 100 four-line predictions published in 1555. Such was the impact of these prophecies at the time – most notably the prediction of the death in 1559 of Henri II of France in a jousting accident – that his fame spread throughout the world. Today, these same prophecies continue to be the subject of universal debate and speculation. Nostradamus's vision of world events in the latter part of the twentieth century is awesome to say the least:

Après grat troche[11] *humain plus grand s'appreste,*
Le grand moteur les siècles renouelle:
pluye, sang, laict, famine, fer and peste,
Au ciel veu feu, courant longue estincelle. [12]
After a great human [military?] exchange another even greater approaches
when the driving power of the centuries is renewed. [13]
It will rain blood, milk, famine, iron and pestilence.
In the sky fire is seen running with long sparks.

Au révolu du grand nombre septième
apparoistra au temps Ieux d'Hacatombe,
non esloigne du grand eage milliesme,
Que les entrés sortiront de leur tombe. [14]
At the completion of the great seventh cycle
it will appear at the time of the great games/eyes of slaughter,
not far from the great age of the millennium
when the buried come out of their graves/those who entered will leave their tomb.

L'an mil neuf cens nonante neuf sept mois
Du ciel viendra un grand Roy deffraieur
Resusciter le grand Roy d'Angolmois.
Avant après Mars régner par bonheur. [15]
In the year 1999, and seven months
from the sky will come the great King of terror.
He will resuscitate the great king of the Mongols.
Before and after war reigns happily.

It is clearly no accident that Nostradamus evokes similar apocalyptic scenarios as the biblical prophets. He was not only living at a time when it was widely believed that human history would last for 7,000 years – a theory originating from the Book of Enoch – but his education and background was steeped in Judaeo-Christian philosophy. To Nostradamus and others of his time, the end of the twentieth century was considered to be the seventh and final millennium, a time of great tribulation which would give way to a new and glorious age. Although some critics of the *Centuries* have suggested that Nostradamus was little more than a clever plagiarizer, it is a matter of historical fact that he was a gifted astrologer, [16] and well versed in Platonic thought, alchemy and the magical arts – hardly an individual whose only source of inspiration lay in the words of earlier prophets. Clearly, his theological background must have acted as a guiding principle in his work, but I am sure that the mainspring for his prophecies was his own divine revelation. As he says in a letter to his son, Caesar, his 'predictions have been made through the inspiration of divine will alone and the spirit of prophecy in particular'. And if the biblical prophets received God's word in this way – and their visions of man's future were correct – why should Nostradamus differ in his perception of events?

One of the greatest problems with Nostradamus's prophecies, and evident in the examples I have chosen, is the translation of the language and the interpretation of the abstruse descriptions. Nostradamus not only used symbolism, metaphor, anagrams, ellipses and other grammatical tricks in his *Centuries* but a mixture of Latin, French and doggerel; he also chose not to place his predictions in chronological order nor, seemingly, in any discernible thematic sequence. Thus, in a great many cases, the quatrains appear to apply to more than one historical event. The reason for this, I imagine, is not that he was 'hedging his bets' but that, in the way of mystics before him, he was anxious to ensure that the truth could only be discerned by those capable of putting such knowledge to good use – had he not been careful to cloak his statements in metaphorical and grammatical mist, the *Centuries* might well have been destroyed by the religious orthodoxy. (Clearly, Nostradamus not only wanted to protect his prophecies – and himself – from being destroyed by the Inquisition, but also perceived that they might also fall foul of future generations.) It is also probable that he set a deliberately hard task for anyone attempting to unravel the prophecies in the way that a master would put his pupil through hoops so that in the process he would acquire knowledge and enlightenment. However, as an astrologer, I must confess that it is extremely puzzling, if not downright irritating, that he placed so few astrological clues within his prophecies. Such phrases as 'Mercury, Mars, Jupiter in France' [17] make very little astrological sense, unless one considers France to be a Leo country, in which case the timing for the 'horrible war in preparation in the West' must be when all these planets are found simultaneously in Leo (1 July 1991). In another quatrain[18] where he states that 'blood will rain on the rocks . . . war near Orgon' when 'the Sun [is] in the East, Saturn in the West' he could be indicating Saturn's position 180 degrees away from the sun at sunrise in Orgon (Oregon?) – an aspect that occurs once every year! Perhaps this quatrain relates to an earlier one[19] where 'At sunrise a great fire . . . noise and light extending towards the North . . . death awaits through weapons, fire and famine.' However, I did locate one specific astrological indication in *Centuries* 9[20]: 'The sun, 20 degrees of Taurus, the earth shall quake.' Although this provides us with a day, 10 May, the actual year is not mentioned – but by some intuitive sleuthing, I did come across an extraordinary coincidence. In *Centuries* 1:51 Nostradamus gives us 'At the height of Aries (*Chef d'Aries*) Jupiter and Saturn, eternal God what upheavals . . .' This has been variously interpreted as a Jupiter–Saturn conjunction in Aries, which is not due to manifest until well into the twenty-second century.[21] There is, however, a Jupiter–Saturn conjunction set to occur a little before that time – on 28 May 2000 – not in Aries but in the next-door sign, Taurus. Even more significantly, on 10 May of that year the Sun is conjunct Saturn at the all-important 20th degree of Taurus. Also, the phrase '*Chef d'Aries*' is intriguing. It actually makes no sense at all, even to astrologers. Chief of Aries? Head of Aries? But bearing in mind Nostradamus's superlative craftsmanship in word play, by placing the first letter of the alphabet in front of the 'head of Aries' the meaning becomes absolutely clear. Not 'a head of Aries', but 'ahead of Aries'.[22] And what is ahead of Aries in the zodiac sequence, but Taurus. Now the two quatrains link satisfactorily to make one clear prediction; the first providing us with the degree of the zodiac and the event, the other revealing the year. And what an astrologically perfect day it is too for an earthquake. On 10 May in the year 2000, the Sun is not only conjunct Saturn at 20° of Taurus but at an exact angle of 90 degrees from earth-moving Uranus and thrown in for good measure are Mercury at 22° of Taurus and Jupiter at 19° of Taurus with the Moon reaching 20° of Leo around 20 hours GMT – what a recipe for a disaster. As if to drive the point well and truly home Nostradamus refers time and time again to May and Easter in connection with earthquakes.[23]

Nostradamus's countdown to the apocalypse follows biblical lines in that seven major events are set to constellate prior to Armageddon: 1) religious deception; 2) internal revolutions; 3) wars; 4) famine; 5) poisoning of the Earth; 6) earthquakes; and 7) plagues and diseases.

Nostradamus, like Daniel and St John, also talks of an Antichrist; indeed in his epistle to Henri II, he refers to three. Most researchers have identified the first two as Napoleon and Hitler and both these men are named in the quatrains – Hitler as Hister[24] and Napoleon as Pav Nay Loron,[25] an anagram of Napoleon Roy. Characteristically, of course, Nostradamus makes identification of an Antichrist *per se* as difficult as possible so that for the main part, we are left to thread our way through the labyrinthian network of stanzas interpreting 'he' in one quatrain to mean Napoleon and in another to mean Hitler, or possibly the Shah of Iran or Saddam Hussein. Quatrain 77 in *Centuries* 8 is typical of the sort of confusion created by Nostradamus: '*L'antechrist trois bien tost annichilez, vingt & sept ans sang durera sa guerre . . .*' – 'The third Antichrist soon annihilates (everything), twenty seven years of blood his war will last . . .' However, this could also be interpreted as the Antichrist soon annihilates three. The other quatrain featuring the word 'antichrist' states:

> *Le chef de Londres par règne Americh,*
> *L'isle d'Escosse tempiera par gellée:*
> *Roy Reb auront un si faux antechrist*
> *Que les mettra trestous dans la meslée.* [26]
> The head of London through American power,
> will temper the Island of Scotland with frost:
> King Reb/Red leader (or an anagram of Roy Reb) will have
> so false an antichrist
> that all three of them will be put in disorder.

Nostradamus leaves us with several possible clues as to the identity of Antichrist III – some of which appear to be anagrams; Aenodarb,[27] Aenobarbe,[28] Mabus[29] and Alus[30]; even more abstrusely we have 'The last but one of the prophet's nickname.'[31] Nostradamus, once again echoing biblical prophecy, also prepares us for an Antichrist from the East: in one quatrain[32] we are told, 'The Arab Prince, Mars, the Sun Venus in Leo . . . nearly a million men will invade Egypt and Byzantium (Turkey). Ver. Serp.'[33] Elsewhere Nostradamus tells us, 'Throughout Asia there will be great proscription . . . blood will flow because of a dark young man full of evil.'[34] This evil man from the East crops up once or twice as 'the man of blood',[35] 'the African leader'[36] and even as 'a man who is reborn from the infernal gods of Hannibal'.[37] There are also some astrological clues: aside from the stellium of planets in Leo, we are told:

De l'aquatic triplicité naistra,
d'un qui fera jeudi pour sa feste:
Son bruit, loz règne, sa puissance croistra,
par terre & mer aux Oriens tempeste.
From the water triplicity (Cancer, Scorpio and Pisces)
will come one who will make Thursday his feast day:
His renown, praise, rule and power will grow by land and sea,
bringing trouble to the East.'[38]

The third Antichrist presents us with possibly Nostradamus's greatest conundrum. Although in the main this man from the East is deemed to be dangerous and bloody, he may also have remarkable, even supernatural, powers. In two quatrains, we discover that 'He will pass through Armenia leaving his bloody rod in Turkey'[39] and 'He will cross through the sky, the seas and the snows and he will strike everyone with his rod.'[40] The interpretation of 'rod' here is crucial. Nostradamus uses the word *gaule* – which could be translated as a Welshman, a Frenchman, or, as some researchers have concluded, General de Gaulle – but somehow leaving a Welshman in Turkey or striking everyone on the head with de Gaulle doesn't sound quite right to me. Clearly rod must be a weapon of some sort or a type of magic wand, even if, ultimately, *gaule* turns out to be a clue to or an anagram of a name. One theory that has been put forward is that 'rod' infers a tax or levy; another possibility is that it could represent a radio mast or a television aerial thereby implying that the man from the East could use radio and telecommunications to powerful effect. Certainly this would apply to any leader – political or religious – on today's world stage. But there is also the very real chance that the 'rod' could be an Hermetic symbol, the caduceus, or the staff of Hermes.[41] Nostradamus was well versed in the Hermetic arts and he could have used no more appropriate yet covert way of telling us about the extraordinary powers of this man than by showing him to have Mercury's rod – a symbol of enlightenment and magical powers. And that with this power, he could either transform and illuminate the world or control and subjugate mankind.

So, is this man from the East with incredible powers one and the same as the Antichrist or are we looking for two men – one distinctly evil and the other an enlightened teacher? At this point, perhaps we need to refer to the Bible for a second opinion. One of the fundamental tenets of Christianity is that Christ will return to Earth and before that time there will be 'wars and rumours of wars . . . famines . . . pestilences and earthquakes' – all familiar ingredients of the Nostradamus quatrains.

Jesus also tells the disciples that before he returns, 'There shall arise false Christs, and false prophets, and shall shew great signs and wonders; insomuch that, if it were possible they shall deceive the very elect.'[42] But while Jesus warns of pretenders, he does not predict one Antichrist more terrible than the rest. That task, as we have seen, was left to St John in Revelations.

As I discussed earlier, Nostradamus does seem to have echoed biblical teachings about the end of the millennia and there is a case to be made for the fact that he included in his *Centuries* all the anticipated ingredients of the apocalypse – antichrists, beasts, and false prophets – in the hopes of some of them materializing. But I firmly believe that he was a great and gifted prophet and if I understand some of his quatrains, he is forewarning us of more than one hugely influential man from the East. In his visions of the future, Nostradamus appears to have clearly foreseen the huge global influence the East would exert and glimpsed the shadows cast by many future leaders from the East, any one of whom could, dependent upon a combination of fate and free will, become the agent of Satan and an ultimate world destroyer. What is remarkable is that Nostradamus lived at a time when the East was considered the seat of infidels, yet he was able to predict that hundreds of years in the future a non-Christian sect and/or its leader would have a world-wide influence.

This certainly seems to be the case today. In the August of 1990, an Iraqi tyrant by the name of Saddam Hussein invaded his oil-rich neighbour, Kuwait, and plunged the entire world into crisis. While the combined weight of the allied forces drove the Iraqi army out of Kuwait, Saddam himself was not overthrown. In an effort to cling on to power, he butchered thousands of his own people – men, women and children – and effectively sentenced to an icy death hundreds of thousands of Kurds as they fled into the mountains to escape his blood-crazed troops.

There is also the Libyan leader Colonel Khaddafi – another charismatic butcher and superlative politician. Either one of these two men could fulfil Nostradamus' prophecies for not only are they capable of bringing the world to a nuclear end, but as far as their own people are concerned they are the embodiment of the spirit of Islam. These are the two men from the East whom we know we have to fear, but there are other more shadowy figures – terrorists like Abu Nidal, Abu Abbas – and, of course, the infamous and thoroughly evil Pol Pot, who has had millions of Cambodians tortured and slaughtered. Then there are the religious gurus – Sun Myung Moon, Sai Baba and the Maharishi Mahesh Yogi for instance – all of whom wield a massive following from East and West.

What may be more important to humanity's destiny, however, is not who the Antichrist is, but what he represents. Even without Nostradamus's foresight, it must have dawned upon today's powers that be that the world would be a safer place without the presence of certain dictators. Yet to remove any one of them would not only create even more antagonism but, in the way of Medusa's heads, as soon as one was eliminated another would spring up to take his place. In a sense, it is as though humanity has projected its inner polarity and conflict out onto the world's stage and while we in the West consider Saddam Hussein or Colonel Khaddafi and Islam to be the Shadow which must be destroyed, to the East, it is President Bush and we ungodly lot who need to be annihilated. In this way, the Antichrist or his alter-egos, the King of Terror and the Beast, are not monsters in the flesh so to speak, nor any one ruler, religion or institution, but the manifestation – in whatever form – of all that is dark and destructive within man's consciousness.

One way or another, we shall surely bring upon ourselves the harvest of man's disharmonious spirit. We are already tasting the bitter fruits of our excessive materialistic labours: the stripping of the rain forests, the burning of fossil fuels, the use of CFCs and all manner of pollution of the atmosphere – actions perpetrated to assuage the insatiable appetite of the consumer generation – have made a gigantic hole in the ozone layer and contributed to climatic changes which in turn are destroying the livelihood and very existence of a large part of the world. So great is the level of the pollution of the Earth that our bodies' immune defence systems are breaking down, rendering us vulnerable to the onslaught of all manner of strange and fatal diseases. We really don't need a nuclear holocaust – Armageddon is all about us.

The manifestations of humanity's darkness may indeed involve the rebellion of the Earth itself – Gaia in revolt.[43] Through man's insensitivity to nature, his inability to respect the Earth that nurtures and sustains him, he has propelled Gaia into such a state of disequilibrium that she has flipped into self-destruct mode. As she endeavours to right the balance, she must be transformed, and that process necessitates elimination on a massive scale. All the ancient prophets speak of huge Earth movements, whether these are inspired by war or by nature herself. In more recent times, many psychics the world over have echoed these predictions – none so impressively, perhaps, as the twentieth-century American prophet Edgar Cayce.

Cayce, the Sleeping Prophet,[44] left us a wealth of information on all manner of spiritual philosophy, and like Nostradamus and the Old

Testament prophets he talked of massive land shifts throughout the world, which he maintained would be triggered by a revolution of the Earth on its axis: '. . . there will be [around the year 2000–1] the shifting then of the poles – so that where there have been those of a frigid or semi-tropical will become more tropical and moss and fern will grow.'[45] Indeed, Cayce's prophecies about mankind's tribulations at the turn of the twentieth century virtually all hinge on the land changes related to a pole shift.

Within the scientific fraternity a schism exists between the catastrophic theory of geological change and the more orthodox concept of uniformitarianism. In 1840 Louis Agassiz was the first person to propose that ice ages, instead of developing gradually over the course of thousands of years, were precipitated suddenly by a global catastrophic event. He never speculated on the nature of that catastrophic event but less than a century later, engineer Hugh Auchincloss Brown theorized that periodically the Earth flipped over on its axis due to the pressure of ice at one or both poles. Admittedly, the great majority of scientists has little time for either the catastrophic theory or the possibility of terrestrial pole shifts, but over the years several renowned individuals have argued the case impressively.[46] In his research for *Worlds in Collision*, for example, Velikovsky scoured ancient literature for evidence of pole shifts. One example that he gives was provided by the writer Pomponius Mela in the first century and echoed later by the historian Herodotus:

The Egyptians pride themselves on being the most ancient people in the world. In their authentic annals . . . one may read that since they have been in existence, the course of the stars has changed direction four times, and that the sun has set twice in that part of the sky where it rises today.[47]

While terrestrial pole shifts may be purely speculative, reversals in the magnetic poles are a fact. But why such magnetic reversals occur – and there have been about five in the last million years – is yet again a mystery. One theory – aside from the result of simple geomagnetic field changes – is that a large cosmic body passing too close to the Earth, or even colliding with it, could cause a reversal of the geomagnetic field. (See Chapter 3, pp.60–1.)

Clearly, the Earth tumbling around in space would be enough to fulfil most prophetic visions of mountains moving and the heavens disappearing like a scroll. Jeffrey Goodman, in his book, *We are the Earthquake Generation*,[48] gives a chilling account of what we might expect:

It is 5pm in Boston and the people rushing home from work hardly notice how the setting sun seems to hang on the horizon. After several hours people start to wonder why darkness is not coming and they start to fear the faint dull roar they hear. Some also begin to feel light on their feet, whether from the giddiness induced by the prolonged twilight or from subtle gravitational and magnetic changes that the earth's shifting in space is creating. Some have that I-could-jump-over-anything feeling. Animals act skittish and then suddenly all start to move or migrate in the same direction. *Then the sky reddens as huge clouds of dust begin to blot out the sun.* Next, a steady wind starts to blow. As the wind strengthens, *the faint dull roar heard earlier grows even louder* as if the source were moving closer. But just then, *a temporary stillness sets in* and the air seems like it is being sucked up by a giant vacuum cleaner. There is no sign of movement; all the animals are gone. After a few minutes, the winds are back even stronger. There are gusts up to a hundred miles an hour. Trees are plucked out of the ground, and railroad trains are tumbled over and over and shuttled along like hockey pucks. As the wind jets up to over 200 miles per hour, buildings and everything above ground are decimated. The air becomes a thick mixture of dirt and debris. Those fortunate enough to be tucked safely away below the ground find the air hard to breathe since it is being drawn by the holocaust above. The wind factor has plummeted the temperature down to just above freezing, even though it is spring. There are almost continual electrical storms. Quakes and volcanoes are set off around the world and a rift opens up as the earth splits in several places to relieve the stress produced by the shift. The holocaust goes on and on as if it is never going to stop: ten hours, fifteen, twenty, forty, forty-eight. Then suddenly the winds subside and material from the sky starts to come crashing down. For a few minutes it seems to be raining automobiles, boats, washing machines and kitchen sinks. The temperature comes back to normal for this time of year, a pleasant 50°F. But this temperature rise continues. By the next day, the third since the start of the shift, the temperature has hit 103°F, just what one would expect in equatorial Africa for this time of year – not Boston. From Boston to St Paul to Seattle to Anchorage, out come the Bermuda shorts. Layers of mud spread for thousands of miles as a grim reminder of the holocaust. The decaying bodies of animals of every size and shape are found in caves where they huddled together in their last moments. [My italics throughout.]

And every island fled away and the mountains were not found.[49]

However attractive Bermuda shorts in Spring may sound, were the Earth to shift on its axis, even less than a full 180 degrees, there wouldn't just be the carcasses of animals decaying in the heat. With the nuclear arsenal stored all over the world, the heaving and shifting Earth would trigger warheads left right and centre. There would be nothing of humanity left at all. Not even an Antichrist.

By and large, according to the prophets both ancient and modern, we don't have much to look forward to, unless, of course, anyone positively relishes a holocaust of global proportions. Yet the essential message most of the prophets tried to put across was that the tribulations to be heaped on humanity were not only God's judgement on our accumulated sins but would pave the way for a new heaven and a new Earth. In his letter to his son, Caesar, Nostradamus talked explicitly of a forthcoming Golden Age:

> The work comprises prophecies from today [1555] to the year 3797 . . .
> [there will be] world-wide conflagration which is to bring so many
> catastrophes and such revolutions that scarcely any lands will not be
> covered by water . . . this is why, before and after these revolutions in
> various countries, the rains will be so diminished and such an abundance
> of fire and fiery missiles that shall fall from the heavens that nothing shall
> escape the holocaust . . . with Almighty God's aid, and before
> completing its [the moon's][50] full cycle, the monarchy will return, then
> the Golden Age. For according to the celestial signs, the Golden Age shall
> return, and after all calculations, with the world near to an all-
> encompassing revolution – from the time of writing 177 years, 3 months
> and 11 days . . . This will be after the visible judgement of heaven, before
> we shall reach the millennium which shall complete all.

The Golden Age will be the subject of my next chapter but before we turn our attention to how we may survive to enter this New Age, I feel I must address two of the perplexing issues raised by Nostradamus in his letter to Caesar. Nostradamus gave many pointers that the great conflagration was to occur at the end of the millennia, yet in his letter he mentions a figure of 177 years, 3 months and 11 days until the time of the arrival of the Golden Age. If we add this figure to the year in which Nostradamus was writing, we arrive at 1732. And perhaps more to the point, Nostradamus stated that his prophecies went on until 3797. So was the Golden Age to have come in before the conflagration, or was this yet another example of Nostradamus' talent for camouflage? Jean-Charles de Fontbrune in his excellent book on the prophecies[51] makes the point that

> . . . the prophecies end with the seventh millennium, which according
> to biblical chronology is the conclusion of the Piscean Age,[52]
> approximately 2000 AD. Hence again, Nostradamus cunningly

concealed this fact: the calculation can only be arrived at using the biblical reckoning he gives in the letter to 'Henry Roy de France Second', as follows:

From Adam, the first man, to Noah	1,242 years
Noah to Abraham	1,080 years
Abraham to Moses	515 years
Moses to David	570 years
David to Jesus Christ	1,350 years
i.e. from Adam to Christ, a total of	**4,757 years**

While this ingeniously solves the mystery of the date of the Golden Age, and brings it on target for the end of the millennia, there is still the curious statement about the monarchy returning prior to the arrival of the New Age.

Initially I found it strange that while Nostradamus concurred almost entirely with the biblical concept of the last days, he made virtually no mention in the quatrains of a Second Coming and, after all, he did have a Judaeo-Christian upbringing. Then my eyes fell on the phrase 'the monarchy will return'. Now, this is Fontbrune's interpretation of Nostradamus's original reference to the Sun returning[53] prior to the Age of Saturn.[54] Implicit in this statement is, I believe, a triple play on words: on the one hand, the Son of Man – the Sun also symbolizes the great solar myth of the hero's rise to glory, his death and resurrection – and on the other, the return of the Merovingian dynasty – the royal bloodline of Jesus Christ.

In *The Holy Blood and the Holy Grail*,[55] Baigent, Leigh and Lincoln make a fascinating, meticulously researched, although much ridiculed, case for the argument that Jesus Christ did not die on the cross; furthermore, that he not only survived well beyond the age of 33, but fathered a royal line of David (brought to Europe by Mary Magdalene) that exists to this day in France. The descendants of the royal line of David were purportedly the Merovingian dynasty which, after the assassination of its last king, Dagobert II (later mysteriously canonized), continued on in the Plantavelu family – the Dukes of Aquitaine – and the house of Lorraine. The authors maintain that this is the great secret held by the Prieuré de Sion – a 'discreet', mystical society dating back to the days of the Templars which boasts of such illustrious Grand Masters as Leonardo da Vinci, Sandro Filipepe (Botticelli), Victor Hugo and Isaac Newton. The present Grand Master is none other than Pierre Plantard de Saint Clair – a direct descendant of Bernard Plantavelu ersatz the Merovingians and the royal house of David.

It is not known if Nostradamus was a member of the Prieuré, but he almost certainly rubbed shoulders with those who were: his grandfather, astrologer, cabalist and physician, Jean de Saint Remy, was a member of the court of René d'Anjou – a Grand Master of the Prieuré between 1418 and 1480. The authors of *The Holy Blood and the Holy Grail* reveal that Nostradamus spent a considerable period of his life in the Duchy of Lorraine:

> . . . this would appear to have been some sort of novitiate, or period of probation, after which he was supposedly 'initiated' into some portentous secret. More specifically he is said to have been shown an ancient and arcane book, on which he based all his own subsequent work. And this book was reportedly divulged to him at a very significant place – the mysterious Abbey of Orval . . . where . . . the Prieuré de Sion may have had its inception.

Baigent, Leigh and Lincoln also maintain that 'there is no question that some of Nostradamus's prophecies were not prophecies but referred, quite explicitly, to the past – to the Knights Templar, the Merovingian dynasty, the history of the house of Lorraine.'

Thus, it is entirely possible that Nostradamus wrote his quatrains not only for the benefit of mankind in the sense of forewarning and forearming – for a great many of his prophecies have been fulfilled over the centuries – but as a means of imparting and maintaining the portentous truth that the bloodline of Jesus Christ and the house of David was coursing through the veins of the Dukes of Aquitaine and Lorraine. And that at the end of the millennia the King of Kings is primed to take up his divine and rightful throne on Earth. (Quite how this all fits in with the Earth's virtual destruction will be the subject of discussion in Chapter 2.) By writing his *Centuries* in the certain expectation of their enduring popularity, Nostradamus, without any official link to the Priory, could ensure the perpetuation of this knowledge in the event of the demise of the Priory. In this way, he was entrusted with one of the most important roles in the history of the Priory: to become its most enduring mouthpiece. Using the technique adopted by mystics across the ages – as, indeed, in biblical parables themselves – he publically addressed anyone and everyone yet at the same time concealed the true meaning from all except those open to perceive such a truth. In a sense, the *Centuries* were conceived as a sort of time bomb in that the prophecies could only be understood when the time was right. That, in 1555, he predicted the time for the return of the monarchy – some four-and-a-half centuries hence – may be due entirely to his own clairvoyant skills or the long-term plans of the Priory itself – possibly bent on fulfilling the Old Testament millenarial prophecies – perhaps a combination of the two. Whatever the case, this knowledge is only now beginning to reveal itself to a larger public – not in 1782 or 3797 but a matter of years before the end of the millennium.

As far as I am concerned, if there is one quatrain more than any other that supports the hypothesis that Nostradamus knew of the re-establishment of the monarchy with a divine bloodline, it is quatrain 70 in *Centuries* 6:

> *Au chef du monde le grand Chyren sera,*
> *Plus oultre*[56] *après ayme, craint, redoubte:*
> *Son bruit & los cieux surpassera*
> *Et du seul titre victeur fort contente.*
> The great Chyren will be chief of the world
> more, ever more, after, loved, feared and dreaded.
> His fame and praise go beyond the heavens
> and he will be greatly satisfied with the sole title of victor.

The key word here is 'Chyren' – often mistakenly assumed to be an anagram of 'Henryc' and applied (correctly in some other stanzas) to various King Henrys. Crucially, however, the present day Grand Master of the Prieuré de Sion, Pierre Plantard de Saint Clair, a direct descendant of the Merovingian kings, uses none other than Chyron as his *nom-de-plume* – whether by accident, design or divine right. And although the prospect is rather alarming that Chyren may be feared and dreaded, the Bible urges us to treat God with awe and fear, and, indeed, any individual who wields power and charisma – no matter how good and true he or she may be – also evokes a certain amount of respect and veneration. Certainly, if we are to understand Baigent, Leigh and Lincoln, M. Plantard moves in exalted political and royal circles and already exerts a low-key but powerful authority and influence – he was most certainly a key figure in securing De Gaulle's return to power in 1958. The authors of *The Holy Blood and the Holy Grail* describe M. Plantard as 'a dignified, courteous man of discreetly aristocratic bearing, unostentatious in appearance, with a gracious, volatile but soft-spoken manner. He displayed enormous erudition and impressive nimbleness of mind – a gift for dry, witty, mischievous but not in any way barbed repartee . . . For all his modest, unassertive manner, he exercised an imposing authority over his companions. And there was a marked quality of asceticism and austerity about him.'

Elsewhere, the authors discuss the ambitious political plans the Priory apparently nurture. According to a journalist, Jean-Luc Chaumeil, who had interviewed M. Plantard for a magazine, 'Within a few years he [M. Chaumeil] asserted, there would be a dramatic change in the French Government – a change that would pave the way for a popular monarchy with a Merovingian ruler on the throne. And Sion, he asserted further, would be behind this change – as it had been behind numerous other changes for centuries.'

I realize, of course, that I could well be weaving a fabulous tapestry from a skein of dubious threads, but there is no escaping the mystery surrounding Nostradamus's connections with the Priory and his subsequent publication of the *Centuries*. In his letter to Caesar he clearly mentions 'the return of the Monarchy' prior to the Golden Age, which is the closest he comes to echoing the biblical prophecies of the Second Coming prior to the realization of a new heaven and a new Earth. Of course, the possibility that Nostradamus actually knew the true nature of the Second Coming casts a rather different complexion on many of the quatrains pertaining to the 'man from the East' – after all, the Merovingian's family roots were in the Holy Land. In light of this new understanding, the 'bloody rod' could be interpreted as royal blood (*sang real*, an anagram of *Sang gaule*) with a double play on the hermetic 'rod', the caduceus – the Merovingian kings were fabled to have extraordinary, supernatural powers. But even if we can identify some of these stanzas as indications of the coming of the earthly King with divine powers, we are still left with all the other formidable quatrains that describe pestilences, earthquakes and wars.

It would be much easier to consider that all the portents of disaster were simply Nostradamian red herrings or metaphors of something not quite so literally Earth shattering but I don't think we can escape some major world-wide catastrophe before the end of this century, whether this emerges in the form of a global economic or ecological cataclysm rather than a third world war or a pole shift. I also believe, along the lines of Cayce and many other modern-day mystics, that humanity will undergo a major spiritual catharsis, whether this is inspired by a divine emissary or a collective spiritual awakening. With this in mind, I will conclude with two slightly different perspectives on the end of the millennium. The first is taken from the last paragraph in *The Holy Blood and the Holy Grail* and the second is a personal insight:

There are many devout Christians who do not hesitate to interpret the Apocalypse as nuclear holocaust. How might the advent of Jesus's lineal descent be interpreted? To a receptive audience, it might be a Second Coming.

In the Autumn of 1978, I spent a weekend working with a group of astrologers and Buddhists at the little town of Rye in Sussex. It was a highly stimulating occasion where there was much spirited discussion on such light and airy topics as the nature of existence and life after death. Not surprisingly in the early hours of the Sunday morning I had a dream.

In the dream I was in bed in my room at Rye. There was an extraordinary sense of waiting for something to happen. I looked out of the window into the darkness, when suddenly, I noticed that it was raining. Then I realized that there was something unusual about the rain: at first I thought it was white rain, then I saw that it was raining stars. All at once the stars became still. They twinkled and hovered. Beautiful as this sight was, it was also menacing. There was a sense that they were only temporarily suspended and that an event of enormous proportions was about to occur.

I woke up in a mixture of sheer terror and elation and recounted the dream immediately to my husband.

As I was working on the prophecies for this chapter I remembered this dream and was able to find it recorded in my journal. I had also noted that on the night in question I had decided not to stay up and watch the film – Ingmar Bergman's *The Seventh Seal*.

And when he had opened the seventh seal, there was a silence in heaven about the space of half an hour . . .

REVELATIONS 8:1

Appendix

1) Peter II, 1:21.
2) Malachi 4:1.
3) Joel 2:5 and 6.
4) Ibid, 2:30 and 31.
5) Ibid, 2:10.
6) Isiah 13:4,6,8,10.
7) Victor Dunstan, author of *The Invisible Hand* (Megiddo Press, 1984) and Gordon Strachan, author of *Christ and the Cosmos* (Element Books, 1985) are among others who believe that there is a code in the Bible and that words such as 'mountain', 'the sea', 'the vine' and 'sheep' and so forth are allegories of such things as kingdoms, the Jews and the Tribes of Israel. They also propose that the Bible contains a time code so that days and weeks are symbolic of years and centuries.
8) Daniel 7:4–8.
9) Ibid, 12:8,9,10,11.
10) Revelations 6:12,13,14.
11) According to Erika Cheetham in *The Final Prophecies of Nostradamus* (Futura, 1989),

troche is taken from the Greek *trikos*, misery. I have opted instead for the French *troc*, exchange.

12) *Centuries* 2:46.

13) The end of the millennium: the turn of the year 2000.

14) *Centuries* 10:74.

15) Ibid, 10:72.

16) Nostradamus was unquestionably an astrologer, which makes it all the more strange that he should apparently include astrologers with the fools and barbarians who are to keep away from interpreting the *Centuries*: '*Omnesque Astrologi, Blenni, Barbari procul sunto . . .*' Jean Fontbrune in *Nostradamus: Countdown to Apocalypse* (Pan, 1983) maintains that Nostradamus is addressing twentieth-century astrologers here since in the sixteenth century the empirical study of the stars (astronomy) had not become separated from its sister science the subjective interpretation of the stars (astrology). This may be true, but I expect this was yet another ruse of Nostradamus to sever all connections with the occult in the event of his being 'detained' by the Inquisition.

17) *Centuries* 9:55.

18) Ibid, 5:62.

19) Ibid, 2:91.

20) Ibid, 9:83.

21) The previous Jupiter–Saturn conjunction in Aries occurred in 1702.

22) I could be accused of taking considerable poetic licence here since the French word for 'ahead' is *en avant*, but maybe – just maybe – Nostradamus left this clue to be unravelled in the twentieth century by an astrologer more familiar with the English language!

23) *Centuries* 9:31; 6:88; 10:67.

24) Ibid, 4:68.

25) Ibid, 8:1.

26) Ibid, 10:66.

27) Ibid, 5:45.

28) Ibid, 5:59.

29) Ibid, 2:62.

30) Ibid, 6:33.

31) Ibid, 2:28. The prophet referred to here could be Nostradamus himself in which case we could perceive a resemblance to Saddam (Hussein).

32) Ibid, 5:25.

33) This is typically confusing. Considering this is one of the quatrains featuring astrology, *ver serp* could well mean 'toward Serpentis'. Serpentis is a fixed star at 19° Scorpio renowned for its dark nature. On the other hand, *ver serp* could refer to the Arab Prince as the true serpent.

34) *Centuries* 3:60.

35) Ibid, 2:89.

36) Ibid, 5:23.

37) Ibid, 2:30.

38) Ibid, 1:50.

39) Ibid, 5:54.

40) Ibid, 2:29.

41) Moses, it might be remembered also had a staff – and a pretty powerful one that parted the Red Sea – and I'm not the first person to propose that Moses knew

a thing or two about Hermeticism, aspects of which have filtered through into Jewish Kabbalism.

42) Matthew 24:24.

43) Gaia – the goddess of the Earth in Greek mythology – is an hypothesis created by Professor James Lovelock suggesting that the Earth too is an organic entity.

44) Cayce was known as the Sleeping Prophet because he gave all his pronouncements in a somnambulistic state.

45) Reading 396:15, 19 January 1934.

46) Charles Hapgood, *Earth's Shifting Crust* (Chilton, New York, 1958). Thomas Gold, 'Instability of the Earth's Axis of Rotation', in *Nature*, 175, 26 March 1975, 526. W. Munk and R. Revelle, 'Sea Level and the Rotation of the Earth', in *American Journal of Science*, 250, November 1952, 829 – 33.

47) Immanuel Velikovsky, *Worlds in Collision* (Doubleday, Garden City, NY, 1950).

48) Jeffrey Goodman, *We are the Earthquake Generation* (ARE Press, 1988).

49) Revelations 16:18.

50) Fontbrune interprets the Moon in Nostradamus's work to imply the republic as opposed to the Sun which symbolizes the monarchy. However, the Moon could symbolize the end of the Piscean Age which gives way to the Age of Aquarius (at that time considered to be ruled by Saturn). Although modern astrologers consider Pisces to be ruled by Neptune, this planet had not been discovered in Nostradamus's time. And while Jupiter was the original ruler of Pisces, in esoteric astrology Neptune is considered the higher octave of the Moon (see Chapter 7, p.164), therefore linking the Moon to Pisces – something Nostradamus as a mystic might well have opted to do.

51) Jean-Charles de Fontbrune, *Nostradamus: Countdown to Apocalypse* (Pan, 1983).

52) For full discussion, see Chapter 2, p.36.

53) See reference 50.

54) Ibid.

55) Baigent, Leigh and Lincoln, *The Holy Blood and The Holy Grail* (Corgi, 1989).

56) Erika Cheetham considers *plus oultre* to represent the device of the Emperor Charles V – *Plus oultre Carol Quint*. In this way the quatrain would read 'Chyren will be ruler of the world after Charles V.' But Cheetham confesses this isn't ideal. She concludes by saying, 'Until Chyren is satisfactorily explained these [Chyren] quatrains are impenetrable.'

2

The Dawn of a New Age

*T*HE SILENCE IN HEAVEN 'FOR ABOUT THE SPACE OF HALF AN HOUR' precedes the great earthquake and the subsequent fire and brimstone. But there is worse. According to John the Divine, even after the third part of all the waters and the Earth, sun and stars have been destroyed and all manner of plagues and unholy spectres heaped on mankind, anyone whose name does not appear in The Book of Life will be cast into the 'lake of fire', presumably for all eternity. On the other hand, those who are fortunate enough to be among the elect can enter the New Jerusalem to live in a state of grace with God. (This, by the way, is rather an oversimplification since before the establishment of the New Jerusalem, various selection processes, including a first death and a second, have to be accomplished – but I will cover this later.) Suffice to say that the first heaven and the first Earth pass away and 'a new heaven and a new Earth' come into being. In other words, as one world ends, another begins.

Almost all 'primitive' cultures across the globe retain a belief that there is more than one world age; and that as each world age passes away a new one is born. The Hopi Indians of North America have a tradition that three worlds existed prior to the one in which we now live: the first was destroyed by ice, the second by fire and the third by water. According to the Hindu tradition, there are also four world ages – each one becoming progressively more negative: first is the *Satya Yuga* (Age of Gold), then the *Treta Yuga* (Age of Silver), third, the *Dvarpara Yuga* (Age of Copper) and finally, the present age, the *Kali Yuga* (Age of Iron). Guatama, the Buddha, declared that the great Wheel of Dharma turned every 25 centuries – with the next revolution calculated to be at the end of this millennium.

The Great Astrological Ages are also cycles of roughly 25,000 years, which are further subdivided into 12 periods of approximately 2,000 years – each of those periods corresponding with a sign of the zodiac.[1] Although astrologers differ about the time the sub-age of Pisces in this Great Year will give way to that of Aquarius, if we consider the Piscean Age to have begun within 100 years or so of the birth of Jesus Christ, we must now be well within the aura of the Age of Aquarius. Indeed, some astrologers consider the stellium of planets in Aquarius on 5 February 1962 to have represented the birth of the Age of Aquarius.[2] One of the most striking characteristics of the Piscean Age[3] has been Christianity itself – a religion that has flourished for 2,000 years. Jesus was known as 'the Fisher of Men' and the secret symbol for the early Christians was the fish. In similar vein, the Age of Aries that preceded that of Pisces was one where the ram was a symbol of worship and before that, the calf, or cow, symbolic of the Age of Taurus. Indeed, each sub-age, or 'month' of the Great Astrological Year, synchronizes with a new expression of spiritual energy. So as we come toward the end of the Piscean Age, a new spirituality is struggling to be born – a spirituality that reflects the qualities of Aquarius.

The transition period between the end of one Age and the beginning of another is considered to be a time of great upheaval; it is as though the energies of one epoch are pitted against the incoming forces of the next, resulting in chaos, confusion and turmoil on all levels. The tribulations referred to in the Bible reflect this concept, as does the Great Purification in the Hopi tradition. This tumult is experienced on a multitude of levels so that the Earth itself quakes, edifices tumble, institutions collapse, economies crumble and people's attitudes, emotions, perceptions and very beings are torn apart. But within this stormy passage is the promise of hope and the expectation of a new Golden Age. And to lead us into that New Age, man needs some help from on high.

Christians, of course, anticipate the Second Coming, when Christ and his angelic host will lead the blessed into the New Jerusalem. For the Hopis, it will be the Great White Spirit who comes back to lead the way and for the followers of Buddha it will be Maitreya. The return of the great king is a mythical theme found in almost all cultures and belief systems – the Western mystery tradition, for instance, speaks of the return of Arthur and Merlin. But before I move on to discuss the traditional concept of the Second Coming and the arrival of a great Master who will lead us triumphantly through into a New Age of Light, I would like to return to one of the ideas – albeit a highly speculative one – discussed in Chapter 1: the return of the actual bloodline of Jesus as opposed to the supernatural resurrection of Christ or the reincarnation of the Messiah.

The authors of *The Holy Blood and the Holy Grail* propose that there is a king in waiting in France – not of the line of the Bourbons but descended from the royal house of David. According to Baigent, Leigh and Lincoln, Jesus Christ was indeed, the King of the Jews – not metaphorically speaking but truly so: he was a direct descendent of King David and of the tribe of Judah; his wife was Mary Magdalene of the tribe of Benjamin. After the crucifixion – which, the authors allege did not result in Jesus's death[4] – Mary Magdalene fled to France where the royal line continued to flourish, albeit underground and intermixing with other Jewish families, Romans, Visigoths and Franks, until it eventually emerged in the Merovingian dynasty in the fifth century AD. Documentary evidence of Jesus's lineage which had been secreted in a temple in Jerusalem was secured and brought back to France by the Knights Templars in the eleventh century. The Templars subsequently became guardians of this secret information which is purportedly maintained to this day by the mysterious order of the Prieuré of Sion. And, if we are to believe the reports of those claiming to have knowledge of the intentions of the Priory, before the end of the millennium, the rightful heir to this most holy and royal dynasty will take up his throne. Such a man will not be the reincarnation of Jesus Christ, nor his resurrection – except in a metaphorical sense – but a descendent of his very blood. Indeed, this evidence of the bloodline of Christ is at the very heart of the mystery of the Holy Grail.

Tales of love and chivalry centring on the quest for the magical object or great treasure (the Grail) that would restore a kingdom to its former glory proliferated in the Middle Ages. But as Baigent, Leigh and Lincoln note, 'During the mid to late twelfth century the originally pagan foundation for the Grail romances underwent a curious and extremely important transformation . . . on the basis of some elusive amalgamation, the Grail became inextricably linked with Jesus.'

In *Roman de l'Estoire dou Saint Graal*, penned by Robert de Boron at the end of the twelfth century, we learn that the Grail is the cup of the Last Supper. This cup passed into the hands of Joseph of Arimathea, who filled it with Christ's blood when he was taken from the cross. (Joseph later brought the Grail to England.) It is because the Grail was used as a container for Christ's blood that magical properties were endowed upon it. According to the authors of *Holy Blood, Holy Grail*, some of the Grail romances are not purely fictional, but stories woven around true events. The connection between knights in shining armour and the Knights Templars is self-evident, but there are other more subtle yet infinitely more powerful allegories. Baigent, Leigh and Lincoln point out that in several versions of *Perceval and the Quest for the Holy Grail*, the writers have gone to great pains to explain Perceval's lineage and his relationship to the mysterious Fisher King. They also describe one case[5] where Perceval comes across a castle housing a conclave of 'initiates' familiar with the Grail where he is received by two 'masters' and joined by 33 others. They comment, 'If the *Perlesvaus* was not actually composed by a Templar, it nevertheless provides a solid basis for linking the Templars with the Grail.'

While the Grail romances, like the biblical parables, make a wonderful story, they may also conceal truly remarkable knowledge and that knowledge is bound up in the very meaning of the term 'Holy Grail'. In many early manuscripts, the Grail is called the *Sangraal* – even Malory, in *Morte d'Arthur*, as late as the fifteenth century, called it the 'Sangreal'. Thus, Baigent, Leigh and Lincoln suggest that this word 'was subsequently broken in the wrong place. In other words "Sangraal" or "Sangreal" may not have been intended to divide into "San Graal" or "San Greal" – but into "Sang Raal" or "Sang Real". Or, to employ the modern spelling, *Sang Royal*, Royal blood.' In this way the Grail can be interpreted both as a vessel that contained the blood of the crucified Christ and the womb of the Magdalene – the receptacle that nurtured Christ's seed and assured the perpetuity of his bloodline.

Fantastic as many people believe *The Holy Blood and the Holy Grail* to be, the possibility that a descendant of Jesus Christ could make his appearance before the end of the century is surely no more incredible than the expectation that Christ will come down from heaven on a cloud with his angelic entourage. And while many historians and theologians would question the authors' interpretation of the evidence they have unearthed, there are still some curious anomalies that defy any other explanation. Certainly the explanation rings true that the Grail became inextricably linked with Jesus in the literature of the Middle Ages because of the Knights Templars' knowledge of the existence of a sacred bloodline. If this is mere coincidence then it is stretched even further by King Arthur's amalgamation with the Holy Grail. There are many curious coincidences between Arthur, Jesus Christ, the Merovingian dynasty and the Priory of Sion. The very name Arthur is derived from *arth*, the Welsh for 'bear' and both the Merovingian kings and the Priory of Sion are associated with *ursus*, the Latin for 'bear'. And although Arthur is a legendary king, he was based on a real King Arthur who lived around the turn of the sixth century – the peak of the Merovingian ascendancy. According to legend, one day King Arthur and/or Merlin will return to lead us into a new age of enlightenment – is the latter, the master magician, perhaps just an echo of the Priory's Grand Masters? And if the legend is based on truth then, perhaps, Pierre Plantard de St Clair (or his equivalent) will emerge the triumphant mediator in the face of an international crisis, declare his sacred heritage and lead us into a new era of global fraternity and enlightenment.

But, the enthronement of a descendant of Jesus notwithstanding, the reappearance of the Messiah or the Great White Spirit will not automatically guarantee entry into the new world – that right is not given unconditionally:

> When the Son of Man shall come in his glory . . . before him shall be gathered all nations: and he shall separate them one from another as a shepherd divideth his sheep from the goats: And he shall set the sheep on his right hand, but the goats on the left. Then shall the king say unto them on his right hand, Come, ye blessed of my Father, inherit the kingdom prepared for you. [6]

As far as fundamentalist Christians are concerned, Jesus will quite literally emerge from the skies and lift up his people – it will be a supernatural event. As Paul says in Thessalonians, 'For the Lord himself shall descend from heaven with a shout . . . and the dead in Christ shall rise first then we . . . shall be caught up together with them in the clouds to meet the Lord in the air: and so shall we ever be with the Lord.' [7] And while Christians consider that all those who believe in Christ and follow the biblical message represent the chosen to be 'caught up', anyone who has any doubts about his or her credentials can seek reassurance in a sign. St John makes the point that 'the servants of God who have been sealed in their foreheads' represent the elect who shall be saved and allowed to enter the 'new heaven and the new earth'. So what might this seal be? And how can we ensure that we have one so that we will be lifted up and not left behind with the goats?

Short of all Christians at some point in the future being forced to carry some kind of mark on their foreheads it is more likely that this 'seal' is not a physical brand but the mark of the believer in the sense that God knows his own. However, this seal could also signify the mystical third eye, which is situated in the centre of the forehead near the pineal gland. [8] While our two physical eyes are concerned with outer vision, according to mystical tradition the third eye is the organ of inner perception. It links with the divine and can be activated in each of us by increasing our sensitivity and awareness. Jesus Christ appears to be talking about the properties of the third eye when he says, 'If thine eye be single, thy whole body shall be full of light.'[9] The third eye must also be implicit in the statement that when the Messiah returns every eye shall see him (for presumably by that time, after the tribulations, telecommunications will be defunct).

It has always seemed to me to be rather simplistic that merely by declaring oneself a Christian, believing the Bible verbatim and attending church services regularly an individual will gain entry into God's kingdom, while those who may spend their lives working with the Light, healing and spreading love, will be denied that right simply because they follow a different religious path – or no declared religion at all. I'm sure that entry into the Kingdom of God first necessitates an opening to the 'God-light' within and that demands practice, effort and awareness, as well as trust and faith – dogma and tunnel vision serve only to obscure the God-light. And this God-light within is nurtured through the channel of the third eye – the 'seal'. Thus to be prepared for the coming of the Lord and the elevation to the New Age, this third eye must be opened – at least to some degree.

Now, it may be that Jesus Christ or Maitreya or the Great White Spirit will indeed appear in the recognizable form of a man, I don't know. And I don't want to offend those who do believe this, but, drawing from my own Western-based Christian tradition, I am much more inclined to believe that it is the Christos *energy* that will be made manifest. As Luke says, 'And when he was demanded of the Pharisees, when the kingdom of God should come, he answered them and said, The kingdom of God cometh not with observation . . . the kingdom of God is within you.'[10] The awareness of the Christ within and the mass development of Christ in consciousness is to my mind what the return of Christ is really all about.

To begin with, I wasn't sure quite how the Christos energy would come in. Would an angel stand at the foot of my bed one night and direct a beam of light toward me? And would this happen to people all over the world? I almost came to distrust the idea completely until extraordinary events in the world at large and in my personal life began to occur – it was as though people were beginning to gain a larger perspective on and an enlightened comprehension of divisive issues and global ecology. Iron-clad barriers – both literal and psychological – were being demolished, corrupt totalitarian regimes were being overthrown, oppressed peoples were at last emerging from their incarceration. As the Iron Curtain was smashed to pieces and East and West were no longer separated by the wall of their political differences, a new spirit of union was born. At this time, in the December of 1989, all around me barriers between individuals were being dismantled and new relationships born out of the ashes of the old – time and again I would hear friends, colleagues and clients saying, 'Something's going on . . . I can feel it.'

A matter of weeks before the frontier between East and West Germany was breached, I received a press release from the United States. It was the sort of thing I would normally heave into the rubbish bin, but since it had been forwarded to me by someone I respect enormously, I decided to give it some serious thought. The press release came in the form of a channelled message from an entity called Amatron:

In your evolution you move into times of extraordinary change, times that are momentous for your history, for your eternity, for your earth. During November 17, 18 & 19 [1989] there will be a puncturing of your reality here as you know it, a Warping of Time. It is the beginning of a grand cycle . . . Understand that you presently have a time pocket, a delay mechanism. Time-space. You have delays that create minutes, months, years, lifetimes, before a manifestation comes into your life. During the November Time Warp there will be a dimensional collapsing of time in which your time pocket will be diminished and literally put on hold. As a result, what you hold in consciousness and feeling is going to manifest faster and without this elongated time pocket. It is going to be an instant mirror for you.

Your Time Warp is being created by a shifting in consciousness. It is an evolutionary process, an expansion of energy. Because you have invoked higher consciousness you have magnetised to you a gravitational field that is now pulling you to a new dimension. . . . Your whole galaxy is expanding in consciousness. It is speeding up in frequency . . .

This is an opportunity for each one of you to get a direct experience of what it is to be in Christed energy, to experience miracles of healing, miracles of joy, miracles of creation, miracles of life. You create from your consciousness and your feelings. You manifest not always according to your pictures but always according to the desires and feelings within you . . . [At this period in November] it is important for you to heal feelings that have been denied. Emotional healings are coming up in your lives at this time, situations that confront your feeling level, providing opportunities to heal old pain, old anger, old anguish, old polarity, old inequality, old unworthiness. You are all preparing on a Soul level to be able to hold willingly the clearest consciousness . . .

All your meditations for planetary peace and healing that are brought forth with purified unconditional feeling are going to have an opportunity to be accelerated and intensified 1,000% during the Time Warp. Every one of you who is aligned at that time in the Now from your heart creating pure love for all things and all peoples will radiate and reverse the negativity of 100 others who are ignorant and asleep.

At this time I was involved in a small healing group and we all decided to 'offer up the light' at the times suggested in the press release. And while we still retained a degree of Anglo-Saxon scepticism about the communication from Amatron, we nevertheless opened our hearts and minds to the possibility. I don't think any of us were prepared for the stupendous events that followed. I remember watching the television broadcasts of the overthrow of the Ceauşescu regime and the opening of the borders between East and West Germany. Small children, their eyes saucer-like with dazed perplexity, watching grown-ups clutch and embrace each other – scenes at once jubilant and traumatic. These events were momentous enough to remain etched in my memory always, but they assumed an even greater significance in a macrocosmic-microcosmic sort of way since I was about to undergo a series of experiences that were to utterly transform my life. There was no need for an angel with a beam of light: I could perceive the new consciousness at work out in the world and I could feel it with my own heart.

While this expansion of consciousness was, and is, almost palpable, I have to take it on trust that it is concurrent with a 'speeding up of frequency'. Amatron is just one voice of many who talk about this change in vibration. In preparation of his book, *We are the Earthquake Generation*, Dr Jeffrey Goodman worked with six gifted American psychics, who independently referred to this concept:

> An entirely new vibrational environment is projected for the earth. In addition to the spiritual changes people initiate, they will become more spiritually aware as a result of the geological changes foreseen because these changes eventually will establish a more harmonious vibrational environment to live in. The earth will undergo a self-cleansing process to overcome the distorted vibrations that man, through his free will, has created over the centuries.

The influence of the new vibration will have a different effect on different people. Hindu philosophy teaches that man's behaviour can be divided into three categories, or *guna*s – *Sattva* (purify), perfection, rhythm, harmony, self-realization and a healthy nature, *Rajas* (inertia), passions, attachment, egocentricity and self-orientation, and *Tamas* (regression), ignorance, darkness, degeneracy and base tendencies. While each of us oscillate between these three states, there is always one that predominates and thus characterizes a basic state of being, or consciousness. Moria Timms in *The Six O'Clock Bus* puts forward the idea that with the increasing light vibration those of predominantly Rajas disposition (the average state of the masses) will suffer dissipation of vital tendencies, becoming restless as negative qualities surface to cause anxiety, disorientation and confusion. Furthermore, basically Tamasic types 'do not have much to look forward to as the higher frequency triggers inertia, delusions, sickness and violence'. On the other hand, primarily Sattvic individuals 'will gain in wisdom and understanding as the vibration continues to increase. It could be said, more simply, that the awakening is like the two-edged sword and that vibrational acceleration nourishes a pure condition but badly over-amps fair to middling characters. *The light that illuminates also blinds.*'

Goodman's psychics, like Cayce and many others, perceive this shift in consciousness to go in tandem with shifts in the Earth. We are given to understand that things must change on a terrestrial level as well as the psychical plane in preparation for existence in a more enlightened state. To go back to the earlier discussion about the tribulations prior to the coming of the Kingdom of God or the new Golden Age, whatever the nature of the turmoil, the experiences must be interpreted as a proving ground for the spirit. While in some Christian quarters it is considered that 'the righteous' will be whisked away before any of the nastiness begins, there are others who believe, rather more along the lines of the Great Purification, that none will escape the term of trial since it is the very experience of the torment that will separate the sheep from the goats.

And in many ways, earthquakes and wars notwithstanding, humanity is already in crisis on a collective and personal level. Famine is decimating a third of humanity, economies throughout the world are in crisis and AIDS is running rife globally – and with no sign of a cure. All these things, and more, have an effect on individual lives and everyone is suffering and fighting for survival in some way.

But, according to many of the New Age communicators, however formidable the tribulations might be, the Earth will not be destroyed completely:

I can tell you that the massive nuclear holocaust that you so fear will never become a reality because the forces of the universe will not allow it . . . [but] while the cosmic forces will not allow nuclear destruction because of the cosmic consequences, they will not prevent physical calamity from touching Earth . . .[11]

Mentally superior beings have always monitored your life behaviours – in a constant surveillance of what earth people are doing – especially in the ever growing insanity of your space race and the invention of advanced weaponry. Since the atomic bomb, they have been particularly positioned around the earth to assure protection to space and the life forms in it; but they have watched for thousands of years. [12]

Jeffrey Goodman maintains that his American group of top psychics insist that spiritual help for mankind is on its way:

Abrahamsen, Karish and Elkins . . . speak movingly of the coming of a messiah. They all speak of the return of 'John the Forerunner' and of Jesus Christ. According to Cayce, by the year 2000 a number of Christ's disciples will be living on earth again. Then John the Baptist will appear, going by the name of John Pineal, and give to the world the new order of things before Christ finally appears. According to Abrahamsen, Christ will bring many spiritual teachers with him. Abrahamsen said that people from outer space will also come to the earth, primarily to observe. He said they are too afraid of what our reactions to them would be to make themselves fully known at this time. [13]

Jeffrey Goodman also poses the question of what happens if the great conflagration does indeed come to pass:

. . . what of those who die? The psychics, who all believe in reincarnation, said that those who perish won't really have lost their lives. They will have many opportunities to reincarnate and live out new lives on earth . . . [And] what of the survivors? . . . [My] psychics feel there is a definite plan for the survivors. They have spoken in mystical terms about a new 'root race' coming into existence with the Aquarian Age . . . the survivors will have the opportunity for true spiritual growth. [They] will learn to give thanks in the midst of catastrophe. The greatest growth will come to the children as they learn to believe in the presence of God and to contact 'higher sources' for information and guidance. [14]

These times in which you live [are] some of the most difficult which the universe as a whole and the earth plane in particular have ever had to face. But do not allow yourselves to be drawn into thinking that time will run out, that the cataclysm will come and many will be flung into outer chaos and confusion. We speak now always of the changes with optimism and joy in our vision of all that is to be. The changes precede an age of gold, and in a large part constitute a slow, learning, growing process which is even now in operation on a very wide scale. The final shift into the fourth dimension will not at the time be pleasant, and there will indeed be many who are not ready to go forward, so many will be taken and many left. Yet do not forget that the light in all its power and strength is tempered with infinite compassion, and not one of those who are left will be forgotten. If they are not ready, then this experience will be part

of their evolution, but there will be those who will watch over them and
guide their steps until they are ready to enter into the new
consciousness. [15]

And the Golden Age itself? What are we to anticipate? Abrahamsen says
the Golden Age 'will take several hundred years to develop fully . . .
government, instead of regulating people, would put its emphasis on
helping people to develop and regulate themselves. Mind-to-mind
communication will be commonplace. While transportation will still be
dominated by the aeroplane, there will be some teleportation . . .
Education will teach people how to tap their inner power. Agriculture
will use prayer to control crops and rainfall. The sun and the earth's
electromagnetic field will be the main sources of energy. Psychics will
be used to guide successful research. Medicine will rely heavily on
healing via colour, often with dramatic results. Cancer will be cured.
There will even be limb regeneration. Crystals are supposed to be used
for healing and energy.' [16]

Before I go on to discuss my own concepts of the New Age and the
nature of the transition period prior to its advent, I would like to
summarize so far. A New Age is upon us and with the dawn comes a
change in 'frequency' which is causing different reactions in humanity
according to individual levels of awareness. This new Golden Age,
astrologically viewed as that of Aquarius, will be a kind of Utopia; prior
to our entry into that glorious time, there will be a great purification
and subsequent weeding out of the elect and the non-elect. In order to
aid humanity's transition from one world to the next, spiritual entities –
possibly Jesus Christ himself – will appear. There is even the possibility
that a flesh and blood descendant of Jesus Christ will instead lead us
through the perilous journey to a new era of peace and understanding.

The more I have pondered on the above scenarios, the less I am
convinced that Jesus Christ, or Maitreya, will return, either in the sense
of the reincarnation of a Great Master or as a supernatural
manifestation. I am much more inclined to believe that Christ, or some
such archetype, will manifest within our consciousness, and it is this
awareness that precipitates our entry into another level of being – a
New Age. While this is not an original concept, I have my own ideas
about the utilization of this new frequency and why it is so vital that
we recognize and open ourselves to its properties.

The Earth is now in such a state of crisis that it may well be that there
is no way in which we can reverse the self-destruct process, no matter
how many damaging chemicals we eliminate, no matter how many trees
we plant. Even if we put a total halt to the creation and usage of nuclear

power, the pollution by nuclear waste – and other deadly chemical waste – of the seas and the atmosphere is already irrevocable. As more and more of the produce of the Earth becomes inedible, as more and more creatures of the Earth are poisoned by the environment and whole species decimated by strange viruses and as the more and more dangerous it becomes to breathe in the oxygen or venture out into the ultra-violet light, the less and less we humans are capable of functioning. It is my belief that, short of a genuine miracle, humanity as it is now simply cannot survive. But I do believe humanity *as it can become*, will.

In short, I believe that if we open ourselves to a higher state of awareness our psyches can become channels for a new powerful stream of consciousness, Christos energy by another name, and in this way we can be borne along on a growing wave of finer consciousness (a higher frequency) into a new, more rarefied state of being. We already know that changes in the emotional or psychic state of an individual trigger changes in the physical body; in the same way, but on a grander scale, this harnessing of greater consciousness will in turn precipitate huge changes in the way our physical bodies function. In higher consciousness we feel a sense of expanding, of rising up and so it is through the route of higher consciousness, of contacting the divine Self, the God within, that we can be 'caught up' as St Paul says, and transported to a new dimension. Let me explain.

Adepts have through the ages been capable of extraordinary feats – levitation, bilocation[17] and teleportation for instance. Such feats are not accomplished by accident or by natural talent alone, but by diligence. Developing the skill to overcome the forces of matter through the power of the mind – the harnessing of spiritual forces and the will to control the material plane – takes considerable time and great discipline. But such skills are available to everyone given the desire and effort to allow them to develop. Among the phenomena familiar to adepts, yogis and shamans alike is the ability to leave the body at will – to separate from the physical body while retaining consciousness elsewhere. Carlos Castaneda's shaman, Don Juan,[18] talks about the 'double body'; elsewhere in occult literature this second body of consciousness is known as the astral body.

Spontaneous out-of-the-body experiences are not uncommon, although they are extraordinary in their nature: to find yourself awake in another place in the full knowledge that you are in bed asleep, or simply beside or above your sleeping form changes your whole perception of reality. Indeed, this is what happened to me. From my first alarming encounter of separation from the body, I discovered that there was nothing to fear from being outside my physical self and instead

I began to look forward to any disembodied forays. As each one occurred, I was able to negotiate my way with increasing confidence and dexterity – sometimes finding myself in busy high streets, at other times in a strange lunar-like landscape with two suns which I came to understand was the Astral Plane. But wherever I was, the quality of light was extraordinarily vivid and there was a luminosity about everything. And although I could not manipulate other living things or aspects of the environment as one might do in a dream, I found I could fly – indeed, it is a skill I've been able to improve over the years. But perfecting a manoeuvre when once in the double body presents far less of a challenge than getting into it in the first place. Leaving the body at will requires an enormous amount of effort and practice; effectively, what must happen is that the body must be sent to sleep while the mind is kept awake.

Now, there is a purpose behind this little excursion into astral projection which will be revealed shortly. First I want to return to the subject of the frequency change and the expansion of consciousness. One of the points raised by Kenneth Ring in *Heading Toward Omega*[19] is that phenomena such as kundalini[20] and NDEs (Near Death Experiences)[21] appear to be on the increase – indeed up until 1984, when the book was published, around eight million Americans were reported to have had NDEs. Since such experiences not only transform people's attitudes and perceptions about life but, in the case of kundalini particularly, precipitate an increase in intellectual functioning and an enhanced state of awareness, Ring hypothesizes that the effect of so many enlightened individuals on the planet will lead to a mass heightening of consciousness. In *Omega*, Ring quotes Gopi Krishna, who says, 'The final target of the [kundalini-mediated] evolutionary process is to carry the whole of mankind toward a higher dimension of consciousness.'[22] Ring himself proposes that 'NDErs – and others who have had similar awakenings – [may] collectively represent an evolutionary thrust toward higher consciousness for humanity at large.' He further suggests that the 'NDE itself is an evolutionary mechanism that has the effect of jump stepping individuals into the next stage of human development by unlocking spiritual potentials previously dormant.' He goes on to speculate, 'Are we seeing in such people – as they mutate from their pre-NDE personalities into more loving and compassionate individuals – the prototype of a new, more advanced strain of the human species striving to come into manifestation? No longer *Homo sapiens* perhaps, but tending toward what John White has called *Homo noeticus*?[23] Could NDErs be, then, an evolutionary bridge to the next step in our destiny as a species . . .?'

To add further support for his hypothesis, Ring quotes from the works of the Jesuit philosopher and paleontologist, Pierre Teilhard de Chardin, who argued that human evolution was headed towards a transhuman state he called 'noo-genesis', the birth of a unified planetary mind aware of its essential divinity. These latter concepts of humanity's thrust toward greater consciousness are not at odds with the ideas discussed earlier of 'a new vibrational environment being projected for the earth', for this frequency change is not something imposed on humanity from 'out there', but something that occurs in tandem with humanity's development. As Amatron says, 'Because you have invoked higher consciousness, you have magnetised to you a gravitational field that is pulling you to a new dimension.' There have always been enlightened individuals who have operated on a higher plane of consciousness than the rest of us; the difference is that now there are more and more people accessing this higher dimension within themselves. And the more and more people there are who do so the more they facilitate higher consciousness for everyone else.

Rupert Sheldrake in *A New Science of Life: The Hypothesis of Formative Causation*[24] proposed that the exact shape of living things and their behaviour is not dependent on DNA and information transmitted from cell to cell, but a response to a previously shaped field – a 'morphogenetic field'. In his book, he uses as an example an experiment conducted by William McDougall, a Harvard psychologist, in 1920. McDougall trained a group of rats to swim through a water maze; he then taught the descendants of these rats the same procedure over 20 generations. As each subsequent generation of rats were taught to negotiate the water maze, the quicker they were to learn how until the last generation picked up the skill 10 times as fast as the first batch. Applying Sheldrake's theory, the first group of rats generated a morphogenetic field for negotiating the water maze that then transmitted itself via 'morphic resonance' to subsequent generations. In this way, we have a working hypothesis of how higher consciousness could manifest within humanity as a whole. As the science writer Peter Russell put it, 'Applying Sheldrake's theory to the development of higher states of consciousness, we might predict that the more individuals begin to raise their own levels of consciousness, the stronger the morphogenetic field for higher states would become, and the easier it would be for others to move in that direction. Society would gather momentum toward enlightenment.'[25]

Morphogenetic resonance could also play a crucial part in other skills that humanity needs to develop. A little earlier I discussed the out-of-the-body state and how this experience tends to occur spontaneously but is much more difficult to achieve at will. But why should humanity need to develop the ability to move out of the physical body? If it is that we are indeed approaching a point where the Earth will not be able to sustain life as we know it or we are to face massive Earth shifts or nuclear war, the ability to vacate the body at will must be an attractive proposition at the very least.

Of course, this begs the question that even if we can leave our bodies to escape the pain and trauma of a holocaust of one sort or another, in the event of our physical bodies being reduced to ashes, or at the very least if our immune systems are in terminal decline, how can we return to those bodies? And if we cannot return to those bodies, doesn't that mean that we are technically dead? Or worse, have we joined the great un-dead? The prospect of roaming around a poisoned, barren Earth until the end of time isn't much of a prospect for anyone. Faced with such a spectre, a sudden violent death has its attractions – straight through the 'tunnel' described by NDErs and into the 'city of light'. But that's just the point – we do not want to go to *that* heaven, we want to create a *heaven on Earth*, albeit in a new dimension, the fourth dimension spoken of by mystics (including Nostradamus) and channelled entities (like Gildas).

Occult and Eastern tradition teach that there are various planes of existence. Theosophy, for instance, teaches of seven – Divine, Monadic, Spiritual, Intuitional, Mental, Astral and the Physical. These worlds beyond the physical are not separate in the way that the planets in the solar system are, but these planes interpenetrate each other; *they depend for their differences upon the relative density of the matter that composes them, and the consequent difference in the rates at which the matter in each world vibrates*. The astral plane, which is the level beyond the physical, is the world to which we have the easiest access and frequently enter in spontaneous out-of-the-body states. At death, according to occult and Eastern thought, the soul sheds its various 'bodies' as it moves from one world to the next. The Christian tradition, of course, teaches only of one world beyond the physical – a heaven and Earth – and even heaven cannot be reached at death, but only when Christ returns to resurrect the dead. The Near Death Experience tends to conflict with this latter view in that many NDErs talk of Jesus Christ, or a being of light, indicating a radiant place they can enter if they decide not to 'go back'. Eastern religions would, in the main, consider this heavenly place not to be Nirvanah, but the Intuitional (*Buddhi*) or Mental (*Manas*) plane; the level at which all the thought-forms of heaven and the various gods exist.

As I perceive it, this new Golden Age is synchronous with humanity's evolution to a new state of being; a new dimension of consciousness.

This not only implies a new state of higher consciousness in the sense of awareness and perception which in turn breeds universal love, harmony and peace, but a new Earth plane. Whether this is because the Earth gradually becomes less and less able to support human existence, or because the planet topples over in space or erupts in a series of earthquakes or explosions, the only way humanity can welcome in a New Age is by an exodus from physical Earth into a fourth-dimensional reality.[26]

Without the transition from the physical body to the second body of consciousness (the astral body or the double body) the death of the physical body would lead to the normal sequence typified by the Near Death Experience – through the 'tunnel' and into the 'city of light'. To circumvent this process and so ensure entry into the fourth-dimensional Earth which represents the New Age of enlightened mankind – *homo noeticus* perhaps – a state, incidentally where there can be no death as we conceptualize it, the ability to move into the second body before death must be achieved. This new enlightened humanity would in effect be a sort of mutation having human shape but comprising an altogether different density of matter due to its level of consciousness.

Now, it may be that many individuals all over the world will begin to access the out-of-the-body-state, initially spontaneously but ultimately at will, and the more this occurs the more other people will experience the same phenomena by means of morphogenetic resonance. Since such an experience automatically forces an individual to change his attitude to reality, there will develop a burgeoning interest in spiritual matters, in meditation or T'ai Ch'i, and a subsequent greater awareness of self and the interconnectedness of all things. Gradually, a perceptible shift in consciousness will take place, in which the world not only begins to look different (perhaps there is a luminous quality to all living things or the sky assumes an iridescent hue), but telepathic communication and other strange phenomena (completing a journey in a fraction of the time than by all laws of motion it should, for example) start to occur, until the higher state accessed only in meditation becomes the normal range of consciousness. At the same time, an individual who experiences this may find that he has developed an infinite supply of compassion for his fellow man and that he identifies with the suffering of others; he can express love without contrivance and feel as never before. He may not be a saint, but he is super-aware, super-conscious. He is also aware through dreams and a profound sense of inner knowing that he is being helped and guided; he may be directly contacted by beings of light or hear their voices. The more he functions in higher consciousness, the more his third eye opens to allow the God-light to enter and slowly filter through his system right down to cellular level. Such an individual is ready for the quantum jump to the next stage of evolution.

It may be that as time goes by the increasing level of consciousness allows the fourth dimension to gradually 'overtake' the existing vibratory rate of the three-dimensional world, so that as each generation increases its level of consciousness, eventually humanity as a whole will become the enlightened, spiritual beings that will characterize the new Golden Age. Or it may be that the propulsion into the fourth-dimensional state of existence will be fairly swift. Either way, the time of preparation is now.

In light of the prophets and the channelled communicators, it would appear that the latter scenario is the more likely. As Gildas says, 'The changes precede an age of gold, and in a large part constitute a slow, learning, growing process which is even now in operation on a very wide scale [1979]. The final shift into the fourth dimension will not at the time be pleasant . . .' We might assume from statements like this that some sort of cataclysm does indeed provoke an almighty shift into another dimension of being. It may be that those who are 'sealed in their forehead', those who are already operating in a permanent or semi-permanent state of higher consciousness, will either have a forewarning that facilitates their exodus from the physical body, or it may be that through their openness and preparedness they are automatically shunted into the incoming dimension. The vision of John the Divine reveals that 144,000 elect will be 'taken up' before the dreadful events precipitated by the opening of the seventh seal.[27] Taking this second scenario, it may be that prior to the 'final conflagration' those whose third eye is indeed open perceive Jesus Christ, or other great Masters, who enable them to move through the frequency veil from one reality to another – their very presence facilitating this process. Those whose level of consciousness is not raised enough simply fail to see the light and transmogrify.

But what will happen to these 'goats'? Gildas says, '. . . there will indeed be many who are not ready to go forward, so many will be taken and many will be left. Yet . . . not one of those who are left will be forgotten.' St John, the originator of the concept of the sheep and goats talks about this process in far more dramatic terms:

And I saw the souls of them that were beheaded for the witness of Jesus and for the word of God . . . and they lived and reigned with Christ a thousand years. But the rest of the dead lived not again until the thousand years were finished. This is the first resurrection. Blessed and holy is he that hath part in the first resurrection: on such the second death hath no power . . . And death and hell were cast into the lake of fire. This is the second death. [28]

In other words, after Armageddon only the righteous souls are resurrected from the dead and taken to join the 144,000 that have already gone ahead into the New Age. Those who are not 'dead in Christ' are not resurrected for 1,000 years and then, if their names do not appear in The Book of Life, they are relegated to a second death – an eternal one. But 'death' may not imply physical death but a state of ignorance, an inability to open to the higher level of consciousness that makes for entry into the 'new Earth'. Thus the 'dead', the remaining goats, still continue to experience the 'normal' process of life and death – unable to recognize their innate potential to become alive in God forever. Even if the cataclysm wipes out the greater part of mankind it may be that a few pockets of people do survive. And although St John can give them no hope, entities like Gildas and Argatha assure us that they will be helped and not forgotten.

Yet entry into the New Age, even for the elect, does not imply an escape from the tribulations. Of the 144,000, John says, 'These are they which came out of great tribulation . . . [but] they shall hunger no more neither thirst any more . . . and God shall wipe away all the tears from their eyes.' [29] In John's sequence of events the chosen who are whisked away before the opening of the seventh seal have nevertheless experienced the heavens departing as a scroll and all manner of continental drifts and assorted catastrophes. To date, of course, we have experienced massive earthquakes in Armenia and China, the eruption of Mount St Helens and many more earthquakes that have registered alarmingly high on the Richter scale – even Britain, normally an earthquake-free zone, has had two (the epicentre of the second, in Wales, was forceful enough to be felt 200 miles away in London), not to mention two hurricanes that devastated the South East of England in as many years. These geological effects combined with all the other aforementioned crises currently facing humanity make it difficult to deny that the tribulations are already upon us. Life, both on the collective front and individually, is continually presenting us with extremes – some extraordinarily high-level events at the same time as some desperately awful ordeals. It does indeed appear that as consciousness increases to a higher level there is a counter-movement in the opposite direction. It also seems that the experiences we are forced to undergo – with no apparent choice or control – are the 'stuff' of transformation. In other words, we are being tested to our limits of endurance, whether in the sense of physical pain, financial hardship or emotional anguish, in order that we may find the route to higher consciousness. This is not a pleasant process, for we are being stripped of everything that has comprised our previous support systems; indeed, it smacks in no uncertain terms of the Great Purification.

I have discussed at length some of the requirements, or rather the effects, of New Age consciousness; in the process I may have inadvertently implied that becoming enlightened demands great spiritual discipline and intellectual feats. But while the mind – not the intellect – is the doorway to higher consciousness, the pathway is through the heart, through love. It is a pathway available to us all. Though our individual tests may involve financial or professional survival, physical or emotional torture, it is the triumph of the spirit above the circumstances that limit us, the transcendence, through love, of the tribulations that beset us that ultimately pushes us through the barrier of our small selves to the Divine within – and thereby grants us our entry to the new Golden Age of greater consciousness. Occasionally we meet our divinity in the joy of union with another person – whether a child, a parent, a friend or a lover – and while this exchange allows us to glimpse the potential God within us, it is all too often only transient. It seems that only through a dark and difficult passage, the heart tried by pain, that we make that assent to a level where we can locate that divinity and sustain it. This time is now.

The dawning of a New Age hinges upon the manifestation of greater consciousness within each individual. This consciousness can be perceived as the Christos energy or simply as a higher vibration of love and awareness. Either way, mankind is on the threshold of a new world. Pierre Teilhard de Chardin believed humanity was headed toward a transhuman state, Robert Graves considered we were moving into a New Age which was neither an epoch where the solar-masculine influence was manifest supreme, nor the lunar-feminine, but an Age of Magic; an age of super-humans. Aquarius is the zodiac's water-bearer – not the water of the feminine, but the ether of spiritual enlightenment. Uranus, Aquarius's ruling planet, symbolizes the upper reaches of the celestial regions and the principle of limitless freedom and thought and spirit. [30] We have everything to look forward to. But before the first light of the New Age can dawn we must pass through the dark hours of the night.

As I began this chapter, I selected a rune, [31] giving as my question: 'The issue is the New Age.' Inguz was the rune that fell into my hands:

The completion of beginnings is what Inguz requires. It may mark a time of joyous deliverance, of new life, a new path . . . The period at or just before birth is often a dangerous one. Movement involves danger. Now is the time to enter the delivery room.[32]

Appendix

1) These astrological Great Ages occur because of the phenomenon of the precession of the equinoxes: the Earth wobbles on its axis as it rotates around the sun; in so doing, the vernal point (the first degree of Aries) moves fractionally (about 50 seconds) every year. In this way, the first point of Aries seems to move backwards through the zodiac taking roughly 25,000 years to complete a full circle of 360 degrees.

2) On 5 February 1962, there was a total solar eclipse at 15° 43" Aquarius; the same day the Sun conjuncted Mercury; Venus conjuncted Jupiter at 18° 42" Aquarius; Mars was also in Aquarius within a degree of conjuncting Saturn at 3° 48" Aquarius. And even if this massive stellium in Aquarius did not herald the New Age, it certainly heralded the era of such Aquarian phenomena as psychedelia and flower-power.

3) Pisces is known as the sign of the Fishes.

4) Baigent, Leigh and Lincoln, authors of *The Holy Blood and the Holy Grail* (Corgi, 1989) hypothesize that Jesus may well have died at Masada in AD 72. More appositely, perhaps, in the April of 1991, a controversial theory that Christ did not die on the cross was put forward by retired physician Trevor Lloyd Davies, and his theologian wife, Margaret. In an article in the *Journal of the Royal College of Physicians*, Davies maintains that the flogging Jesus received led to his premature collapse on the cross: Jesus may well only have lost consciousness because of diminished blood supply to the brain 'and is more likely to have been resuscitated than resurrected'. (Taken from a report in *The Times*: 27 April 1991.)

5) *Perlesvaus* was penned by an anonymous author whom the authors of *The Holy Blood and the Holy Grail* believe to have been a Templar – they quote as a reference *Knight and Chivalry* by R. Barber (Ipswich, 1974) 2nd edition.

6) Matthew 25:31.

7) Thessalonians 4:16,17.

8) The pineal gland is a small organ in the centre of the brain whose function still remains somewhat of a mystery to scientists. According to Dr Douglas Baker in his book *The Opening of the Third Eye* (The Aquarian Press, 1977):

> The human pineal is made up of two types of cells – pineocytes and astrocytes – the latter are found throughout the nervous system, but they are not present in any other gland in the human body. The pineal, therefore, appears to be a gland which also acts as nerve tissue . . . a situation that has given the scientist quite a headache, because theoretically it just isn't possible . . . Although the pineal gland is linked with the brain, it is not activated by the nerve cells that surround it. It appears, in fact, to be activated by 'messages' that reach it from the eyes . . . messages conveyed by the pupils rather than retinal images.

9) Matthew 6:2.

10) Luke 17:20, 21.

11) Meredith Young, *Argatha – a Course in Cosmic Awareness* (Gateway, 1987). Extract quoted by D. M. A. Leggett in *Facing the Future* (Pilgrim Books, 1990).

12) Virginian Essene, *New Teachings for an Awakening Humanity* (SEE Publishing Company, USA, 1986).

13) Jeffrey Goodman, *We are the Earthquake Generation* (ARE Press, 1988).

14) Ibid.

15) Ruth White, *The Healing Spectrum* (Neville Spearman, 1979).

16) Ibid.

17) Bilocation is a phenomenon whereby an individual is seen simultaneously in two places.

18) Carlos Castaneda has written eight books to date on his experiences of shamanism: *The Teachings of Don Juan: A Yaqui Way of Knowledge*; *A Separate Reality: Further Conversations with Don Juan*; *Journey To Ixtlan: The Lessons of Don Juan*; *Tales of Power*; *The Second Ring of Power*; *The Eagle's Gift*; *The Fire from Within* and *The Power of Silence: Further Lessons of Don Juan* (Simon & Schuster).

19) Kenneth Ring, *Heading Toward Omega* (Quill, New York, 1985).

20) In Sanskrit, *kundalini* means 'coiled up' (like a serpent). Kundalini energy lies at the base of the spine; when this energy is activated it travels up the spine energizing all the chakras. In some cases, the experience of raising kundalini is similar to an extraordinarily intense orgasm: to begin with the sensation is that of an exquisite orgasm, but the orgasm gathers an increasing intensity that ultimately permeates the whole of the body – the energy can be perceived to extend out beyond the body; it is at one stage ecstatic yet as it rises to flood the brain, the sensation is painful – rather like a series of electric shocks. Kundalini is one of the most beautiful ways of gaining enlightenment. Ring says:

> . . . however the actual process of kundalini arousal may be experienced, it is held that this energy it draws upon has the capacity to catapult the individual into a higher state of consciousness . . . The idea that this energy, which is held to be both divine and divinizing, is responsible for humanity's evolution toward higher consciousness is called *the kundalini hypothesis*.

21) Since the early 1970s – initially through Elisabeth Kübler Ross and her work with terminally ill patients and later through Dr Raymond Moody and others – increasing literature has emerged on the Near Death Experience. People who have been pronounced clinically dead and later resuscitated have reported that they have left the body and undergone a series of events that convinced them that there was, indeed, life after death. Intriguingly, regardless of race, socio-economic, age or religion, NDErs recount similar core experiences – for instance, travelling through a tunnel, entering light and being shown (by one or more spiritual beings) a city of light in the distance. I have discussed this phenomenon at length in *The Forces of Destiny* (Weidenfeld, 1990).

22) Gopi Krishna, *The Awakening of Kundalini*, as quoted by Kenneth Ring in *Heading Toward Omega*.

23) From John White, *Jesus, Evolution and the Future of Humanity*, as quoted by Kenneth Ring in *Heading Toward Omega*:

> *Homo noeticus* is the name I [John White] give to the emerging form of humanity. 'Noetics' is a term meaning the study of consciousness, and that

activity is a primary characteristic of members of the new breed . . . Their changed psychology is based on expression of feeling, not suppression. The motivation is cooperative and loving, not competitive and aggressive. Their logic is multilevel/integrated/simultaneous, not linear/sequential/either-or. Their sense of identity is embracing-collective, not isolated-individual. Their psychic abilities are used for benevolent and ethical purposes . . . They seek a culture founded in higher consciousness, a culture whose institutions are based on love and wisdom, a culture that fulfils the perennial philosophy.

24) Rupert Sheldrake, *A New Science of Life: The Hypothesis of Formative Causation* (Paladin, 1988).
25) Peter Russell, *The Global Brain* (J.P. Tarcher, Los Angeles, 1983).
26) Lewis Spence, *An Encyclopaedia of Occultism* (Citadel Press, 1960):

There are three known dimensions in space typified in the three geometric figures – a line, having length, a surface, [having] length and breadth [and] a cube [having] length, breadth and thickness. It has been conjectured that a fourth dimension may exist in addition to length, breadth and thickness. Spiritualists have claimed to find proof of a fourth dimension in certain of the physical phenomena of the séance room such as the tying of knots in endless cords, and the passage of matter through matter.

27) Revelations 7:4.
28) Ibid, 20:6,14.
29) Ibid, 7:14,16,17.
30) The positive and higher side of Aquarius breeds an enlightened society – all for one and one for all, the brotherhood of man. But the negative aspect of Aquarius is typified by the inhuman face of communism. It makes a certain sense that the 'sheep' will access the higher aspect of Aquarius while the 'goats' will experience the lower.
31) The runes are an ancient alphabetical script used in the main part for divination purposes. Each hieroglyph – most often inscribed on a smooth piece of stone – imparts information, yet for the true wisdom of the runes to be revealed intuition must be employed.
32) Ralph Blum, *The Book of Runes* (Michael Joseph, 1984).

3

Planetary Consciousness

*O*NE OF THE MOST FASCINATING ASPECTS TO THE DISCOVERIES OF THE trans-Saturnian planets is that their mythological names (chosen by astronomers) reflect their characteristics as perceived by astrologers. But, more importantly, perhaps, events in the world at the time of each planet's discovery synchronize with the qualities of that planet. It is as though man's ability to perceive a new planet – which, after all, has always been there – depends on his increased awareness. In other words, the sighting of a new planet indicates a widening of man's horizons on all levels – a leap in consciousness. Considering the enormous changes in our lives since the 1960s – space travel, for instance, and the way computers and advanced communication systems have come to dominate all aspects of existence – and, more appositely, the huge movement toward higher consciousness, the discovery of a new planet must surely be imminent. It is the advent of a new planetary flagship for the New Age that is the subject of this chapter, but before I move into the realms of yet more hypothesis, I would like to go over some old trans-Saturnian ground.

Until the latter part of the eighteenth century, the solar system (excluding Earth) comprised five planets – Mercury, Venus, Mars, Jupiter and Saturn. Then, in March 1781, William Herschel discovered Uranus. He named his discovery Georgium Sidus (after the reigning monarch, George III); later it was known as Herschel and ultimately as Uranus. Of course, the discovery of Uranus was not achieved in a blinding flash – no matter how appropriate – since it had been observed 22 times previously by various scientists. Astrologers, who invariably work just as well with hypothesis as scientific fact, had already been incorporating in their studies a hypothetical planet they had named Ouranos.

Right from the outset, Uranus proved to be a tricky customer. With its axial inclination at 98° to the perpendicular to the plane of its orbit, each of its poles takes it in turns to have a 'night' of 21 Earth years. No other planet has such an extravagant tilt and, reflecting this idiosyncrasy, Uranus is synonymous with the eccentric, the unusual and the downright disturbing. Astrologers had intuitively named this planet after the Greek sky god Ouranos, and when it was officially discovered in 1781, it was synchronous with the French, American and industrial revolutions. Since man had reached a point where the old ways of life, old attitudes and old values were no longer appropriate, radical and dramatic change was required – nothing less than an entire revolution, in intellectual, cultural and socio-economic terms.

Less than a century later, in September 1846, the planet Neptune was discovered. And, as befits a planet named after the most chaotic and duplicitious of gods, its discovery was veiled in confusion and political 'fog'. Although technically, d'Arrest and Galle actually located Neptune, this was only made possible by the calculations of two other astronomers, Adams and Leverrier. Even so, this planet had already been observed, although mistakenly assumed to be a star, in 1795 by Lalande. While the discovery of Uranus coincided with a revolutionary thrust toward a 'brave new world', Neptune's shift in consciousness was less earth-shattering and synchronized with a universal reaching out, for the sublime, the transcendent and the mystical. This was the period of the great Romantic movement – vividly captured by such composers as Liszt, Chopin and Tchaikovsky and by the Impressionist painters. In the mid-1800s there was a resurgence of interest in Eastern mysticism and life after death: the Theosophical and Spiritualist movements swept the globe and, in medicine, similar reality-escaping phenomena such as anaesthesia and hypnosis were developed.

Half a century after its discovery, astronomers noted that Neptune appeared to be wandering from its predicted orbit, thus they speculated that the cause was another unknown planet. They were right. Until his death in 1916, Percival Lowell, together with William Pickering, conducted a search for this ninth planet. Sadly he was to die without actually finding it, although he had established its existence mathematically. Eventually, in January 1930, 'Planet X' was officially discovered. Astrologers, once again at the forefront of speculation, had already been referring to this planet as Pluto and although scientists initially named it Lowell-Pluto, it soon became simply Pluto.

Not that anything could be simple about this planet. Pluto's orbit is the largest and most elliptical of all the planets: so elliptical in fact that at perihelion[1] it comes within the orbit of Neptune – therefore rendering Neptune the farthest planet from the sun. To add mystery to the complexity, according to its estimated size, mass and orbit Pluto should not, by the laws of physics, have the apparent effect on Neptune that it does. Some scientists have speculated that its surface is covered with ice so all that can be seen of it is the sun's reflection on the ice – a factor that renders much of Pluto invisible. In keeping with Pluto's Underworld theme, at the time of its discovery depth psychology was in the ascendancy; various underground movements and secret organizations, like the Mafia, were gaining momentum; fascism was on the rise and, of course, Plutonium was discovered.

Initially it was the irregularities in Uranus's orbit that propelled astronomers to look for another planet, and when, after Neptune's discovery, there were further irregularities in both these planets' orbits yet another planet was sought to explain these 'residuals'. But even Pluto's existence cannot explain all the problems in the motion of Uranus and Neptune: Pluto simply isn't massive enough to cause the irregularities in these planets. And so, it would seem – at least to some astronomers – that there is a planet to be discovered beyond Pluto.

Currently engaged in searching for 'Planet X' are Thomas C. Van Flandern and Robert S. Harrington,[2] Daniel P. Whitmire and John J. Maltese,[3] John D. Anderson[4] and Conley Powell.[5] And while all these scientists have come to the conclusion by very different routes that a tenth planet must exist, their estimations of what that planet might be like are remarkably similar. As Mark Littmann says in his prize-winning book, *Planets Beyond*:

> No object in the solar system has caused more trouble. Imagine a Most Wanted poster for this fugitive planet:

WANTED

on cosmic charges:

- Disturbing the motion of Uranus and Neptune.
- Smuggling short period comets (like Halley's) into the inner solar system.
- Suspected of trespassing at Neptune, driving Triton and Nereid berserk, and kidnapping Pluto.
- Repeated assaults on Earth with deadly comets, causing periodic mass extinctions of life.

DESCRIPTION of fugitive:

One to five Earth masses; eccentric, with odd inclination; likes to leave subtle clues to tantalize astronomers; lives in trans-Plutonia, constantly on the move, no known address, might repeat movements every 700 years; knows how to hide.[6]

While the general consensus of opinion is that Planet X's orbit is between 700 to 1,000 years (although Powell and Gomes[7] put it within 500) and its magnitude is 14, its location is considered variously in Virgo, Scorpio, Gemini and Cancer. And while Van Flandern believes Humphrey or Zorba to be a fitting name, Powell – clearly an intuitive astronomer – has opted for Persephone.

The anomalies that led most of the astronomers to consider the possible existence of a tenth planet were the irregularities in the orbits of Uranus and Neptune, the reversal in the motion of Triton[8] and the kidnapping of Pluto,[9] but Whitmire and Maltese – active in the controversy over the reason for mass extinctions on Earth – were drawn to this possibility by a different route.

In 1980, Luis and Walter Alvarez, Frank Asaro and Helen Michel proposed that some 65 million years ago a collision involving an asteroid some six miles in diameter had generated so much dust in the atmosphere that the sun had become completely obliterated from view:

It was black as night for months. In the dark and cold, plants died. Animals that depended on the plants died. Animals that depended on other animals died. More than half the species of plants and animals on Earth [including the dinosaurs, of course] perished at that time.[10]

One of the problems with this hypothesis when related to a Planet X was that Earth has experienced a series of mass extinctions over the past 250 million years and at regular intervals of approximately every 28 million years, and there is no way that asteroids could collide with Earth with any sort of regularity. However, although asteroids may be out of the question, comets aren't – if something like an unseen star or planet disturbs them. Initially, Davis, Hut and Muller[11] proposed that the culprit was a companion star to our sun which they named, somewhat appropriately, Nemesis. However, Whitmire and Maltese thought a more likely culprit to be a planet: a planet that could disturb a cluster of comets[12] thought to lie in the plane of the solar system with orbits not far beyond Neptune and Pluto. And although no planet could reasonably take 28 million years to orbit the sun, it is possible that the gravitational effects of the neighbouring planets could cause the whole orbit of this planet to precess, and such a precession could conceivably take 28 million years. At a certain point in its orbit, Planet X may indeed upset a disk of comets, accelerating some of them out of the solar system but decelerating others, forcing them to fall closer to the sun so that one or more hit the Earth with cataclysmic consequences. In this way, Planet X would inadvertently be responsible for the periodic 'death' of life on

Earth – a process symbolized not so much by Nemesis, but Persephone.

But before I expand on Persephone and her mythical origins, a word about Chiron. In 1977, a new planetary body was discovered and named Chiron after the centaur and healer of Greek myth. Astrologers were over the moon. But what precisely was Chiron – a planetoid, an asteroid, or what? By 1990, Chiron has been deemed to be a comet – which certainly casts some doubt on all the various interpretations thrust upon it by astrologers. However Chiron is no mean comet. It is 10,000 times bigger than Halley's comet and, according to astronomers at Manchester university,[13] it was probably some of the 'lumps of material' discarded by Chiron when its orbit was closer to the sun that collided with Earth and precipitated the last ice age, the demise of the dinosaurs et al. But even if the finger can be pointed at Chiron for actually wielding a body blow to life on Earth, the reason for the disturbance in its orbit clearly lies elsewhere, which brings us back to Planet X, or as I feel compelled to call it, Persephone.

The myth of Persephone is one of the best known and best loved:

Persephone was the beautiful and adored daughter of Demeter, the goddess of the Earth. One day, as Persephone was picking flowers, Pluto, the god of the Underworld, burst forth from a fissure in the ground and carried her off to his kingdom. Demeter was distraught and wandered across the Earth in search of her daughter. In the meantime, the Earth withered and died. Eventually, Zeus intervened and ordered Pluto to return Persephone to her mother. However, Persephone had eaten the sacred pomegranate, which meant that she was bound to the Underworld. This made a compromise necessary whereby Persephone remained half a year with Pluto in the Underworld, during which time the Earth mourned her loss, and six months with her mother on the Earth when nature celebrated her return by renewing and replenishing itself.

As I mentioned earlier, astrologers invariably sense the drumbeat of a new planet long before it officially arrives and accurately intuit its name. And while there have been several contenders for the tenth planet I don't want to confuse the issue by exploring all their potentials; I would rather concentrate on Persephone. (Interested readers can turn to the Appendix to this chapter for a full discussion on all the hypothetical planets.[14])

We can certainly learn something of the nature of Persephone from both the myth and its behaviour in the solar system. Astronomers are already suggesting that a tenth planet is the likely culprit for the extinction of life on Earth and allegorically Persephone was linked to the death of nature. Somewhat ironically, the tenth planet is thought to have been responsible for the kidnapping of Pluto[15] – a sort of cosmic role reversal. But as with the discoveries of the other trans-Saturnian planets, synchronous events on Earth also tell us much about the nature of a new planet.

December 1989 was momentous on several counts: the barriers between East and West Germany disintegrated almost overnight; the Rumanian people rose up against their corrupt and cruel dictatorship resulting in the execution of President Ceauşescu and his wife by the end of the year; although the USSR bowed under the weight of internal political dilemmas and splits, its President, Mikhail Gorbachev, was hailed as a world peace-maker and a new level of accord, understanding and mutual regard reigned between America, Europe and the USSR. *Perestroika* – renewal – became the new catch-phrase on both sides of the almost non-existent Iron Curtain. Such an extraordinary crossing of boundaries – a sense of unity unparalleled in human history – must surely be the signature of Persephone, a goddess who crossed the boundary between Earth and the Underworld and was synonymous with the cycle of death and renewal. Yet within nine months of these uplifting events and within weeks of the signing of the formal treaty uniting East and West Germany, an Iraqi dictator called Saddam Hussein swept into the neighbouring oil-rich state of Kuwait and brought the prospect of Armageddon just that little bit nearer. And this is where the less familiar side to Persephone comes in.

Persephone, or Kore as she was also known, was considerably older than the Eleusinian myth I outlined earlier. She was, in fact, Queen of the Underworld long before the myth arose of Pluto's abduction of her. Orphic mystics worshipped her as the goddess of the blessed dead, and she ruled the Underworld as Destroying Mother Kali ruled it under the name of Prisni. Indeed, like Kali the Destroyer, Persephone was the basic Death-Goddess. Beautiful, yes, but terrifyingly powerful: she personified the power of death over life yet in her hands lay also the power to renew the life force.

Accordingly, inasmuch as Persephone unites, so she destroys. And as we learn more and more about the cause of the cataclysms that have periodically decimated the Earth, as we face the very real threat of nuclear war, and as humanity takes more and more steps toward global unity, our awareness draws us ever more nearer to sighting this planetary flagship of a new era. *Inasmuch as Persephone unites, so she destroys* – that is, she represents the next evolutionary step for mankind but what we may have to learn from her is that we cannot move forward into a state of perfect union and harmony until we have destroyed the old ways. A new heaven and a new Earth necessitate the passing away of the old.

As I discussed in the last chapter, mankind is already accessing a higher state of consciousness which will ultimately provide the route to a new humanity. This higher state of awareness is reflected in the increased understanding of the power of the mind and the spirit over matter: the New Age movement and its companions, the alternative health and ecology (Green) movements are gradually wearing down the die-hard traditionalists and in their wake reducing all the unacceptable profit and material excesses of the consumer society. And with the awakening to the God within, or the Christ consciousness, comes the need to free ourselves from the strictures of organized religion and so end the needless wars that have plagued so much of human history. And, most important of all, with the higher awareness comes a greater capacity for love. All this, I believe, is the hallmark of Persephone. And her influence is manifesting with increasing intensity as we draw ever nearer to the end of the millennium. When Persephone ultimately reveals herself, we shall be no longer on the threshold of the New Age, we shall be entering it – and perhaps through the cataclysmic doorway envisioned by prophets both ancient and modern. I will talk more of Persephone later, but for the moment we will leave her.

The growing wave of higher consciousness is not only paving the way for mankind's quantum leap into a new era – which is in turn reflected in the awareness of another planet way beyond the sphere of Pluto – but is also changing our perception and experience of the other trans-Saturnian planets. As we learn more about their astronomical characteristics, so we experience a greater appreciation of the qualities of Uranus, Neptune and Pluto. Ask most astrologers about the nature of these three planets and they will tell you that they represent a generational influence – they are collective 'energies' and cannot be experienced personally. I believe this is changing. As we move into higher states of awareness, we can appreciate the finer 'energies' of these planets and so experience them personally. Humanity has already progressed to a point where the new in 1781, 1846 and even 1930 is part of our fabric of consciousness. We can no longer disown Uranus, Neptune and Pluto as being 'out there', out of our personal grasp – as though the changes and effects they characterize are foisted upon us by the great sweep of collective fate. Uranus, Neptune and Pluto address us directly and demand that we expand our awareness so that we can incorporate them fully in our consciousness and into our life.

One of the points that I made in my previous book, *The Forces of Destiny*, was that the development and dominance of the ego in the individual psyche inhibits access to the dimensions of consciousness symbolized by Uranus, Neptune and Pluto; only by sustaining a higher level of awareness can the individual respond to the higher nature, experience or expression of these outer planets. Thus as the new consciousness sweeps through humanity, it is as though the resonances of Uranus, Neptune and Pluto can be more directly appreciated. And to a certain extent as our instruments (our bodies and our psyches) adjust to these purer resonances we can expect to undergo a degree of discomfort – a process of trial and error – until we achieve the correct pitch.

In astrology, Uranus has represented the principle of revolution. Since this planet passes through one sign in seven years, it is thought to be too general to have meaning in the individual sense: only by its position in the diurnal circle (its house position) and its aspects to the personal 'planets' (Sun, Moon, Mercury, Venus and Mars) and the angles (Ascendant, Descendant, Midheaven and Nadir) is it thought to bring its revolutionary message into the individual's life. In its passage around the birth chart (reflecting its orbit around the sun) when Uranus meets one of the personal planets or any of the angles he brings sudden change. He is astrology's great awakener. However, in his higher aspect – the level we meet in higher consciousness – he represents the Higher Self. Ouranos was the great sky god and allegorically, Uranus provides us with a bird's eye, or celestial, view of life. Instead of blindly hacking our way through life's vicissitudes, we are transported by Uranus to a high mountain top where we can see the whole panorama spread out in front of us. By accessing the Higher Self we can perceive the greater situation and so make the correct moves and changes – or allow them to happen – in the certain knowledge that they are appropriate for us.

The more the new consciousness filters through to each individual, the greater the facility each person will have to access his Higher Self and operate from that lofty position. This means that his decisions can be based upon a complete perception of all the issues and potential outcomes involved in any situation – rather like seeing every move on a chess board in a matter of seconds. An individual accessing his Higher Self is a much larger human being in the psychological and spiritual sense. And since astrologers have also come to understand that Uranus's field of experience includes such things as telepathy and other paranormal phenomena, like telekinesis for example,[16] an individual accessing his Higher Self will be able to use mind-to-mind communication and perform other mind-bending tasks. He will not need to wait until Uranus reaches a crucial position in his birth chart to awaken such potential because it already 'lives' within him, but such a transit might well synchronize with the conscious connection to the Higher Self. And, of course, this awakening to the Higher Self represents the doorway to all the other high-level functions of the other trans-Saturnian planets. So as soon as an individual is aware he is operating from and co-operating with his Higher Self – which must in turn mean that he has apprehended the new wave of consciousness – all the other higher dimensions of the outer planets – divine love (Neptune) and transmogrification (Pluto) – are available to him.

In *The Forces of Destiny* I tell the story of 'Peter', who was astounded to find a figure of light standing at the foot of his bed one night who informed him that he could heal and so changed his whole life direction; this experience happened under a transit of Uranus to his radical Mars. But this is not an isolated story. It seems to me that there is a huge increase in the amount of people who are being visited by beings of light or, perhaps more dramatically as in the case of American author Whitley Strieber,[17] by extra-terrestrials. There is also a massive channelling movement (especially in the United States): sensitives, or mediums, are receiving communications from discarnate entities who claim variously to come from other dimensions. Unlike the mediums of the late nineteenth century – and indeed up to and including many present-day mediums – the 'new wave' channelled entities do not bring news of 'cousin Fred from the other side who has news for someone called Flo' but instead they provide teachings about the human soul and about the future of mankind. This movement, somewhat predictably, has come under intense criticism from sceptics who consider the sensitives to be nothing more than good actors keen 'to make a buck or two'. Nevertheless, the teachings supplied by these entities strike meaningful chords with those receptive to them. In response to such criticism, it might be worth mentioning that even if these entities are purely and simply manifestations of the medium's personality, they clearly know a lot more about the nature and purpose of our lives and exhibit far more laudable attitudes and a great deal more sympathy and love for humanity than the 'average' individual. And, in turn, by becoming a channel for such enlightened information, the medium becomes a 'better' human being. In a sense, these entities are equally as valid whether they do indeed come from another dimension of time and space or whether they are personifications of the medium's Higher Self. But as far as I am concerned, I am altogether more comfortable with the concept that it is the Higher Self that dons a definite identity to impart information not readily accessible to the normal range of consciousness. On the other hand, given the extraordinary powers of consciousness to create form, it may be that man's belief that his salvation rests in a higher power outside himself has created thought-forms in the shape of entities from outer space or beings of light.

Whatever the legitimacy of such claims the communication from a higher source is quintessentially Uranian. And, as many of these channelled entities have espoused, each and everyone of us can become channels for higher information. Thus to prevent ourselves from becoming prey to the idea of possession by spirits or abduction by extra-terrestrials perhaps it is a good thing that we do consider our communicator to be our Higher Self. And as I mentioned earlier, this recognition of the Higher Self and the ability to maintain a level of connection with this dimension of consciousness opens the doorway to enlightenment – our passport to the New Age.

I feel I must add a word here for those astrologers who, if they accept the concept of Uranus representing the Higher Self, may consider that the sign, house position and aspects of Uranus must therefore describe the Higher Self. I am sure that there are astrologers who could make a good case for this, but what I am concerned to put across is that as soon as one is tuning into these higher octave 'energies' one has crossed the boundary of the ego, thereby rendering any aspect of personality, or typing, as such redundant.

Nowhere does the dissolution of the boundaries of the ego seem more applicable than in the sphere of Neptune – a planet synonymous with the nebulous and the transcendent. Ever since it was discovered, Neptune has been a source of mixed feelings as far as astrologers were concerned: on the one hand, this planet provides inspiration and on the other, sheer escapism and chaos. Neptune in a birth chart designates to where and to what the individual can aspire yet also wherein lies his downfall; by transit, Neptune all too often brings confusion, betrayal and illusion. Yet through the doorway of the Higher Self and by the renunciation of the ego, the little 'I' that says, 'I want, I need, I hurt' is transcended, and the divine 'I' encountered. As Uranus, when met in a higher vibration, hoists the individual up into the higher reaches of his consciousness whereby he can gain a panoramic view and come to an understanding of his real Self, when resonating with Neptune on a higher plane, the individual can experience infinite compassion and a sense of connectedness with all-that-is.

The traditional concept of Neptune is bound up with suffering and sacrifice. Jesus Christ was the archetypal manifestation of Neptune – a saviour, the Son of God, a man of divine origins who was crucified and suffered for humanity. His life and death – whether a myth or a reality – stand testament to the concept that the divine is not out of reach of mankind. But so far, most of us have missed the point: we are isolated from our divine source; we seek ecstasy in the arms of another human being, or through drugs, even through pushing ourselves beyond the limits of physical endurance or in a musical or theatrical experience and then we wonder why the sense of bliss is so transient and insubstantial. We feel betrayed and thus tend to dismiss such an experience as the stuff of unreality, of illusion. Why seek such an opiate when it serves only to distract us from the real world? Indeed, until we have made that leap into a higher realm of consciousness, Neptune merely tantalizes us, shows us a glimpse of what we might know, if only . . . Through the doorway of the Higher Self, Neptune allows us to experience the God within – and to sustain that sensation of at-oneness. No longer is feeling the stuff of the emotions, but a quality of expanded consciousness: gone is the sense of isolation and in its place is a sense of being at one with the universe; gone is the 'narrow little bargaining love', for it has been superseded by a *limitless* capacity to feel and love. This is truly the stuff of Neptune.

As the higher level of consciousness manifests in more and more people, and this state of consciousness becomes the 'norm', clairvoyance – the ability to actually see images on another vibratory level and perceive events in a future time slot – will become another feature of 'everyday' consciousness. Appositely, Neptune's higher resonance synchronizes with the opening of the third eye. Indeed, many people describe the opening of the third eye in terms of the action of a shutter in a camera. This was very much the case with my own first experience; I even heard the 'click' of the shutter and was relieved to find the only images that were presented were patterns and mandalas. More recently, I had the experience of seeing events as if through a telephoto lens. Perception is a thoroughly Neptunian concept and with the change in resonance, the intellectual realization that matter is not solid but at the sub-atomic level simply energy can become a springboard to the ability to interpenetrate other levels of reality. While the use of drugs to transport the psyche into other realms can reduce the experience to nothing more than a chemical aberration, with the opening to the higher frequency, such an experience can be sustained and repeated at will so that we can truly comprehend what mystics have long claimed – that it is the material world that is *maya*, or illusion. In many ways, the higher frequency of Neptune represents the thinning of the veil so often mentioned by mystics and clairvoyants. As this veil between one reality and another diminishes, what we understand as heavenly or angelic influences can stream through and be actively felt and responded to by those whose third eye or Higher Self has been activated. It is, of course, in this heightened level of consciousness that the appearance of Christ and his host can be perceived and any transition to a 'new heaven and a new Earth' facilitated.

If, with the heightening of consciousness, Uranus offers us access to the Higher Self and if the higher frequency of Neptune leads us to experience the God-light within and achieve that sense of connectedness with all-that-is, what does Pluto's individual experience offer us at this level?

Pluto spends, on average, 20 years in each sign of the zodiac[18] and in this way carves its signature on a whole generation. Until recently, Plutonic influence has come to us individually through Pluto's aspects to the personal planets and angles in a birth chart, and when it transits a strategic radical point. But as the level of consciousness is raised in each individual the higher dimension of its transformational nature is made accessible.

Pluto's rule over all things of an underground nature is pre-eminent in astrology. In the realms of mythical Hades lay riches beyond man's imagination, but only through death could one find them. In death, one went naked – stripped of one's assets – into the Afterlife to be judged and if found wanting relegated to torment in Tartarus or to bliss in the Elysian Fields. We, as individuals, have almost certainly experienced, or will experience, this 'death' and 'judgement' at some point in our lives when we are stripped of a resource we thought we could not live without and subsequent events either raise us to greater heights or plummet us into the depths.

As I write these words, on 22 November 1990, Margaret Thatcher has just resigned the premiership of Great Britain, thus bringing to an end one of the most transformative political regimes in British history. For over 11 years she had dominated the world stage and to many people's minds she was inviolable, if not immortal; but, in a strategically planned campaign to oust her from power, she was forced to resign. It was obvious to one and all that she had been stabbed in the back by colleagues she trusted and relied upon – and at a time of world crisis in which she had a crucial role to play.

But later she turned humiliation into triumph when, on the day following her resignation, she gave her last speech to the House of Commons. It was a moment of supreme victory in defeat – her words so powerfully and eloquently delivered, her humour, her strength and her style in glittering array. And at the end of the day there were few who would not admit that the Tory Party had probably made the biggest mistake of its political life.

The events in Mrs Thatcher's life at this time were the hallmark of Pluto: underground movements – of which she was entirely unaware –

had brought about her political death. Not only did such a death mean the departure from a job she adored but from an entire way of life. No longer a world voice but a back-seat influence, her role had been utterly transformed. By no mean coincidence, when she came into power in 1979, Pluto, by transit, had reached her Sun, and throughout the eleven-and-a-half years of her leadership, it had moved relentlessly toward her Ascendant and Saturn. Inasmuch as Pluto had brought her into power and changed her from a mere politician to an international titan, so he transformed her role – and, indeed her whole being – yet again a decade or so later. But the outer events of such Plutonic experience are not the most important ones: while it seemed she had been plunged into a situation not of her making – impelled by the force of fate to relinquish the reins of power in no uncertain terms – from the metaphysical perspective, such a situation had been Self created so that an even greater journey of transformation could begin.

Indeed, this cycle of rise and fall is most meaningful viewed through the lens of the psyche for it is a process whereby an individual is forced to let go of the trappings of his ego, make a journey into the depths of his subconscious, his past, and find treasure in a buried or repressed experience that becomes the key to his transformation. But this journey is not without danger, for it may lead to transformation or decimation, enlightenment or insanity. This process is very much akin to Jung's concept of individuation – the inner journey to realize the Self – which we will discuss later in connection with Persephone. We can also perceive this process as a series of stages reflected in each of the outer planets: by opening to the higher Self (Uranus), and renouncing the ego (Neptune) one can find the treasure – the power of regeneration and transmogrification (Pluto).

The higher resonance of Pluto offers us the experience of total transformation right down to cellular level: as I discussed in the last chapter, the opening of the third eye allows the God-light to stream into the system so that we can achieve the sort of enlightenment known only to advanced spiritual masters. Of course, one of the routes to enlightenment is through kundalini and the Near Death Experience itself – both archetypically Plutonic. Kundalini is linked to the sexual chakra, and if there's one area of life other than death synonymous with Pluto, it is sexuality – the Near Death Experience speaks for itself. As I mentioned in the previous chapter, Kenneth Ring believes these extraordinary experiences are becoming more and more common and may, in fact, be leading to the development of an advanced species of human being. If finding the God within is the stuff of Neptune, then gaining enlightenment and transforming the self – mind, body and spirit – is the quintessence of Pluto.

Certainly the higher frequency of Pluto has much to do with spiritual power and the power of the mind over the body. So far we have touched on communications from discarnate entities (or messages from the Higher Self), clairvoyance and the perception of other realities. Plutonic experience takes us one stage further – the ability to change our material form and to manipulate matter.

Ask anyone who has spent any length of time with Sai Baba, or, indeed, any great mystic, and he will tell you of the extraordinary feats accomplished by these enlightened souls – live butterflies produced from the breath and the mystic himself being seen, touched and spoken to in two locations at the same time. And then there are fantastic psychic surgeons who perform major surgery without any surgical instruments or anaesthetic. The writer Margot Grey had a firsthand experience of the power of supernatural healing when she visited the Magus of Strovalos in Cyprus. The Magus asked her to feel the backbone of an elderly woman with curvature of the spine. Margot drew her hand along the length of the backbone, feeling the skeletal structure and noting its deformity. The Magus then passed his hand over the spine – without touching it – and asked Margot to once again feel the backbone. This time, to her amazement, what had formerly been a rigid structure was now a jelly-like mass. The Magus then began to rearrange the bones and when he had finished, passed his hands above the body once again. Margot was requested to feel the spine for the third time: it was completely solid and perfectly formed.

Such spectacular gifts may be beyond the range of most of us now, but as the higher consciousness increases, the development of extraordinary powers will become increasingly available. Indeed, the ability to affect change within the biological system itself will be a prerequisite in the transition from the three-dimensional world to that of the fourth. Perceiving the new heaven and the new Earth is one thing, changing one's form in order to enter it is quite another – and it is this process that is fundamentally akin to the higher resonance of Pluto. And at the risk of repeating myself *ad nauseam*, it is the raising of the level of awareness that allows us to apprehend and bring into full consciousness the higher dimensions of experience represented by the three outer planets. And this process is synchronous with our development into the enlightened beings who can make the transition to a new epoch.

But this transition period is surely the most difficult so far faced by humanity. And the beginning of its end – or the end of its beginning – can be traced to the December of 1979 when Pluto moved within the orbit of Neptune, thereby bringing Pluto's transformational properties closer to us and allegorically marking the countdown to the New Age. This Plutonic message was reinforced by Pluto's entry into the sign of its rulership, Scorpio, in 1983. Since this time, AIDS and other immune system diseases like ME[19] have emerged in full force, not to mention the awareness of the ecological time bomb. Within eight weeks of Pluto's entry into Scorpio, Neptune moved into Capricorn, symbolizing the erosion of all the Saturnian principles of structure and the establishment. By February 1988, Uranus had joined forces with Neptune and also entered Capricorn, heralding more upheaval and change to established orders. To make this powerful double act a truly formidable trio, Saturn joined the fray later in 1988. More than any other planetary factor, it has been this cluster of 'heavy duty' planets in the powerful, cardinal sign of Capricorn that has brought the concept of the tribulations fairly and squarely home to us all. The year 1990 will surely go down in history as one of the most relentlessly difficult for much of humanity. I will refrain from mentioning all the global events once again, but emphasize that people, ordinary people, the world over have been faced with financial, psychological, material, physical or emotional hardship, the like of which they have never before known. While this relentless hardship, upheaval and erosion is designated by the situation of Saturn and the trans-Saturnian planets, in synchronicity with this astrological state of affairs humanity is undergoing a baptism of fire evoked by the raising of the level of consciousness.

This heightening of consciousness is not an overnight event and, by the same token, neither can we experience the higher resonance of the outer planets in one full sweep – and sustain it. We are at this point in time in a process of *becoming* – a precarious and volatile state that is in turn reflected both in the vicissitudes of our individual lives and on the collective front. As I have mentioned already, our level of awareness – the rate at which we resonate – dictates how we will respond to the influence of the 'increasing light vibration'. According to Hindu philosophy, the basic level of humanity up to this time has been predominantly Rajas (passions, attachments and egocentricity), with a proportion of individuals falling well below this category into the Tamas state (ignorance, darkness and degeneration). Thus, as the light vibration becomes finer, the resonances of the planets, or rather, the way in which we can respond to their intrinsic qualities, also becomes refined.[20] This is one crucial reason why so many individuals feel as if they are characters in a schizophrenic nightmare: as the barometrical pressure of their psyches dips and dives they rise one moment to the Sattvic level of expanded consciousness and the next fall back into the

Rajas state where passions and attachment cloud perception. And, I imagine, this schizophrenic process will continue until we have fully acclimatized to the higher resonance. Even then, there are those who will simply not be able to get there. We can also see this vicissitudinous process mirrored by the planets: since hardly any of us are functioning in a permanent Sattvic state we must seemingly undergo both the high and low-level experience presented by Saturn and any one of the trans-Saturnians.

Our inner tribulations, like the continuing planetary drama, are unfolding for a purpose. And as we meet our personal crises and our collective fate, we move ever nearer to that new era, allowing these very trials to pitchfork us into a new state of awareness. Unless we do so, the prospect of global cataclysm is almost certainly our destiny. In January 1996, Uranus enters its own sign of Aquarius, a matter of weeks after Pluto changes sign into Sagittarius. Whatever outer events we must meet with this planetary transition, we can be certain that it will synchronize with another massive upward shift in consciousness – maybe one that will allow us to perceive Persephone in the 'flesh'. For now, on this journey to greater consciousness, we can but *sense* her presence. And it is awesome.

Appendix

1) The point in a planet's orbit at which it draws nearest to the sun.
2) Thomas C. Van Flandern and Robert S. Harrington: US Naval Observatory.
3) Daniel P. Whitmire and John J. Maltese: University of South Western Louisiana.
4) John D. Anderson: Jet Propulsion Laboratory (NASA).
5) Conley Powell: Aerospace engineer for Teledene-Brown Engineering, Huntersville, Alabama.
6) Mark Littmann, *Planets Beyond* (Wiley, 1988).
7) Rodney S. Gomes: Brazil (quoted in *Planets Beyond*).
8) At one time, there was a generally held view that Pluto was originally a moon of Neptune, along with Triton and Nereid, and that a gravitational encounter between Triton and Pluto had reversed the motion of Triton and hurled Pluto out into its own orbit around the sun. But the more up-to-date view is that Pluto simply doesn't have the mass to turn Triton around and that this cosmic reshuffle is probably due to the presence of Planet X.
9) See reference 8.
10) Mark Littmann, op.cit.
11) Marc Davis, Piet Hut and Richard Muller comprised the other team to Whitmire and Jackson working on the reason for the periodic asteroid collisions with Earth.
12) The Oort Cloud of comets.
13) *The Times* newspaper – 9/11/90 – reporting on an article by Gerhard Hahn and Mark Bailey in *Nature* magazine.

14) According to Charles Harvey in *Recent Advances in Natal Astrology* (compiled by Geoffrey Dean and published by The Astrological Association of Great Britain, 1977), 'There are now perhaps in excess of 100 hypothetical planets proposed and testified to by astrologers of some standing . . .' Of these 100, there are at least 25 hypothetical planets for which ephemerides have been published:

Lilith of Sepharial in the UK, later of Jacobson-Goldstein in the USA, said to be an invisible satellite of the Earth.
Vulcan of Weston in the USA, an intramercurial planet.
Jason of Wemyss in Scotland, said to lie between the orbits of Saturn and Uranus; and **Dido**, **Hercules** and **Wemyss-Pluto**, all trans-Plutonian.
Cupido, **Hades**, **Zeus**, **Kronos**, **Apollon**, **Admetos**, **Vulkanus** and **Poseidon** of Witte's Hamburg School in Germany, all trans-Neptunian.
Transpluto of Landscheidt and Hausmann in Germany.
Persephone, **Hermes** and **Demeter** of RAM in Holland, all trans-Plutonian and not to be confused with asteroids of the same name.
Pan, **Isis**, **Hermes**, **Osiris**, **Midas**, **Lion** and **Moraya**, all collated by Jayne in the USA and all trans-Plutonian.

Dean comments in *Recent Advances* that astronomical calculations by RAM for Persephone fall 'within the most recent (1976) astronomical limits for a trans-Plutonian planet'. However, RAM's calculations that Persephone is by now (1991) in Pisces does not agree at all with current astronomical thought which places Planet X anywhere between Gemini and Scorpio.

15) See reference 8.
16) A paranormal phenomenon whereby objects are moved by the power of the mind.
17) Whitley Strieber, *Communion* (Century Hutchinson, 1986). In his book, Strieber recounts some extraordinary episodes where he is 'kidnapped' by extra-terrestrials. He provides a very plausible and detailed account of his experiences and underwent stringent medical and psychological tests to validate his story.
18) Pluto takes roughly 248 years to orbit the sun and due to the changes in its motion and its elliptical orbit it spends some 30 years in Taurus yet only 13 in Scorpio.
19) *Myalgic encephalitis*, also known as Post Viral syndrome and more colloquially as 'Yuppy Flu'.
20) Most contemporary astrologers consider that the planets synchronize with human behaviour and events rather than causing them. However, there is a view, which I espouse, that we resonate with the planets; a view that would support the concept that as consciousness is raised we respond to the higher frequencies, or pitch, of the planets. The theory of planetary resonances was developed by Dr Percy Seymour and is the subject of his book *Astrology: The Evidence of Science* (Penguin, 1990). Pythagoras and Kepler considered that there was a divine harmony at work within the universe and that man resonated with the planets and indeed, the cosmos as a whole. Seymour has posited a scientific explanation for this mystical view: that the planets resonate with the sun's magnetic canals and in turn those resonances are pitched (via solar wind) into Earth's magnetic field. Since the human body also has an electromagnetic field, we too respond to these resonances. Indeed, our

nervous system acts as both a receiver and transmitter for geomagnetic waves, ersatz planetary resonances.

I have covered these ideas at length in *The Forces of Destiny* (Weidenfeld, 1990).

4

Persephone

TO DEDICATE AN ENTIRE CHAPTER TO A PLANET WHICH MAY NOT EVEN
exist may appear to be the greatest folly to which an astrologer can
succumb. But while astronomers may be searching for Persephone's
objective reality, which will in turn provide a new horoscopic influence
for astrologers to incorporate in their work, I would suggest that her
archetype is alive and well within us all and that it is already manifesting
in events in the world at large and in our individual lives. Some of the
ground work has already been laid in the previous chapter – for
instance, Persephone's hallmark of unity and destruction which, since
December 1989, has become increasingly evident – and in this chapter
I will fully explore her meaning and her potential. I realize, of course,
that some would argue that events over the last two years could be seen
to be reflected by other planetary dimensions – ones we already know
about. All I ask in this case is that you keep an open mind for the next
few pages, and maybe – just maybe – by the end of the chapter you will
be able to accept that Persephone, certainly as an archetype, if not a
planet, has a more than valid place in our psyches and in our lives.

As I was preparing to write this chapter, I tried to recall the first
moment that I 'tuned into' Persephone. It wasn't exactly a moment of
Eureka, but I do remember suddenly making the connection between
the truly extraordinary world events of the previous fortnight, which
seemed to be an outer manifestation of a gigantic leap in consciousness,
and the idea that these momentous changes ought to be reflected by the
discovery of a trans-Plutonic planet. It was just before Christmas and
I was sitting by the fireside with some friends – considerably mellowed
by several glasses of sloe gin. The conversation had moved from the
unification of Germany and the Rumanian uprising to what might

Figure 1: Persephone
I have assembled this glyph of Persephone by combining those of Venus (♀)
and Pluto (♇). Curiously, several of the shapes that unaccountably appeared
'overnight' (apparently created by no human hand) in the cornfields of
England in 1990 bore a strong resemblance to the above glyph. But when you
consider that Persephone's mother, Demeter, was the goddess of the harvest,
perhaps it's not so strange . . . Yet another synchronicity?

loosely be termed as gossip. It transpired that we all knew of couples whose established relationships had been suddenly upended in the past three weeks because one partner had fallen ecstatically in love with someone else and the level of feeling generated by the new alliance was such that there could be no turning back. All the people involved in these upheavals had claimed that they had been rendered powerless in the face of fate. What I felt unable to share with any of them, however, was that I was also among this hapless number, for I too had met someone who seemed set to change the course of my life.

At that time, I was frantically preparing a series of lectures and workshops to give in Australia the following two months: much of the material was on relationships and the force of fate – the latter the subject of a book, *The Forces of Destiny*, in which I used hypnotic regression and astrology to demonstrate how understanding and processing past trauma could lead to dramatic change and healing in a present life. I had decided to use one couple as a sort of continuing case history that could be examined from different astrological perspectives in the various lectures and workshops. The couple in question had had the most passionate and all-consuming love affair that had propelled them both into therapy when it collapsed. The relationship dramatically changed both their lives and forced them to look into their mutual past lives to try to come to terms with, and ultimately transcend, the ties that kept binding them and destroying them. What a strange synchronicity, I mused, that I should have chosen such a fated relationship to discuss when I was in the throes of a similarly passionate experience. I immediately put aside the thought that the relationship I was involved in would end up tearing more than just the two of us apart. It couldn't happen to me.

On the day I left for Australia, two great friends – who had been there on the day I had first mentioned Persephone – gave me a book, *On the Way to the Wedding* by Linda Leonard. I read it from cover to cover through the long flight to Perth, identifying many of its themes with astrological symbolism – much of which is included in the next chapters. In Perth I was to stay with Barbara and Peter Brackley who I had been assured would treat me as a daughter. And indeed they did. These were not the only two people with whom I was to form a powerful bond.

I saw eight clients in Perth, each one of whom mirrored aspects of my own current situation. By extraordinary synchronicity, one of those clients was even called Persephone. Although some years older than myself, Persephone had a chart strikingly similar to mine. Her life had been a journey in consciousness and many of its events and themes uncannily reflected mine. By the time I gave my first lecture in Perth, I felt compelled to talk about the prospect of a new planet called Persephone. Many of the audience were receptive to the idea – although I had not yet explored her potential – indeed, one man declared that he had just christened his new racehorse Persephone.

Although I had only a few ideas formed about Persephone's meaning, I felt personally touched by her advancing presence. It seemed, by the synchronous events, that she had something to do with union and with fated alliances. As luck, or serendipity, would have it, also living with Barbara and Peter was Barbara's mother, Rix Weaver, one of Australia's most celebrated women, then 87 years of age. She had been one of Jung's pupils and later one of Marie Louise von Franz's. After spending some years at the Jung Institute in Switzerland, she had returned to Australia, not only becoming acclaimed as an analyst but also as an author. Rix was in very poor health at the time, and sadly she was to die some eight months later, but her mind was as sharp as the proverbial rapier and we struck up an immediate rapport with each other. During my stay in Perth she was to help me unravel an important dream and we discussed many aspects of symbolism and divination. On my last evening there she took me by the hands and said, 'Few are called to greater consciousness, my dear. It's a painful path but the rewards are beyond riches.' At the time, I felt poised on the threshold of a new life with all the hope and excitement such a prospect can generate. I didn't want to know about pain.

Australia proved to be one of the most pivotal experiences of my life. I had left a grey and depressed England one January morning and less than 24 hours later landed in the shimmering splendour of Perth. It was as if a magic carpet had transported me to fairyland. The very being of Australia emphasized this quantum leap from one reality to another: stark contemporary architecture towered over ornate Victorian buildings – a striking contrast in their own right, but stunning set amidst the vast raw beauty of the land itself. Not only was Australia a feast in visual terms, but the stimulus of meeting new people and being exposed to fresh ideas and attitudes – not to mention being wined and dined on an exotic scale – proved a heady mix for a pioneering Aries spirit. Not only this, but 10 days after my arrival in Australia I was joined by the man I loved. It was as though the gods had chosen not only to smile on us but to bestow us with all their divine gifts – and we indulged ourselves in no uncertain terms.

My relationship with Damon had opened doors that neither of us had believed possible. We enjoyed a mutual involvement in metaphysics and a passion for the Taurean things of life – a highly sensory affair on all levels; but above and beyond this there were moments when we would experience such a sense of ecstatic unity that the world literally seemed to stand still. We had known from the first moment that there was no turning back, and by the time we reached Singapore on the last leg of our journey before coming home marriage was an inevitability.

Four weeks later he had vanished from my life.

I didn't want to know about pain. But here it was in all its glory. I had been forcibly ejected from Mount Everest and plunged to the bottom of Niagara Falls – almost overnight. The shock was all but fatal. I was numb and disoriented; my life was in total disarray. What, a mere month before in Australia, had promised to be the overture to a new life had ground to a discordant halt before the first movement was barely underway. The sheer physical loss of someone I had been so close to was appalling. There had been no warning, no gradual drawing apart; one moment I was wrapped in his arms and the next he was gone. No apology. No sugar to sweeten the pill of his bitter departure. The only acceptable anaesthetic was to move into my Higher Self.

I had been meditating somewhat spasmodically for many years but during a course I had been undertaking on hypnotherapy and psychotherapy, I had been accessing altered states in a more active way. Now, as I pulled the mundane strands of my life together, once the domestic chores were completed, I would escape for as much of the day as possible into a higher space. There I found a temporary respite from the pain and isolation; I felt a palpable link with something or someone who understood the reason for such things and who supported and sustained me. In this way I rose above the small self that was in such a state of turmoil. For three months I coped superbly. Friends and family were relieved and impressed that my life had not fallen apart: deadlines were met, appearances kept up and my children thrived. Only those who knew me well were aware that I was on 'automatic pilot' – in a limbo land where the ghost of the real me hovered in and out of everyday reality. Then I made a decision. I realized that I could not go on taking the anaesthetic for much longer without suffering some serious consequences. I knew that by removing myself from the hurt, I was not working through an essential process, and by suppressing the emotional pain I was paving the way for those unacknowledged feelings to erupt in a physical way, perhaps through cancer or an ulcer – at the very least, a nervous breakdown. It was a decision that precipitated a descent into the Underworld.

Any descent into the darkness is to be feared, since it is invariably precipitated by a psychological death. The ancients, who knew a thing or two about the psyche, were only too aware of this. In myth, the Underworld and its rulers were always held in awe and fear, which is why Persephone's abduction can never be taken at face value. Persephone is never totally a bright creature of the sun; she is also a dark sister of the moon. Her parentage is given in many myths as Zeus and Styx rather than Zeus and Demeter, thereby planting her roots ever more firmly in the Underworld. Like her counterparts in other mythical traditions, Kore, for instance or Prosperine, she was the dread goddess of the Underworld: it was her more than Hades himself who controlled the activities of the spirits of the dead. Persephone was she-who-must-be-obeyed. And you crossed her at your peril.

Persephone's descent into the Underworld and her annual return to Earth not only reflected the cycle of nature but the life cycle itself. We find similar parallels in myths of all cultures, but the one I find most revealing is that of Babylonian Ishtar. Ishtar is a personification of that force in nature which shows itself in the giving and taking of life. Like all Great Mother (moon) goddesses she has a two-fold character – the creator of life and the destroyer:

Ishtar, the Queen of Heaven had a son, Tammuz (also known as Urikitter, the Green One) whom she condemned to death on his arrival at manhood. At the summer solstice he was ritually slain and taken to the Underworld. All women, including Ishtar, wept for him. Eventually Ishtar alone undertook the dangerous journey into the Underworld to look for him. At each of the six gates of the Underworld, her jewels were systematically stripped from her until, naked and defenceless, she met and fought her sister Allatu for possession of Tammuz. Victorious, Ishtar returned to Earth with her beloved Tammuz. But while Ishtar pursued her perilous quest, the Earth was consumed by a terrible depression and despair: 'Nothing could be conceived. Neither man nor beast nor plants nor trees could propagate, and worse than ever they could not even want to propagate. The whole world is described as being sunk in a kind of hopeless inactivity mourning for her return.'[1]

Ishtar's sister, Allatu, the Queen of the Underworld, is but another aspect of Ishtar. While Ishtar, as Queen of Heaven, was worshipped as the Great Mother who brought fruitfulness and fecundity to the Earth and its inhabitants, as Allatu she was feared as the Terrible Mother, the goddess of the terrors of the night, and of storms and war. As Queen of the Underworld she effectively destroyed all that she had created in the upper world. Yet each aspect of her divinity formed part of the great cycle of life itself. Of course, the Queen of the Underworld was not all 'bad', even if she was terrifying: she was also known as the giver of dreams and omens, of revelation and of understanding of those things that are hidden. 'It was through her magic that men could obtain power and knowledge, often illicit knowledge, of hidden and secret things whose understanding brings power itself.'[2]

Ishtar's journey into the Underworld to regain that which was most precious to her, yet that which she had knowingly destroyed, is not just an allegory of the cycle of nature, but an allegory of the journey we must at some time willingly undertake into the depths of our unconscious. Ishtar, by descending into the Underworld and confronting her dark twin, claimed her precious possession and returned, renewed and replenished into the light; so too in our individual journeys in consciousness – what by the Jungian route would be termed the individuation process – must we wrestle with the darkness if we are to open and flower in the light: to become enlightened beings. In her bright and dark aspects, Ishtar reflects the changing face of the moon and the phases of womanhood: in the waxing cycle, she becomes fertile, procreates and nurtures her offspring; as the moon peaks at its fullness, the process of waning is begun; the moon loses her light, her power, like a dark star, collapses inward – and, like a dark star, destroys anything in her path. Esther Harding, in *Woman's Mysteries*, makes the eloquent point, 'To women she is the very principle of their being, to men the mediator between themselves and the secret spring of life hidden in the depths of the unconscious.'

I was not consciously aware that my decision to meet the pain that I had been so successfully avoiding would involve such a journey into the darkness, nor that by this descent I would be acknowledging an archetypal process personified by Ishtar, or her Greek counterpart, Persephone. I made the decision to leave the sanctuary of the higher self when I returned from a week's stay with a close friend who lived in Majorca. Somehow, by distancing myself physically from my home, I had gained a new perspective on all the issues. Or so I thought. I felt stronger and ready to face whatever might be ahead.

Synchronicities abounded at every turn of the way. One of the reasons I had taken a break was to complete a mini-thesis on Jung for the psychotherapy course I was doing. Without any conscious association, I began to discuss the individuation process. The more I wrote, the more I realized I was addressing myself . . .

The process of individuation comprises two main parts – the first half, 'the initiation into outward reality' and the second, 'the initiation into inner reality'. And while these two parts can be neatly fitted into the first and second halves of life, *the call toward the inner path is usually prompted by a wounding of the personality* which can occur at any stage of adult life.

By the end of the week, I had not only finished my paper on Jung, but had amassed much of the material for the latter part of this book. Within days of my return from Majorca I was contacted by a distraught client who had been suddenly abandoned by a man for whom she had left her husband and children. I saw her immediately and throughout the months that followed, by helping her through this major life crisis to make sense of what had happened and reorient her life, I in turn was helped myself (see Chapter 8).

Certainly the months that followed were the bleakest of my life. There were days when I felt so lost, so consumed with grief that I teetered on the edge of suicide. I was in such a state of self-absorbed pain that I could think neither what my action would mean for those who loved me, particularly my children, nor what such an action would mean in spiritual terms. I just wanted oblivion. There seemed to be no route I hadn't tried, no therapy I hadn't explored. Not even the extraordinary love and support of my husband could penetrate the aching void within. Despite the glorious summer weather and the many normally fulfilling aspects of my life, everything seemed grey. I longed for the summer to be over and the dank days of Autumn more suited to my mood to arrive. If ever I had been in a tunnel with no seeming light at the end, I was in it.

Encountering the despair of the small self did not mean that I lost complete contact with the Higher Self. I merely stopped using the higher level as an *escape*. Now, I realize that it might seem a somewhat masochistic gesture to deliberately stop accessing an altered state which gave me so much support and insight, but because I was too undeveloped to function constantly in the Higher Self, I found the experience of going up and down in consciousness rather destabilizing – a bit like living permanently in an elevator. Also, rightly or wrongly, I felt that this constant recharging of my psychic batteries was preventing me from 'moving on' and ultimately endangering my physical health, as I explained earlier.

However, my Higher Self was functioning quite well without my constant attention and kept me in touch with affairs from a loftier perspective through dreams and synchronicities. In the months that followed I had several dreams about precious stones; I was given lapis lazuli and amethysts by my estranged lover with the words, 'Happy Birthday for the beginning of your new life . . .' Later on in the summer, my jewels were stolen from the boot of my car; in September I lost them in the ocean – and recovered them because the water was so clear. I had dreams about weddings and veils and in many of these dreams I appeared to be not quite ready or prepared for the events. It was only later, when I began the process of writing this book, that the real significance of these dreams and visualizations started to emerge. I began to see that working through the grief and pain had been – and, indeed, still was – a journey in itself. And that this journey comprised a series of initiations. I was only able to perceive this in retrospect, however: my psyche was presenting me with images to which I could only then directly relate. These images were to be found in the archetypal realm of myth.

At the beginning of my relationship with Damon, I had experienced a visualization in which I was presented with a scroll. A hand indicated that I should sign my name and I did so directly under Damon's signature. As soon as this was done, Damon himself appeared and together we walked toward a low boat on a narrow underground canal. We lay in the punt, which moved slowly through the darkness until we came to a lock. The way ahead was blocked by a portcullis and as we stepped onto the quay another portcullis dropped behind us. At the time it struck me that there was an aura of initiation about the experience, although I could not understand what it portended. With hindsight I came to understand that the ecstatic dimension of the union with Damon and all that it had released in the way of the heart had marked the first stage and initiation of the journey itself – the abandonment represented the second. And as I moved ever deeper into the pain, my resources, like Ishtar's jewels, were being depleted bit by bit, as all through the months that followed I battled to keep my financial and domestic ship afloat under the constant battering of an emotional tempest.

Then in the August of 1990 I took part in a channelling course run by a Canadian channeller, Michelle Vezeau. A powerful and gifted medium and healer, Michelle provided yet another lamp with which to illuminate my descent. In a group meditation I found myself beside the sea on an empty beach. It was night and the moon was full and bright. Lying on the beach was a sarcophagus. I went towards it and saw that it was not a coffin but the body, or rather the empty shell, of Damon. I laid myself on the 'shell' endeavouring to draw down the moon's light and pour it into him.

Although at first I interpreted this visualization as my trying to nourish the empty or 'dead' feminine aspect of Damon's psyche, I was also reminded of the myth of Isis and her husband Osiris. It wasn't until I began to put together all the material for this chapter that it began to make sense as yet another dimension of the descent into the Underworld and Persephone. Isis is yet another goddess linked to the Underworld:

Set, the brother of Osiris, was so jealous of him that he decided to kill him. First, he designed a wooden chest that would fit Osiris exactly, then he invited Osiris to a banquet at which he offered the chest to any of the guests who could fit into it precisely. As soon as Osiris lay in the chest, Set's accomplices slammed down the lid trapping Osiris inside. Later they carried the chest to the sea and let the water bear it away.

On hearing of his death, Isis went in search of Osiris and upon finding his dead body in the chest threw herself onto it and conceived Osiris's son, Horus (the Younger). She then returned to Egypt with the chest and hid it in the marshes of the Nile Delta. But the wicked Set discovered the coffin and immediately cut the body of Osiris into 14 pieces. Once again, Isis set out to recover her husband and finding each piece, bar one, of his precious body, she magically brought him back to life. As soon as Osiris was pieced together the gods appointed him the King of the Underworld.

Osiris' first task was to take revenge on Set. He appeared from the Underworld to his son Horus (the Elder) and prepared him for the bloody task. After a fearsome fight, Horus defeated Set, but when he brought him before Isis, she refused to allow him to be killed and instead released him. In a fury, Horus turned on his mother, tearing off her crown and, in some versions, beheading her. Upon hearing this, Thoth, the scribe to the Underworld, made her a crown of cow horns.

Isis, both as an emblem of the cycle of nature and that of the moon, is like all Great Mother goddesses, both creator and destroyer. (The fall of Isis and the gift of the horns is, of course, an allegory of the moon's cycle: Isis loses her light as the moon wanes but retrieves her radiance as the moon waxes.[3]) Her image, with the young Horus at her breast, was worshipped throughout Egypt – and beyond – long before and after the time of Christ and clearly synchronized, if not gave birth, to the Christian reverence of the Virgin and Child. Indeed, it is more than likely that many of the shrines to the Black Virgin in Europe are in reality statues of Black Isis.

The 'black' destroying nature of Isis is personified by her twin sister Nepthys who is described in similar terms as any Queen of the Underworld: 'Terrible one, lady of the rain storm, destroyer of the souls of men, orderer, producer, and maker of slaughter'.[4] But Isis as Mother Nature is both good and bad. She is both just and cruel. The cycle of nature is a ceaseless cycle of growth and decay. According to Esther Harding, Isis decreed that 'there should not be perpetual harmony, with the good always in the ascendant' but that 'there should always be a conflict between the powers of growth and those of destruction'.[5] Yet Black Isis was not entirely destructive, for she was also revered as a goddess of healing and, somewhat appropriately, believed to have power and control over love affairs.

It was in rediscovering Isis that more and more of Persephone's archetypal meaning began to emerge. In several of my dreams, curtains – often thin and transparent, like net – would half-conceal the scene behind; in many others I would find myself in a small boat on a lake or the sea. The Six of Swords unfailingly turned up in any spread of the Tarot cards. In the Waite pack this card depicts a hooded woman and child being ferried in a punt across a calm stretch of water: among its many interpretations, this card is thought to represent a journey in consciousness. Isis in her little boat searching for her lost Osiris is a poignant yet courageous image which, like the appropriation of Ishtar's jewels in her quest for Tammuz, symbolizes the search against all the odds for that which is inestimably precious and that which can only be found by submitting oneself to the darkness and the unknown.

The symbolism of the curtain can also be seen to be connected to Isis and the journey in consciousness. The many-coloured veil of Isis is synonymous with the veil of *maya*, illusion. The veil of Isis 'is the ever-changing form of nature, whose beauty and tragedy veil the spirit from our eyes. This perpetual interplay in the manifest world, which includes external objects, trees and hills and the sea, as well as other human beings, and also ourselves, our own bodies, our own emotional reactions even, the whole drama of the world, seems to have such an absolute reality that we do not question it. Yet in moments of insight, induced, perhaps, by pain and suffering or great joy, we may suddenly realize that this which makes up the obvious form of the world, is not true, the real. The real, the eternal is a different kind of reality.'

The veil of Isis also has other implications: 'It is said that the living being is caught in the net or veil of Isis . . . and that we all get entangled or caught in the net of nature. This net of nature is the same as the web of fate or circumstance.' And although we may resent being caught up with our fate and 'long to be free to follow our own devices', 'if [our divine spirit] were not captured in this way it would wander free and would never have an opportunity to transform. The spirit of man must necessarily be caught in the net of Isis or it cannot be carried in her boat to the next phase of experience.'[6]

At one time myths and religion were inextricably linked – as, indeed, some would argue they are today. So intricately interwoven in fact that aspects of these archetypal stories were enacted in the way of religious rites of passage – as initiations. *The Egyptian Book of the Dead* is in effect a 'handbook' of the various stages of initiation as described by an initiate, Teta. Not only did the initiation bestow the gift of immortality but acted as a guide to the traveller in the Other World. In the mystery cult of Isis that flourished throughout Egypt and the Greek peninsula, initiation involved a dramatic reconstruction of the story of Osiris; by experiencing the grief and joy of Isis and achieving a state of emotional ecstasy, the initiate underwent redemption and became at one with God. One of the most crucial parts of the initiation process was the candidate's identification with and personification of Set – or to use his more familiar Greek name, Typhon. Typhon was the god of lust and 'desirousness' and in his ordeal, the initiate, already weak from days of fasting, had to withstand continual provocation and temptation until he passed through the equivalent of a pain barrier. The purpose of this aspect of initiation was to allow the initiate to fully experience his basest instincts while simultaneously having to exert complete control over them; this effectively brought him to the limits of his sanity and certainly to physical and emotional collapse. After this 'death' the initiate was brought back to consciousness – to life – by the power of Isis. By the impersonation of Typhon, Esther Harding maintains that the initiate experienced his own lustfulness 'until he realized its utter inability to satisfy his human need. The truly human part of him, the spirit, was, as it were, killed by the domination of the Typhonic spirit, just as Osiris had been killed by Set. Then, and not until then, could the love of Isis and his longing for her regenerate him. By her power and grace, he was restored to life, not any longer as a brute beast, but as a man, redeemed from his own animal passions . . . This rebirth, however, could only be achieved by lifting the veil of Isis . . . It is by the power of Isis, through her love, that the man sunk in lust and passion is raised to the spiritual life.'[7]

Before I go on to discuss further aspects of Persephone in the sense of a planetary archetype, perhaps we should review what we have so far. Persephone would seem to have dominion over union, especially in its divine sense, and over fated alliances; she has a dual nature – both creator and destroyer – and it is through her inspiration that we make a descent into the abyss: a descent that strips away all the trappings of the ego and the material resources (*maya*) that blind us to our divine reality, a descent that acts as a process of purification in order that we may find the most precious essence of all, our true Self. Only when we submit ourselves to this process in absolute humility can we be reborn and illuminated. Most crucially, Persephone's journey is not through the intellect but through the heart. Through Ishtar and Isis we comprehend that love and pain inspire both the descent into the darkness and the resurrection. And so it is that the heart tried by pain engenders transformation and gives birth to a capacity for love of an altogether higher nature: it is through the opening of the heart chakra[8] that personal transformation is realized.

And if this sounds like the stuff of Pluto, think again. Allegorically,

Pluto's realm is the Underworld of the unconscious; but this realm is also ruled by his consort, Persephone. Pluto is the masculine aspect of transformation, which to a certain extent is almost entirely related to the intellect on the one hand and 'animal' passion, on the other. (After all, in the Eleusinian myth, it is Pluto's rapacious nature that compels him to abduct Persephone, and in the Osirian myth, Set, or Typhon, embodies lust and 'desirousness'.) And while Pluto may lend his name to the Underworld, its rites of passage are conducted by Persephone, and only by the power of love, not knowledge, can 'death' be transcended and transformation occur.

Until now, astrological Pluto has ruled omnipotently over the subterranean world of the unconscious. 'He' represents all the dark and taboo aspects of life – sex, death and fate. Yet Pluto does not rule alone, he shares his realm with his Queen, Persephone. And while Pluto's realm continues to represent, astrologically, the vast Underworld of the unconscious and, indeed the compelling attraction of the dark and the forbidden, its all-important dimension of creation and destruction is personified by Persephone, not Pluto. Pluto is not a Mother-Goddess archetype – he is male. It is through Persephone that the descent into the darkness is inspired – almost always by a 'wounding of the personality'; and this wound is invariably inflicted by the hand of fate – by a totally unanticipated and life-changing event. Yet fate is not a random force but ultimately something self, or rather soul, created – a process that embodies karma, the spiritual law of cause and effect, the law of divine retribution.

In *The Forces of Destiny*, I discussed the nature of fate at length. I mentioned that in times long past, fate, as a deity, was almost always personified by a goddess – and usually in triplicate (the Scandinavian Norns – Urdi, Vedani and Skuld – the Weird Sisters, the Furies, the Morrigan and the Graeae). The Triple Goddess of fate symbolized the three phases of the moon, 'life as a mystical thread was spun by the Virgin (waxing phase), sustained by the Mother (full moon) and cut by the Crone (the waning, dark of the moon)'; in other words, fate was the territory of the Great Mother (moon) goddesses – Kore, Isis, Ishtar and Persephone. As Esther Harding says of Ishtar, 'the Fate of everything she holds in her hands'. Thus it is not Pluto himself who carries the astrological banner for fate but his consort, Persephone. But if we continue to conceptualize fate as a blind force we miss the point of Persephone: she is concerned with divine justice; like all Mother-Goddess archetypes she represents the eternal momentum of cause and effect; she presides over our just deserts and in this way takes on the cloak of Nemesis.

Also in *The Forces of Destiny*, I discussed the role of Mercury in connection with Pluto. I consider Mercury to be the lower octave[9] of Pluto: in myth Mercury is linked to Pluto since he ferried the souls of the dead to Hades and was the only being (other than Persephone, of course) to be able to enter and leave the Underworld at will. Mercury's staff, the caduceus, is dominated by the intertwining of two serpents which represent kundalini – something we shall again refer to shortly. These connecting principles between Mercury and Pluto serve to illustrate the point that the Mercurial world of thought leads to the Plutonic realm of the unconscious. In an altered state of consciousness, achieved through meditation or hypnotic states, the individual can dip into vaults of the unconscious and so bring to light deeply buried issues that hold the key to many of his problems and complexes. In this way Mercury, as the astrological principle of the intellect and the logical mind, leads to Plutonic enlightenment. *But not to divine transformation.*

Divine transformation must involve the heart and if there is one known planet synonymous with affairs of the heart, it is Venus. Mythological Venus, Greek Aphrodite, was the goddess of erotic love. She was renowned for her countless love affairs with both mortals and gods and she was tireless in her desire to help young lovers. But Aphrodite was a late-comer to Olympus. Prior to her incorporation as a Greek deity, she was an Asiatic goddess. 'There is little doubt that Aphrodite . . . was originally a mother goddess of a type almost universally worshipped in the Near East and perhaps best known under the name of Ishtar or Astarte.'[10] Certainly from the Greek point of view Aphrodite held much sway in the affairs of men and gods, but by the time the Greeks had adopted her, her role as goddess of love became pre-eminent and any vestiges of the Mother Goddess with her creating-destroying nature had been swept away. Aphrodite's origins may indeed have been in Mother-Goddess soil but her branches were wafting in the honeyed scent of erotic love. Aphrodite was, of course, quite capable of wreaking vengeance on those who failed to do her bidding, but she could never be perceived as a black goddess. Nevertheless, through the labyrinthine world of myth we can trace the origins and connections of all the deities and one of the ways in which the Greeks perpetuated the links between Aphrodite and the dark environs of the Underworld was through the myth of Adonis:

Aphrodite, jealous of the beauty of the mortal, Myrrha, caused her to be suddenly smitten with love for her own father, King Cinyras. The result of this union was Adonis. Aphrodite promptly fell in love with Adonis and, placing him in a chest, gave him to Persephone for safe keeping. Persephone, in due course, also fell in love with Adonis and refused to return him to Aphrodite. Eventually the matter was resolved by Zeus who decreed that Adonis should spend part of the year with Persephone and another with Aphrodite.

This, of course, is yet another variation on the theme of the cycle of nature and the division between the fertile months of the year and the barren ones.

But while Aphrodite personifies the erotic aspect of love, she in no way embodies its deeper, more powerful quality: divine love, the love of Ishtar and Isis that transforms and regenerates. But Venus and Persephone are inextricably linked, for it is through the portals of Venus that Persephone's realm can be approached: through the Venusian experience of erotic love – of falling in love – the earthly individual glimpses the divine. But for this glimpse to remain a sustained experience a journey into the depths of his being must be undertaken. And so it is that when the time has come for the individual to take the step toward the divine he unconsciously seeks, Venus and Persephone will conspire to bring about an encounter with fate.

And so we can comprehend the connection between astrological Venus and Persephone: Venus, as the lower octave of Persephone, represents an experience of love almost all of us can relate to – a love of beauty and the things of the Earth, of desires and earthly passions and sometimes the divine, but all too ephemeral nature of eros – but Persephone's love is of a higher resonance. The connection between Venus and Persephone also resolves the problem of the rulership of the sign of Libra. Venus has always been considered the ruling planet of Libra, yet she also rules the sensuous, artistic and rustic sign of Taurus. Dual rulership is a deeply unsatisfactory situation for astrologers to contend with, and while Taurus happily embodies all the more fleshly and substantial aspects of Venus, these earthly concerns are totally unsuited to Libra. Libra certainly concerns itself with love, beauty and relating, but there is also an extraordinary attraction for highly destructive relationships – and we only have to consider the significance of Libra in Hitler's, Churchill's and Thatcher's charts, not to mention that of the Second World War, to ponder how such a loving sign could exhibit such a thirst for war. Persephone, the dread goddess of the Underworld, the creator-destroyer, supplies a reason, not because she relishes death and destruction, but because she comprehends that the balance must be eternally maintained between 'the powers of growth and those of destruction'. In the Eleusinian myth, after Persephone had eaten the pomegranate that bound her to the Underworld, the only way she could return to Earth and her mother, Demeter, was through a compromise negotiated by Zeus – a compromise that allowed her to spend six months on the Earth and the other half of the year underground with Pluto. Libra is the quintessence of compromise and balance and it is Persephone who personifies these principles, not Venus.

From an astronomical perspective, unlike the other constellations (against which the 30 equal divisions of the zodiac roughly fit), Libra shares most of its territory with Virgo and Scorpio – the former ruled by Mercury and the latter by Pluto. Factors that drive the astrological case for Persephone's rulership of Libra well and truly home. Also, considering the horoscopic circle with its 12 house divisions: proceeding anticlockwise from the Ascendant, all the signs in the first half (lower hemisphere) are ruled by the 'personal' planets[11] while those in the upper hemisphere are governed by the trans-personal planets – that is, with the exception of Libra. By designating Persephone as the ruler of Libra, this anomaly disappears.

I have left until last the spiritual dimension of Persephone which has so much bearing on today's change in consciousness. In Chapter 2, I mentioned that the experience of kundalini appeared to be on the increase and that Kenneth Ring had speculated that this increase represented an evolutionary thrust toward a new and enlightened form of the human race – *homo noeticus*. In my earlier writings I had related the experience of kundalini, through astrological symbolism, to Pluto. I now believe that kundalini is the essence of Persephone.

Kundalini, as man's spiritual power, has been a central concept – albeit by various names – of almost all religions and spiritual disciplines. The Gnostic Gospels talk of a divine power existing in everyone in a latent condition; the Masons speak of the energy, or Spirit Fire, that rises up through the 32 degrees, or segments, of the spinal column and ultimately enters the skull. The Hopis believe that each human being is created in the image of God, but from the moment of birth the 'door' (the third eye) at the top of the head gradually closes and man falls from grace. Man then has to work his way up through the chakral centres until the 'door' at the crown re-opens. The Cabbalic Tree of Life with its various stations is but yet another representation of the steps to kundalini enlightenment. The ancient peoples of Mexico worshipped the serpent god, Quetzalcoatl – a clear parallel with the god-like power of the sleeping serpent, kundalini. Indeed, the serpent power even makes its appearance in the Bible, although in a much altered form as 'the devil in disguise'[12] who tempts Adam and Eve to taste the fruit of knowledge and so inspires their ejection from paradise. A considerable reversal of the truth, it would seem.

In the ancient yogic traditions, Kundalini was a goddess. She was portrayed as perennially young and playful yet her play was nothing less than the creation, sustenance and dissolution of the world. In Siddha Yoga she is given different names depending upon the aspect of power she evokes:

She is called Saraswati when she gives knowledge and wisdom [and] when she gives inner experience of the Truth. She is called Shri Lakshmi when she takes the form of good fortune and abundance . . . She is called Durga or Kali when she destroys all that must be destroyed in you, all that is holding you back. [13]

According to Swami Kripananda,

. . . known as the Goddess, or the Divine Mother, as the serpent power or Mahamaya, Kundalini is our potential to know ourselves as God. From ancient times it has been known that this mysterious power sleeps in each human being as a coiled energy at the base of the spine, until that moment in a person's evolution when it is time for self-knowledge to arise. For centuries the great spiritual Masters bestowed Shaktipat, the gift of grace that awakens this power, on only a few initiates.

Now, through the grace of such modern day gurus as Gurumayi Chidvilasananda more and more people have been given the grace (*Shaktipat*) to awaken kundalini. Swami Kripananda goes on to say:

When Kundalini lies asleep, she takes the form of the world illusion, maya, the illusion of multiplicity and separateness . . . When she is awakened . . . she goes to battle against the inner demons: desire, anger, greed, pride, delusion, jealousy. She is ultimately victorious. She is the divine force of transformation. Rising through a subtle channel in the body, she pierces and purifies the energy centres strung like jewels on a thread along her path, destroying our ignorance and misunderstanding about who we are and what the world is. [14]

So many of these attributes of the goddess Kundalini are but echoes of those we have encountered through the course of this chapter. But Kundalini is more than an archetypal theme she is the divine energy alive within us all. And all we have to do is awaken her. And we begin to sense her stirring through the opening of the heart:

There is a space in the heart which is most extraordinary, and it is well worth visiting. There is a lotus, a beautiful lotus inside, and if your awareness could travel along the petals of that lotus, you could see the whole cosmos . . . That fascinating lotus in the heart is the kingdom of God. That inner Shakti, Kundalini, leads the mind, the intellect, the awareness to that place of divinity in the heart . . . If you were to reach that divine space in your heart you would be able to perceive all those things which lie out of the range of your senses . . . As one approaches that space in the heart one is overcome by a delicious bliss, by unearthly sweetness. This is what happens when one is blessed by the inner Shakti, Kundalini. [15]

In many ways, to me, this chapter has seemed like a journey in itself. As I wrote the sequence of events that introduced Persephone to me and traced the experiences that led me to the rim of the abyss and my subsequent plunge into the darkness I was able to synthesize my fragmentary perceptions of Persephone and comprehend the greater meaning of my descent – and why. I came to see that at some unconscious level I had inspired the events that led to my 'downfall'. I found it difficult to accept that I was only receiving my just deserts but could perceive that it was a necessary 'evil'. And through the process of writing, the pain gradually fell away. For my own part, Persephone has been the most powerful lesson in synchronicity anyone could wish to have. Into my own small and insignificant life, Persephone entered like a titanic Furie. As the passionate spark was ignited between Damon and I, Kali quite literally raged. In the outer world, storms plucked the trees from the earth and brought down telephone and electricity lines; and within the lives of our respective families the emotional torrent raged unabated. But, in the eye of the hurricane, Damon and I basked under the spell of Eros: Venus was preparing the ground for Persephone. When the cataclysm finally struck home, I was decimated on all fronts. I might have died, but instead I experienced a psychological death. Eventually, I came to understand that without such a devastating experience I would never have begun the inner journey: only the death of one of my children could have equalled the impact of losing Damon. And ultimately, I came to be grateful. I finally perceived that the pain and grief had had a purpose and that the suffering was, in effect, an initiation. I know there is still a long way to go before I can return victorious with my 'Tammuz'; but at least I can look back and see how far I have come.

This, of course, is a personal experience of Persephone; but the collective one is all about us. Persephone is both creator and destroyer: in the previous chapter we explored her astronomical potential to bring cataclysm to the Earth; her apocalyptic signature must also be on the current events in the Middle East. In many ways, these events more than any other in recent world history bring home to us that Persephone is Nemesis by another name – the goddess of retribution. While, in the January and February of 1991, the might of the allied forces pitted itself against Saddam Hussein in Iraq, the irony remained that it was we in the West who, under the banner of entrepreneurialism, had supplied him with all his phenomenal war machinery – an arsenal with the capability not only to decimate any aggressor or any neighbouring state but the entire world. And although the Iraqi army was successfully driven out of Kuwait, the Middle East continues to be a cauldron of trouble and dissension threatening to bubble over into an Armageddon-like conflict at any moment. There may be little comfort in the knowledge that Persephone is merely presiding over the eternal momentum of cause and effect and ensuring that the balance is maintained between growth and decay but within this concept is the certain understanding that out of the death throes of the old, the new is beginning to emerge – *perestroika*, renewal, also bears the signature of Persephone. And for this there is much to celebrate.

Above all, Persephone's way is through the heart. And with the raising of planetary consciousness, that route to the divine becomes ever more open to us even if, at the opposite end of the spectrum, the capacity for evil and destruction also soars. Persephone, as the higher octave of Venus, promises a love of an infinite and eternal nature, the love of the higher Self as opposed to the little self – the love that transcends the boundaries of the ego; as kundalini, Persephone offers all of us a route to our divinity; a route to the New Age when man can once again walk among the gods.

Appendix

1) M. Esther Harding, *Woman's Mysteries* (Rider, 1982).
2) Ibid.
3) The maiming of Isis and the gift of the cow horns is also an allegory of the way Isis, as the Egyptian Moon Goddess, was restored to life as the Horned Crescent, Hathor. Hathor also represented the dark destroying aspect of the lunar goddess in the same way as Nepthys.
4) *The Egyptian Book of the Dead* as quoted by Barbara Walker in *The Woman's Encyclopaedia of Myths and Secrets* (Harper and Row, 1983).
5) *Woman's Mysteries*, op cit.
6) Ibid.
7) Ibid.
8) The word *chakra* means 'wheel': just as in the physical body there are the plexuses located along the spine, so too in the subtle (or psychic) body there are energy

centres known as the chakras. There are seven main chakras (and in some systems five): the first at the base of the spine, the second in the sacrum area, the third at the naval, the fourth at the heart, the fifth at the throat, the sixth between the eyebrows, and the seventh at the crown of the head.

9) In esoteric astrology, the trans-Saturnian planets are considered to represent another octave of experience. Thus each one of these outer planets represents a higher vibration of one of the personal planets. Uranus is considered to be the higher octave of the Sun, Neptune the higher dimension of the Moon, and Pluto that of Mercury.

10) Edward Tripp, *Classical Mythology* (Collins, 1970).

11) The Sun, Moon, Mercury, Venus and Mars.

12) In the *Cipher of Genesis*, Carlo Suares maintains that Genesis is in fact a cabalistic script and that such people as Adam and Eve represent abstract formulas of cosmic energy focused in the human psyche. Concerning the serpent in the Garden of Eden he states, 'In certain [traditions] his name is kundalini.' He also maintains that when Eve is questioned about tasting the 'forbidden' fruit she does not say, 'The serpent beguiled me', but replies that the serpent blends his earthly fire with her lost heavenly fire which comes to life again: he breathes the cosmic breath of life into her.

13) From a talk by Gurumayi Chidvilasananda quoted in *Darshan* vol 41/2, 1990.

14) Ibid.

15) From a talk given by Baba Muktananda in California on 17 April 1974: 'A Million Times Brighter than the Sun'.

5

The Ring of Saturn

RELATIONSHIPS HAVE BEEN THE MAINSPRING OF MY ADULT LIFE. AND, cliché of clichés, I suppose I have sought to find myself through partnerships – as if through the mirrors of different people I have been able to glimpse and develop various facets of my being. Far from losing myself in another person I have found that a close and symbiotic relationship actually provides a launching pad for my aspirations – it inspires me to extend my personal frontiers and makes those achievements even more worthwhile and fulfilling. Another aspect of love, in a way. But more than this, I have always believed in the power of love to transform the most ordinary life into something magnificent. If I look back in time, I can see that I was busy preparing the ground for my future quest – my Holy Grail – for the perfect, divine relationship fairly early on. I was an only child and so spent much of my time creating a fantasy world in which I could assume various characters. I had my favourites, of course, but best of all I liked to be the princess – beautiful and serene, if not a little autocratic – who always found her prince and lived happily ever after. Real life was to prove somewhat of a disappointment.

If I hadn't questioned my needs, my expectations and my motives before, I certainly began to do so after the débâcle of Damon. One enlightened friend commented that Damon represented my 'Cosmic Man' – a sort of prototype – in that he combined the characteristics – both physical and temperamental – of the three most important men in my life – my first love, my first husband and my second. Damon's chart also contained features (aspects, signs and degree areas) common to the horoscopes of the other three. Clearly, I was attracted to certain qualities in men because of my astrological and psychological make-up for karmic reasons, and these qualities revealed themselves time and again in the charts of the men I chose. As I looked back on these relationships, I could see that, with the exception of my late husband, Michael, I had been drawn into each relationship through the portals of Venus–Neptune – in other words through the doorway of eros. And while I had been lucky enough to experience that sense of soul contact with both my second husband and with Damon, on each of these occasions something had gone badly wrong. Effectively, although I was drawn in by Neptune, what I ended up with was Saturn.

Now, when I say I ended up with Saturn, I mean that despite all signs to the contrary at the outset of my relationships, ultimately I was presented with all those experiences I least wanted and found most heart-wearying, all those experiences that were quintessentially Saturn. In the place of love, tenderness, joy and compassion came material problems, emotional alienation and relentless hardship and toil and, in the case of Damon, cruelty, rejection and the denial of all that I stood for. Like the physician who must heal himself, I had to face the fact that there was something about Saturn that I was simply not dealing with. And until I did, I knew that I could not hope to reach a level where the divine in a relationship could be sustained.

I've called this chapter 'The Ring of Saturn' for two reasons. First, because of the wedding ring which is a symbol of the bond between two people and their commitment to each other, and second, because while a circle protects it can also imprison. So, on the one hand, while Saturn can be seen to represent the ties that bind two people together, this planet can equally well restrain a couple. Yet this chapter is not about Saturnian contacts between two charts and how they may manifest in a relationship, but rather about Saturn as an archetype and therefore a process we must deal with, an entity we must encounter, in one form or another, 'on the way to the wedding' – on the way to making the marriage within which must occur before we can experience true union with another.

Saturn represents the border country between earthly experience, and therefore the earthy dimensions of relationship, and the loftier regions of the trans-personal planets in which the divine nature of love can be found. But we cannot inhabit these rarefied zones until we have gained our 'exit visa' from Saturn. Until that time we may merely enjoy short stays among their pleasure palaces; we can only set up home on the Olympian heights of Uranus, Neptune and Pluto when we have fully integrated Saturn and thus relinquished the hold he has on us.

Saturn represents all those things which bind us to the Earth and ensure that we remain focused on the realities of life. Saturn stands for all those principles that make us solid citizens, pillars of society. If we fail to pay our taxes or our debts, the law will force us to do so and, if we behave in an anti-social fashion, if we break the rules, we will be punished. And if these aspects of life sound somewhat grim, remember that Saturn is often portrayed as the Grim Reaper – always there to remind us that we have a limited time on Earth. While we can ensure that Saturn is obeyed in practical terms, by not getting into the red, by paying our debts, by keeping within our limits and never crossing the boundary of the letter of the law, there is also the spiritual perspective to take into consideration. Saturn ensures that we repay our karmic debts and that we receive precisely what we deserve from any previous life's efforts. Saturn also sees to it that we keep within the limits of our cosmic blueprint and if we flagrantly dismiss his brief, we shall have to surrender to the inexorable justice of Persephone. But, perhaps the most important aspect of Saturn to grasp is that he represents the shell of the ego and until we learn to dissolve that barrier, until the ego is transcended, we cannot experience the truly supernal qualities of the outer planets. Saturn effectively stands for all those things that keep us trapped within the confines of our ego – all the factors that ultimately deny us the freedom to know the divine. Yet the ego cannot be transcended until it has been fully formed, just as in the individuation process the inner journey can only begin once the ego has been consolidated. There is no Saturnian by-pass on the route to the divine.

The ego is conscientiously built up by the concepts and behaviour that we believe protect and support us. Until we are strong enough and self-aware enough we cannot demolish this, otherwise our world, our support structure, would fall apart. But as soon as the dawn of realization pierces the dimly lit prison of the ego we can see that the key to our liberation lies within our grasp. And by reaching out for that key we open ourselves up to illumination of the true Self, the divine Self. So although Saturn may appear to be a planet that may deny us so much in life, in truth he represents the passport to the higher regions. He becomes, instead of the Grim Reaper, the Dweller on the Threshold.

These Saturnian factors that keep us trapped within the ego are primarily our fears, doubts and negativity, our personal rules and regulations and our need to control. Sometimes these Saturnian limitations are built up through our own experience of the world, but a great many are forced upon us by society and by our cultural and religious bias and, perhaps most important of all, by our parents. Liz Greene was one of the first astrologers to directly relate the Jungian concept of the Shadow with Saturn. In this way, like the archetype of the Shadow, Saturn becomes the dumping ground for all those aspects of ourselves that we feel inferior about and any behaviour that we don't like. It is impossible for us to take up permanent residency in the upper reaches of consciousness and pick the fruit from those orchards if we are loaded with Saturnian baggage. All our doubts, fears and negativity must be confronted, brought into the light, because it is only when we can see what lies in the darkness that we can start to sift through the shrapnel of the ego for any nuggets of gold. Also, to really live the spiritual life, to access those lofty states of consciousness and maintain them, unless we have come to terms with the material world and accounted to Saturn, what we have is merely illusion and pretension.

All the planetary symbols reveal a hierarchy of meaning – in other words, each planet correlates to many, many themes on various levels of consciousness. So, on one level of reality, Saturn represents taxes, debts, responsibilities and obligations in the most material sense, on another level he represents those aspects of our being of which we are most fearful, and on yet another level, he stands for the karmic fruits of our labours and our karmic duties and ties. In the main, Saturn is well and truly 'heavy duty' material, but if we take into regard his exaltation in Libra, we can see that his sort of justice is fair and that sometimes we can do very well from a Saturnian harvest. In *The Forces of Destiny* I discussed Saturn in regard to making one's mark in life, and this is certainly a positive attribute of this otherwise difficult planetary archetype.

We all have Saturn somewhere in our charts, and usually aspected to one or more of the personal planets or the angles, so we cannot escape his influence any more than we can prevent ourselves constructing our individual world view and salting away all our unwanted and negative behaviour. Thus the task of integrating Saturn in one's life and in one's psyche must be accomplished on all levels. The opportunity to come to grips with Saturnian influence on any or all the levels so far discussed arrives when this planet forms angles to its original position or transits another planet or point in the birth chart. It is at these times that Saturn tweaks our Achilles heel and does his best to insist that we confront our obligations and duties and all those things we feel most negative about. Likewise, when we meet Saturn in another person – when contacts between Saturn are exchanged between the charts of two individuals – the opportunity arises to get down to some serious Saturnian business, perhaps related to several lifetimes before, and, hopefully, to resolve those issues.

Saturnian contacts between one chart and another may indeed represent the karmic ties that bind two individuals together, the ties that must be transcended if a true relationship is to be found – one free of any vestige of karmic debris. One of the ways to discover what this karmic debris may be is by accessing a shared past through hypnotic regression. If one cannot consciously understand the reasons why a relationship has come about, why there seem to be so many innate problems and how resolution may be achieved, the answer is not to walk away but to set about the task of clearing one's own Saturnian back yard. With patience, acceptance and love, old Saturnian threads simply fade away.

It is absolutely vital that we fully integrate Saturn, because when we have, we have no further need to project all our negativity onto others or to experience those unacknowledged aspects of Saturn through other people. Also, once we have faced our deepest fears and anxieties, we are free to experience real intimacy in a relationship and therefore begin to find true union with another person. The task of Saturn in relationships is to recognize where the barriers exist – both individually and as a couple – then work to transcend them.

I have already mentioned the concept that until we have made the inner marriage, that is, integrated the many processes within our psyches, we cannot hope to find true and lasting union in an outer relationship. We all have these inner images and processes and our task is to discover how they have been built up and how they interfere with the real experience of another individual. I have known other psychologists and astrologers to condemn these inner images because of the power they exert in falsely projecting themselves onto others. But while it is essential to understand what these projections are, where they come from and why they may be totally inappropriate in some cases – in other words, when the person we project a certain image onto cannot in any way meet those requirements – I would say that without an inner image to draw upon, we would never experience eros – that romantic-divine state which forms the prelude to true union – the engagement that leads to the wedding. In a sense, when such a person truly personifies the archetypal material, we are close to finding a true marriage. Put another way, when we have encountered these images within our psyche and understood them, our partners may truly be found to personify all those qualities. Thus I would not reduce any of the archetypes that we will meet in this book through Uranus, Neptune and Pluto to mere manifestations of the psyche that must be overcome so much as profound themes that haunt us until one day we can fully experience their music and bask in their blissful resonance.

Annoyingly, or happily, depending upon your point of view, very few of us live out only one archetypal theme on the way to the wedding. After all, we all have Saturn, Neptune, Uranus and Pluto in our charts and all of them are likely to make some contact with one of the personal planets or angles of the chart. But clearly when we have a pattern repeating itself time and again with the people we fall in love with or with whom we enter into relationship, then this will resound loudly and clearly in the birth chart.

A little earlier on I admitted that there was something about Saturn that I was obviously failing to deal with: it took me some hypnotherapy sessions to discover what it was. Using the hypnotic state I eventually tracked down the negative little person who lived within me. I was shocked to see how much masochistic pleasure she gained from being hard done by. Worse, that besides this martyr who thrived inside my psyche was a tyrant who drew a perverted satisfaction from nailing her partner to the cross of his failures – no matter how small. I also discovered that this pattern had been established in my subconscious at an early age. I perceived that my father, while consciously presenting me with the image of the successful man-in-charge, was nevertheless unconsciously convinced – through his own family pattern – that he had never achieved the success and recognition that he deserved. In a sense, despite all signs to the contrary – for he had, indeed, received considerable financial and professional rewards for his talents – he believed he had failed, and I, like all small children, was far more responsive to the unconscious message than the overt one. And while I loved him deeply, somewhere along the line I was also deeply affected by his frustration and his sense of inadequacy. This unconscious message had two big effects: first, as an only child and heir to my father's ambitions, I determined to make a success of my own life, and in the process I came to attach no value to myself as a person – I unconsciously believed that I could only be loved for what I could do, not who I was. In this way, while I invariably succeeded at what I did, it didn't make me feel worthwhile. Second, the men I entered into a relationship with also suffered from some deep frustration with their material standing in the world and although I was drawn to them because of this 'wound' I also despised them for their inadequacy. In a way I was getting back at myself through my partners and perpetuating a pattern I consciously did not want.

These realizations are hard to write about but not as painful as they were to experience. No encounter with the Shadow is pleasant. But it was with these truly felt realizations that healing could occur and Saturn begin to be integrated. There was no point in blaming my husband or Damon for the suffering they had inflicted upon me through lack of care and value for me as a person: unconsciously, this is what I had come to expect. Only when this had been fully comprehended and accepted by the unconscious[1] could the 'habits' of a lifetime be transformed.

Linda Leonard brings the archetype of Saturn to life through her discussion of Prince Charming and the Special Princess.[2] Women who resonate primarily with this archetype of the Special Princess yearn to be rescued from their imprisonment; they search for a 'prince' who will take them away from their isolation or their persecutors, a prince who will care for them and support them. Prince Charming, the counterpart of the Special Princess, feels he must constantly rescue women and then continue to protect them and provide them with all his worldly goods. This must be, of course, the most common stereotype of all and one whose very principles form the cornerstones of the marriage vows. Yet both these familiar roles are laden with potential time bombs. The Special Princess and Prince Charming invariably become trapped in the outer manifestations of their roles – he the provider and protector and she the protected – yet effectively they are both caged creatures since it is only the outer trappings of relationship that are being met: until each has encountered his own vulnerability, his fears and his pain, neither is whole enough to relate freely, openly and deeply to another. As Leonard says, 'Many women in our culture . . . have been enchanted by this figure and have married men who they hoped would rescue them from a difficult situation in their lives, thus never looking within to deal with their inner conflicts or looking without to see who was the man they married. Others, with this ideal in mind, remain alone and isolated, unable to find their Prince Charming.'[3] Leonard uses the fairy-tale of *Rapunzel* to convey the archetypal theme of Prince Charming and the Special Princess:

Once upon a time there lived a man and wife who longed for a child, but the wife was barren. The husband loved his wife and did all in his power to fulfil her every wish. One day, as the wife was looking out of a window, she saw some radishes in the next-door garden and begged her husband to get them for her. Dutifully, the husband clambered through the thicket into the garden and picked the radishes. But just as he was leaving, he was caught by the owner – none other than a powerful witch. The husband fell to his knees and begged for his life, but the witch would only let him go if he promised to give her his first child. This the husband did, in the certain knowledge that his wife could not conceive. But, nine months later, his wife gave birth to a daughter. Then the witch demanded her dues and carried the baby – who had been named Rapunzel – away with her.

Rapunzel grew up to be the most beautiful girl; so beautiful that the witch placed her in a high tower which only she could enter. There were no doors, merely one window. Every day Rapunzel would sit at the window of the tower looking out on the world. Since she knew no other life, she was not aware of her imprisonment and, indeed, the witch was good and kind to her. Every day, the witch would come to the bottom of the tower and call up to her, 'Rapunzel, Rapunzel, let down your hair.'

And Rapunzel would release her long golden tresses that fell to the ground so that the witch could climb up to her.

One day, a young, handsome prince wandered into the woods where the tower stood and saw the beautiful Rapunzel sitting by the window. He then heard the witch calling her name and watched her climb up Rapunzel's hair. The following day, he returned to the tower in the forest and called, 'Rapunzel, Rapunzel, let down your hair.'

And when she did he clambered up to her.

Needless to say, Rapunzel was at first terrified of the handsome prince since she had never been in close proximity to any man. But the prince reassured her and soon she began to trust and love him. He visited the tower every day and it wasn't long before Rapunzel agreed to be his wife: together they planned her escape. But the wicked witch overheard their plans and when the prince had gone, she cut off Rapunzel's long tresses and banished her to the wilderness. Then, transforming herself into the likeness of Rapunzel, she waited at the window. But just as the prince had clambered to the top of the window, she released the tresses sending him plummeting to the earth. He fell into a bush of thorns which pierced his eyes.

In utter despair, the prince wandered the Earth blindly searching for Rapunzel. After many years he found himself in the wilderness and heard the weeping Rapunzel. When Rapunzel saw him, she rushed into his arms and in their embrace two of her tears fell onto his eyes allowing him at last to see.

And the prince and the princess lived happily ever after.

There are many themes of Saturnian interest here but the 'happy ending' is a beautiful allegory of the way so many of us search blindly in the wilderness of unfulfilling relationships for a love that is lost or unreachable; a love that can only be truly found when we have made that lonely quest to our inner being. As far as Saturn is concerned, until we recognize that our salvation does not depend on another person but in ourselves, we merely replace one prison sentence for another. Only when we have confronted our inner sense of isolation and found that we are indeed prepared to love and heal ourselves can we avoid incarceration in a marriage that is hollow. It is only through freeing ourselves from our own Saturnian chains that we gain the ability to truly relate.

Rapunzel is redolent with Saturnian symbolism – the barren wife, the punishment, the imprisonment, blindness and abandonment. And while there are lessons for both the Special Princess and Prince Charming in regard to the theme of breaking the chains that bind us to a limited capacity to love and a life-long sentence of romantic unfulfilment, there is, perhaps more for the woman to gain in the way of understanding from this story.

Linda Leonard suggests that Rapunzel is 'the story of many women who are locked away in a tower, cut off from relationship by a devouring, possessive enchantress-like mother. Although they may long for relationship, like Rapunzel they often give their chances away by speaking of the man to the mother, who then attempts to destroy the relationship. And like Rapunzel, often they must leave the mother and go off on their own journey, consciously suffering through life's experience, entering the desert of emptiness and wounds, the dark night of the soul, before they are independent and ready for the hard work of relationship.'[4]

Not only do we find a 'devouring mother' in this fairy-tale, but an absent father – so often twin themes of Saturn in regard to relationships. While most astrologers would agree with relating Saturn to father, especially an absent or cruel one, only a few consider Saturn to be a symbol of mother.[5] Certainly, I have preferred to interpret Saturn as a masculine principle, yet the tenth house of the horoscope, which is ruled by Saturn, invariably characterizes mother. This can be explained by the way that it is almost always the mother who influences the child's view of the world, his social behaviour and his expectations: from Day One, the baby in his mother's arms learns what he can do to satisfy his needs and, dependent upon his conditioning, begins to form his beliefs and assumptions about the way the world works and the role that is thrust upon him. It is through the mother that his ego starts to develop. So the mother, if she is the parent who has daily care and control of the child, has a far more formative influence on him than the father. In this way, it is possible to see that an individual working through a Saturnian theme in his relationships of the Special Princess or Prince Charming may indeed have an imprisoning mother at the root of his problem. And while I don't want to limit myself to specific astrological principles, this theme is more likely to be responded to if the individual has Saturn in, or Capricorn ruling, the tenth or seventh house or the Moon or Venus aspected by Saturn.

I remember some years ago being deeply affected by a television play about a young adolescent girl who had psychological problems. These problems were amplified by her parents, particularly her mother, who was over-protective to the point of emotional and psychological suffocation. Each time the girl tried to assert her independence, the mother would pull her back by subtly playing on her Achilles heel of insecurity and self-doubt. This girl eventually met a boy who loved her and was prepared to protect her. She ran away from home and lived with her boyfriend, through whom she gradually began to gain her strength and confidence. Her parents, naturally distraught, sought police help in finding her. When their daughter was taken back home, she promptly had a nervous breakdown and was taken into a psychiatric hospital. She withdrew further and further into herself until she became entirely cataleptic. It seemed that the only way she could escape the parental bonds that crushed her independence as a woman was by shutting out the world and retreating into madness.

Of course there are individuals, particularly girls, who are not permitted to lead their own lives and make their own choices because of parental demands. And when it comes to boyfriends, parental criticism and displeasure is only too evident. But more often than not, these parental pressures are far more subtle. Conditioning begins in early life with the mother who gives the daughter signals – both overt and covert – about her own femininity and her attitude toward the opposite sex. She may overtly or covertly point out her daughter's faults with subtle remarks like 'You may not be perfect but a nose like yours has real character – and we'll always love you even if no one else does' or 'Men only go for a pretty face . . . they only want one thing.' If the father does not positively confirm his daughter's attractions and gifts either, she will grow up to feel unattractive and unlovable, and if this is carried too far, she may never be able to make a successful adult relationship. On the one hand she seeks to be rescued by a prince who will love her for herself, yet on the other, she knows she isn't worthy.

For a man it is different. A Prince Charming, perhaps through a missing father and a lack of masculine guidance or support for his developing manhood, feels at sea about his male role. Thus, he too is utterly dependent on his mother's positive reinforcement of his attributes. If he has a weak or inadequate or absent father, or one who is cruel, especially to the mother, he may grow up to feel that his role is to continue to support his mother, who will have become the centre of his emotional world. Even if he marries, he may not be able to successfully cut the cords of his maternal bond. At the root of these dilemmas for both male and female is the lack of value for who they are themselves and therefore an inability to relate truly intimately with another person. Added to this is a deep-seated, often much resented, obligation to the parent(s) who they subconsciously feel are their only protectors.

'Sabina' and 'Theo' became clients of mine shortly after their marriage. Each had come to me for entirely different therapeutic reasons: Theo because it appeared that severe stress with his business had propelled him into a depression and Sabina because she was failing to become pregnant.

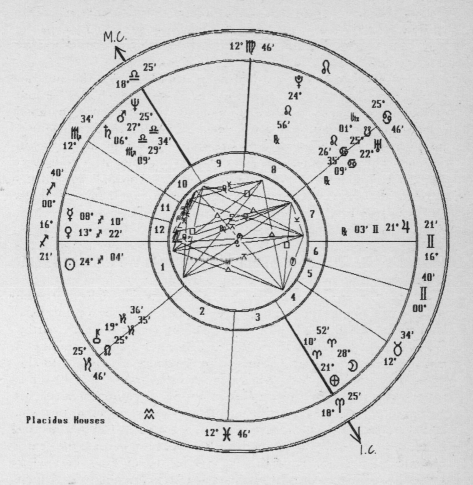

Figure 2: Sabina

Sabina was a highly intelligent, attractive woman of 37. She and Theo had been through the appropriate medical tests to establish if either of them was infertile, but they had both been given the physical 'all clear'. Sabina was thus only too aware that the reason for her failure to become pregnant lay in the psyche. In her early sessions with me she continually apologized for being a 'bad' subject and worried that I might be upset because she was not responding to hypnosis. She also kept apologizing for not being able to stop crying every time I tried to 'put her under'.

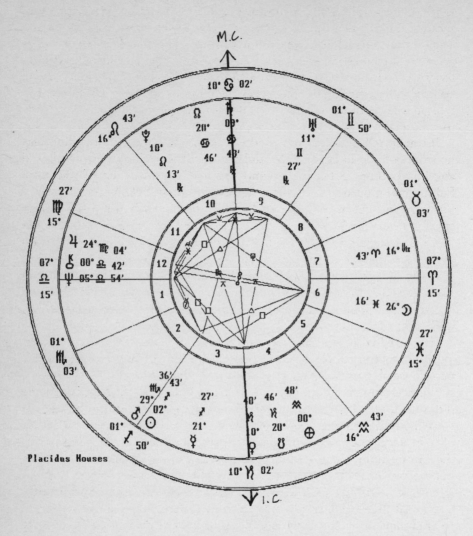

Figure 3: Theo

Of course her psyche was responding splendidly under hypnosis and revealing that under the confident, happy exterior lay some deep unhappiness.

The birth chart gave me a clear idea where the trouble lay. Her Moon – the essence of her femininity and among many other themes a symbol of her mother and her ability to nurture – was strongly placed in its own house of the horoscope related to home and family. But it was under heavy 'ammunition' from Mars, Neptune and Saturn in the tenth house – an area, as I have already discussed, descriptive of mother. This difficult planetary set-up made even more tricky by a 90° angle to Uranus in the seventh house of relationships – in other words a classic T-square formation in the cardinal signs. It will be glaringly obvious to any astrologer that Sabina was likely to experience some considerable emotional upheaval in her life and that her relationship with mother – both in the sense of her own mother and her own attitude to mothering – would be fraught with difficulty.

It transpired that Sabina's mother, a strongly Virgoan character, was neurotic and demanding. Throughout childhood, Sabina remembered continual scenes between her and her mother, and even by the time Sabina had moved to London to begin a successful career as a model – putting some 200 miles between her and the family home – there were spasmodic eruptions with subsequent silences, occasionally lasting some months. According to Sabina, her mother was a perfectionist who would argue the toss at every available opportunity. In keeping with her strongly fiery nature (Sun, Moon, Ascendant, Mercury and Venus in fire signs) Sabina learned how to mount a successful outer defence by answering back but it was her vulnerable inner core that was sustaining the brunt of the damage.

Sabina's first love affair was with a man 10 years older than herself. Within a matter of weeks of meeting 'Kenneth' she had moved into his penthouse apartment. All was well for some months until, like Pandora, she forced opened a cupboard to which only he had the key: when she did, out tumbled packs of nappies, baby clothes, bottles and booties. It turned out that Kenneth was not only very much married but the father of twin baby girls who were spending six months with their mother in the family home in Australia. Somewhat burned by this experience, Sabina put on a brave face and threw herself into her career.

For the next 15 years, she experienced one disastrous love affair after another. While her men all *looked* entirely different they nevertheless all treated her in a similarly appalling manner, invariably ultimately rejecting her in the most technicolour of scenarios. It was during the period of 1982 to 1988, when volatile Uranus transited Sagittarius, as well as Saturn (late 1985 to 1988), that she experienced almost non-stop upheaval in relationships. Then, as Jupiter rocketed into Gemini in 1989 and triggered all the seventh house potential for marriage, she met Theo. By the October they were married.

Sabina had fallen very much in love with Theo, yet right up to the wedding day she experienced wave after wave of doubt and uncertainty. During the engagement period, she was unsure whether Theo really loved her. And even if he did, she worried, would it last? Even by the time she was married and consulting me about becoming pregnant, she would ask if I believed she was the source of Theo's depression. It was abundantly clear that while Sabina looked 'a million dollars' and had all the outer trappings of a successful marriage and an enviable life style, inside was a deeply insecure little girl who truly believed that she wasn't worth very much, let alone worthy of being loved by someone as special as Theo.

Gradually, with the aid of hypnotic regression, Sabina began to bring to the surface more and more of the unconscious memories of her childhood. Copious tears were shed when she re-experienced herself as a two-year-old standing up in her cot in the middle of the night crying for someone to come. It must be said, in her mother's defence, that Sabina was an exceedingly demanding infant who sought constant attention at all times of the day and night and it would take more than a Virgoan martyr of a mother to attend to her needs constantly. However, from babyhood, in fact even while she was in her mother's womb, Sabina had unconsciously picked up the message that her mother was none too happy with mothering. And therefore none too happy about Sabina. And while this impression might have been altered by a father's positive reinforcement of her value, Sabina's father tended always to side with her mother, thereby unconsciously failing to give Sabina the support she needed. 'I can hear my mother saying time after time, especially when I did something wrong and even in front of other people, "Who'd have children – they're nothing but trouble . . . When you grow up, Sabina, have dogs instead." '

With this message deeply embedded in the unconscious it was no surprise that Sabina was unable to become pregnant. Not only did she doubt her own ability to be a good mother, but her unconscious instruction was 'Don't have children.'

While it was possible to reach the unconscious mind and replace this instruction with a different message, there was still much ground work to be done on building up Sabina's value as a woman. And until this was done, not only was her ability to become pregnant in jeopardy, but her marriage to Theo.

Sabina had fallen into the classic pattern of the Special Princess and, ironically, one of the things that upset her most before she married Theo were the words of an 'old' boyfriend: 'I guess you always wanted to be a Jewish Princess.' In all of her relationships, Sabina had sought out men-of-the-world, men with status and a high income – men who could support her financially. Yet these men were at the same time incapable of supporting her emotionally. While consciously Sabina was able to find a man to play the role of protector, a Prince Charming, unconsciously she was also seeking a man who could *not* support her emotionally – a belief fed to her by her mother and her experience as a child. Despite Sabina's insistence on her independence as far as her life style was concerned, she was unable to find her independence as a woman because a part of that womanhood was deeply wounded. Mistakenly, she sought to be healed, or rather rid, of this wound through the love of a man. Like Rapunzel she was locked away in an edifice built up of her fears and insecurities about herself; an edifice that not only kept others at bay, and thus prevented her from experiencing true intimacy, but also denied her the key to her own freedom. Far from being independent, she was utterly dependent on men for their love, approval and support. Deeply insecure about her own self-worth, she was constantly vulnerable to feelings of insecurity within a relationship. After all, if she wasn't worth loving how could anyone truly love her? Like Rapunzel, Sabina was under the spell of an enchantress-like mother who had taken away her power to be a whole woman.

When Sabina met Theo, she had already gone some way along the path to resolving the conflict with her mother and finding her self-esteem through a short span of therapy. Theo had won her mother's approval and it seemed that with her marriage, Sabina had acquired equal 'professional' status to her mother, which enabled her mother's attitude toward her to soften. While there were still the odd squalls, there seemed to be different ways to resolve them. All this progress was encouraging, although there remained some distance to go for Sabina to really free herself from the parental patterning and to discover her true value and gain the trust and security in herself necessary to make an outer relationship secure and free from fears.

A large part of my work with Sabina was in allowing her, via the hypnotic state, to return to scenes of her childhood and to comfort the small Sabina who was so insecure about who she was and what she had to give. She brought to little Sabina the knowledge that she was beautiful and lovable and, in this way, trust in herself and the world began to replace the old doubts and insecurities. The change in Sabina was not an overnight event, but gradually she became calmer and her life less frenetic. She found that in place of the previous 'nervous butterfly' syndrome that always accompanied any period spent quietly on her own was a sense of comfort and a growing feeling of centredness. She stopped worrying about Theo's therapy and no longer assumed that she was the root cause of any of his unhappiness or dissatisfaction. She was on the way to finding true independence and freedom by resolving the patterns that had previously prevented her from establishing true and lasting relationship – one built on mutual trust and shared intimacy. She was on the way to the wedding.

Prince Charming was also on his way.

Theo gave the impression of an easy-going, optimistic and successful man – a man at ease with himself and his place in the world, but a series of distressing physical symptoms had caused him to worry that he was seriously ill. However, after extensive tests, he was pronounced physically in good shape, but suffering from reactive depression. He could think of no reason why he should be depressed – his work was going well and he was happily married; there had been no recent incident to spark off a sudden depression. So, since there was no conscious explanation for the depression, we had to question the unconscious.

Theo proved to be an excellent hypnotic subject. He went immediately into deep trance and I was able to ask the unconscious to provide us with a reason for the depression. What came up was synchronistic as far as this chapter is concerned. Theo described a ring of light that encircled him. Yet there seemed to be no protective purpose to this ring. Theo wished only to get out of it. I tried all manner of suggestions as to how this might be achieved – diminishing the light until it disappeared, making it larger, smaller, higher or lower – but he remained trapped. Theo expressed a great deal of distress about this feeling of being imprisoned by this ring of light. My only remaining option was to order him out of it. Much to my relief, this worked. Later Theo was to explain that while I was giving him the countdown to jump his conscious mind was saying, 'This'll never work . . . I can't jump out of here' – and then suddenly on the count of five he found himself jettisoned out of the circle. This proved to be a major breakthrough. Out of the ring of the depression, he was able to search through his past to retrieve memories and experiences that had contributed to an increasing sense of being weighed down by obligations and responsibilities and an assumption that there was no way out. His depression was the accumulation of years of relentless catering to other people's needs and expectations.

If Sabina's chart was redolent with a Saturnian message, Theo's was overshadowed by one. This bouncy, resilient and optimistic Sagittarian with a forceful and assertive Sun–Mars conjunction was held in the grip of a Venus–Saturn opposition that straddled his MC–IC axis – a horoscopic feature designating his life direction and the roots of his existence. Saturn placed in the maternal sign of Cancer precisely on the Midheaven degree – and at the opposite point to Venus in Capricorn spoke volumes about a mother problem. Yet in questioning Theo, it seemed as if father was the greater problem.

Theo had an elder sister and two younger brothers – one of whom had died in his thirties and the other of whom had become estranged from the family. According to Theo, while the family experienced no material difficulties, he personally considered his childhood somewhat unhappy. This unhappiness seemed to stem from Theo's two major bouts of ill health – one at the age of two and the other between the ages of seven and nine. The onset of glandular fever at seven rendered Theo, already rather small for his age, quite weak and painfully thin. One of his most upsetting memories was hearing a consultant respond to his father's concern for his son's future by saying, 'We don't know if he'll ever be really strong.' It seemed that Theo could never fulfil his father's hopes for his eldest son: his father berated him for his faults and his weaknesses and Theo became inwardly angrier and angrier. He kept all his feelings to himself, never approaching his mother for any comfort since he perceived that she was 'on his father's side'. In his teens he was abandoned by the family, who moved down to London, leaving him to be looked after by a friend of the family in order that he might complete his education in Edinburgh. While Theo considered that he had come to terms with this, it was only his conscious mind that had reasoned things out: unconsciously he was deeply wounded by this act of abandonment. The already harsh Saturnian theme of rejection that had resounded throughout his childhood years was well and truly punched home by this long period of separation – and at a particularly sensitive time of adolescence. Like many Saturnian types, Theo determined to make his life a success without considering his inner needs. With his father's death, when Theo was only 21, it fell to him to father the younger boys and to take over the helm where his mother was concerned. If the seeds of Prince Charming had been sown by his Saturnian experience of childhood, by his twenties they were ready to burgeon forth.

It had never occurred to Theo to do anything but support and protect the women in his life. He was generous, considerate and anxious to make sure that his relationship with them would prove lasting and secure. He remained in his first marriage for 11 years – the bulk of them in misery but with an ingrained sense of responsibility and duty binding him no matter what the cost in emotional terms. Eventually it was his first wife who rejected him. Once he had met Sabina, he was determined that nothing would undermine their love for each other – even if it cost him everything he had. At the same time, not only was he supporting and protecting Sabina but also his mother, his sister and his ex-wife, as well as continually nurturing his clients in his business. His depression was a major indication that this pattern could no longer continue. Were he not to make some way toward resolving his impulse to be all things to all people at the expense of his inner needs his psyche would react by presenting him with a physically debilitating condition or a mental one.

I mentioned earlier that in Theo's case the astrology would point to a mother problem more than a father problem. Initially, Theo simply could not see this. After all, it was his father who had been 'the tyrant' and who had driven home the message to him that he would never be any good at anything because he was weak and inadequate. Yet the writing was on the wall where the 'devouring mother' was concerned: at 50 years of age, his sister still lived with their mother and had done so since the collapse of her marriage some 16 years previously. (His mother had disapproved of the marriage in the first place and it only lasted five years.) Theo could not perceive how his mother's passive dependency on her children had enabled her to wield a Titanic power over them. While she had approved in principle of Theo's two marriages, she certainly made life as difficult as possible for his two wives. Barely a week passed without some drama that necessitated Theo's immediate departure to her home to sort matters out. On each of the two occasions where there had been a major family upset, Theo refused to confront his mother's part in the situation nor how he felt about her. He just did not speak to her for six years.

All this was symptomatic of a man who needed to be in control of everything and everybody in order to feel secure, yet whose world was beginning to crumble because of a fundamental weakness or wound at his inner core. And one that he could not face because it involved meeting all those needs and lacks that had not been met in childhood. No matter how much he compensated in material terms and outer ways for his childhood wound, unconsciously he felt angry about his mother's lack of support and unconditional love for him. He loved and needed her yet he despised that dependency. Like so many Saturnian types, by assuming responsibility for others, by rescuing them from life's vicissitudes, he outwardly compensated for his own needs. But at the same time he avoided looking within himself for fear that his vulnerability would overwhelm him.

Like Sabina, Theo desperately needed to heal that small child within so that he could begin to change a pattern that was potentially capable of destroying him and certainly capable of destroying a marriage. Using hypnotic regression I took him back to the age of seven and talked to the young Theo. I explained that adults sometimes said the harshest things to those they loved most and that 'big Theo' had proved just how strong and successful he could be. Theo himself then took over the process, visualizing himself talking to his younger self and giving him love, confidence and support. We continued to work this way for more sessions, each time strengthening the 'little Theo' inside and healing the wounds of almost a lifetime.

Within a year, the most dramatic change had occurred to Theo and Sabina. Theo wound up two of his businesses, leaving a third to be run by trusted colleagues. He and Sabina decided to spend a year in 'tax exile' removing themselves from the pressures of the rat race and, best of all, Sabina became pregnant. But, in the way of all the best fairy-tales, would the prince and princess live happily ever after?

Linda Leonard sums up the dilemma of the Saturnian theme of the Special Princess and Prince Charming by saying:

> [They] are identities that reduce the whole person to an It, to a controllable object, a 'thing' which can be dealt with in the practical world. While this sort of identity makes life easier to handle, even makes us feel secure and comfortable, the price we pay is the loss of mystery . . . The irony is that both Prince Charming and the Special Princess seek the unique mystery of relation. They seek each other as a Thou, but in wanting to be secure and settled, to be in control, they give themselves away as objects of possession and restrict themselves to only parts of a whole being.[6]

The problem of the Saturnian archetype in relationships – that is to say the problem of those individuals who have a powerful Saturnian theme in their charts[7] or those who have identified primarily with Saturn in regard to their mode of relating – is that such individuals seek security and the outer trappings of a relationship at the expense of inner connectedness. This is why so many people with Saturn in the seventh house or personal planet links to Saturn feel unloved, unappreciated and rejected in relationships. With so much fear and mistrust of themselves, how can they begin to even pierce the mystery of true union?

More than any other astrological theme, it is the Saturnian one that urges the individual to conform to the collective ideas of what marriages should be like – and with such an emphasis placed on the accepted way the roles should be played there is little acknowledgement of the real nature of union. Some find it too demanding to move beyond the barrier of their Saturnian stereotype: by conforming they gain a certain satisfaction and security, yet inwardly they are often lonely. But however cut off they may be from loving and being loved they do not attempt to bridge the gulf that lies between them and their partner, for in order to do that they must be prepared for honesty and intimacy – not sexual intimacy, but the unveiling of feelings and needs. And for that to happen trust must be there. For in revealing such feelings one is utterly vulnerable and exposed to the risk of hurt and rejection from an other. Trust is at the root of intimacy and it is the one factor with which Saturn has so much difficulty – all those fears and self-doubts. Yet if confronted, these Saturnian blocks pave the way for release from isolation from the imprisoning tower of self-hate and self-doubt. To trust oneself because one knows oneself to be worthy of love is to open the doorway of trust to another.

The Special Princesses and the Prince Charmings among us must at some point find that trust so that the true intimacy between them can begin. Sabina and Theo have already moved some distance on that painful path of self-awareness; they are stripping away the outer expectations of their roles and beginning to relate from the heart. In gaining independence from their past and becoming whole in themselves they can meet each other as true lovers. And, perhaps, they can, indeed, live happily ever after.

Saturn is the most testing part of the journey toward the divine encounter. For in breaking through those boundaries the whole gamut of the higher level of experience in love and relating is revealed. By respecting the ring of Saturn and its lessons, by facing the internal doubts and fears that prevent us from opening to another, we can move toward the ineffable mystery of union.

Appendix

1) While the conscious mind may be convinced that a certain behaviour or attitude is wrong or unnecessary, if the unconscious mind does not agree, the condition will persist. If you want to change a pattern of behaviour or an ingrained perception, the conscious mind must be by-passed and the unconscious addressed. Using the hypnotic state, one can communicate with the unconscious and 'the habits of a life time' can be transformed.
2) Linda Schierse Leonard, *On the Way to the Wedding* (Shambhala, 1986).
3) Ibid.
4) Ibid.
5) In the Huber system of astrology, Saturn is considered the principle of mother.
6) *On the Way to the Wedding*, op.cit.
7) A powerful Saturn theme occurs when there are conjunctions (1–8°), squares (90°) and oppositions (180°) between Saturn and the Moon, the Sun or Venus, or any configuration where Saturn becomes a pivotal point – i.e. at the apex of a T-square, or the 'handle' of a 'bucket' chart shaping – or Saturn is conjunct the MC or Ascendant, IC or Descendant or linked to the tenth or seventh house.

6

Uranus: The Shining

*M*OST ASTROLOGERS WOULD BALK AT THE IDEA THAT URANUS, AND THE other trans-Saturnian planets, Neptune and Pluto, could in any way be personalized. As Liz Greene said in 1977, 'The urges which the three known outer planets symbolise are rarely available to the consciousness of the individual . . .'[1] but, as I explained in Chapter 3, as consciousness is raised, so our ability to resonate with the outer planets increases so that we experience them not as a purely collective force, but as elements of our personal consciousness. And for those who find such a concept unpalatable, consider instead that Uranus, in common with all the outer planets, represents specific archetypal themes; as such, they have a psychic life within each of us which, in turn, is reflected in our outer experience.

Since I have already discussed the nature of Uranus and its role in jump-stepping us to a higher reality of our Selves, here, in keeping with the theme of divine encounters, I would like to expand on the expression of Uranus in relationships and how, by encountering what this planet represents to us internally, we may raise it to conscious awareness and ultimately find its divine properties.

Linda Leonard's book *On the Way to the Wedding* was in its own way a Uranian awakening for me: her descriptions of the inner obstacles that block the way to a fulfilling outer relationship were redolent with astrological symbolism. As I sat in the plane, high above the clouds, winging my way to the other side of the world, suddenly a whole new astrological panorama began to take shape in my mind. I had always considered the planets to reveal a hierarchy of meaning in that each planet symbolizes many things, from objects to experiences, personal characteristics to life events, but I had not conceptualized the planets –

or rather, the outer planets – as epic journeys in consciousness. I had gone along with the general consensus that because the outer planets were so out of reach, they were effectively beyond personal grasp, remaining instead in the vast ocean of collective experience; and because they were so unconscious, what they had to offer tended to erupt in a disturbing and negative way in situations not of our making. But as consciousness expands in the individual there is a more conscious connection with and attunement to these archetypal realms. I would not say that they become more under our control, but because they are more accessible, we can be more aware of their intrinsic natures and therefore less at the mercy of their destructive power.

In her book, Linda Leonard discusses the importance of meeting these archetypal themes within us because, unless we relate to them, they remain unintegrated in our psyche and play havoc with our relationships. In the same way, over the course of the next three chapters, I will draw these archetypal themes with an astrological pen so that, by understanding the planetary archetypes, we may increase our comprehension of and our relationship to the outer planets. We can all relate to universal themes though we each have a unique perception of them; likewise we all have the outer planets in our charts so we must learn what they represent to us individually. We are drawn by these outer planets as moths to the flame, but in our small selves we run into danger at the edge of their realms, fighting the terrifying shadows cast by their mountainous interiors. Only when we grow in consciousness can we move out of the darkness and appreciate their divine nature; just as, when we confront the shadows lurking in our unconscious, we are free to perceive the radiance of our true, divine selves.

In 'The Ring of Saturn' I explained the way Saturn represents the fears, doubts and negativity that keep us bound to the ego – limit us to the confines of the small-self – and how, in regard to relationships, developing trust leads to honesty and intimacy which in turn open us to the deeper levels of relating and the mysteries of love. Once through the ring of Saturn, we are exposed to the transformative power of the outer planets. We must bring those themes that have lurked in our unconscious into awareness so that in the light of consciousness they lose their destructive power and instead illuminate our path.

Although Uranus marks a progression from Saturn in terms of consciousness, the planets beyond Uranus do not become increasingly superior: each planet represents a dimension of experience whose properties are neither superior nor inferior to any other trans-Saturnian – they are, simply, all different. However, there is a slight anomaly with Uranus since the lower reaches of Uranian experience have a Saturnian shadow hanging over them which, on the one hand, can be perceived in the way some Saturnian themes seem to repeat with Uranus and, on the other, is demonstrated in the mythical bond between the two planets:

Saturn's counterpart in Greek mythology, Cronos, was the son of Ouranos, the sky god. Ouranos was a tyrant who kept some of his children, the Titans, imprisoned in the earth. Not unnaturally this upset their mother, Gaea, who begged Cronos to do something about the situation. Cronos promptly took on his father, castrated him and usurped his throne. He then carried on a thoroughly autocratic rule of his own and continued to keep the Titans locked in the earth. While, superficially, this may appear to be an act of cruelty and suppression, the reason why the Titans were kept in the dark was that if they were released from captivity, the light would surely blind them.

And so it is that Saturn becomes our jailer, not only because his rule must be obeyed, but also for our own protection against the blinding illumination of Uranus: until we have worked through the barriers of our fears – pierced the egoic shell – we cannot appreciate the divine nature of Uranus. Indeed, there is a close astrological relationship between Saturn and Uranus, although these two planetary archetypes are polar opposites, since the sign of Aquarius is ruled by both these planets.

Uranus can be the most breathtakingly exciting planetary experience; individuals who resonate strongly with this planet – perhaps because Uranus is the chart ruler or placed on an angle or because this planet forms close aspects[2] with one or more of the personal planets – are invariably innovative and creative; Uranus in its higher resonance produces visionary genius and spiritual mastery. Uranians tend to be the humanitarians, outer and inner space pioneers and the high fliers of this world. When Uranus transits a strategic point in our charts, we are released from a long-term sentence – all too often one spent in a Saturnian prison of our own making – we experience an extraordinary event that changes the course of our lives or we are suddenly awakened in some way. Yet Uranus may also wreak havoc in our lives; he not only jolts us out of our safe little ruts but blasts a hole in the very pillars of our life edifice; in the lower register of Uranus, we find upheaval, catastrophe and anarchy. Those who wander within Uranus's lower plane become the delinquents, the drop-outs, the dissidents and sometimes the tyrants of this world.

Women, of course, are just as capable of tyrannical behaviour as men, but history reveals that tyranny, in its most brutish and bullying sense, is more often the province of the male sex than the female: tyrants across history – from Attila the Hun to Mussolini, Caligula to Stalin – have been men. And although today we still have tyrants on the world stage in the form of dictators like Saddam Hussein, many ordinary homes from Baghdad to Minneapolis have their very own tyrants in the form of husbands and fathers – men who may appear to be thoroughly upright citizens but in the privacy of their own homes preside over a reign of terror. In *Romancing The Stars*,[3] I discussed a group of individuals who fall into the category of Right Men. I had come across this psychological type in a book by Colin Wilson and had immediately noted that the qualities allotted to the Right Man had a distinctly Aquarian ring to them. This is what Colin Wilson had to say about the Right Man:

> He has a strong desire for truth, but the story of his life is an unconsciously distorted version, which shows him to have been a hundred percent right and everyone else to have been wrong. And paradoxically enough, this 'strong desire for truth' may make the Right Man a good scientist or philosopher. It is only where he is concerned that his perception of truth is distorted: besides which, the pursuit of abstract knowledge provides a welcome relief from his obsession with himself.[4]

I went on to add:

> In his relationships the Right Man can be exceedingly jealous while often a philanderer himself: he may have a puritanical streak yet sexual conquest is extremely important to him. It is also essential for the Right Man to gain total submission from his partner. At home he acts like the school bully, and while he insists on freedom for himself, his wife must display a slave-like devotion to him.[5]

I considered the Right Man, as a psychological type, to fall most easily into the Aquarian category because of the connection of both Saturn and Uranus with this sign: both these planets are associated with the need to control and the tendency toward autocracy; they also tend to manifest as great fear of intimacy and inability to trust. And although I consider the following discussion on misogynism to fall under the province of Uranus, there is nonetheless a Saturnian dimension to it.

In my work as an astrologer I would from time to time come into contact with wives and lovers of Right Men and, while they may not all have been Aquarian 'wizards' or strong on the intellectual, entrepreneurial or inventive front, they were remarkably consistent in their patterns of emotional behaviour; and while these men did not always have a strong Aquarian content in their charts, they invariably displayed a powerful Uranian theme – Uranus as the chart ruler, Uranus on an angle, or close aspects from the personal planets to Uranus. Then I chanced upon a remarkable book by Dr Susan Forward[6] who classified these men not as Right Men, but as misogynists. Dr Forward discusses a type of man who is basically a misogynist:

> Although it was the woman who usually sought my help, it was the behaviour of the men that claimed my attention. As their partners described them, they were often charming and even loving, but they were able to switch to cruel, critical and insulting behaviour at a moment's notice. Their behaviour covered a wide spectrum, from obvious intimidation and threats to more subtle, covert attacks which took the form of constant put-downs or erosive criticism. Whatever the style, the results were the same. The men gained control by grinding the woman down. These men also refused to take any responsibility for how their attacks made their partners feel. Instead they blamed their wives or lovers for any and every unpleasant event . . . Rather than getting emotional or sexual pleasure from a partner's pain, as the sadist does, the man I was attempting to define felt both threatened and enraged by his partner's suffering . . . As I listened to my clients, I asked myself: Is this the way you treat someone you really love? Isn't this in fact the way you treat someone you hate?[7]

Forward's misogynists demonstrated a somewhat Uranian proclivity for whirlwind romance: they tended to sweep a woman off her feet and their disarming honesty about the strength of their feelings and their open adulation for her make them almost irresistible. However, with such men the speed and intensity of the affair conceals a certain underlying panic that if they don't 'move in' quickly enough their adored woman will move on. But once the misogynist has hooked the woman, it is only a matter of time before his true colours start to emerge – and sometimes the courtship is conducted at such fever pitch that this Uranian character has actually married his love object before the star-dust of eros has worn off[8] so that his dark side does not emerge until it is too late. The first sign that there is a Mr Hyde lurking behind Dr Jekyll is when this previously besotted man suddenly turns on his beloved for some seemingly innocuous incident, or even without any provocation whatsoever. This first outburst is usually followed by assurances that it won't happen again. But, effectively, this is the beginning of the end. The misogynist must have total control of the woman he 'loves', which means eliminating any potential threat in the form of friends, family, job or talent that might take her away from him. This he achieves by overtly or covertly preventing her from pursuing such relationships or interests and/or by unrelenting criticism of those things she loves or excels at, and by systematically stripping away her self-confidence. In his defence, the misogynist is not consciously aware that he wants to imprison his lady, nor does he consciously conduct a reign of terror; he does not recognize that his deep-seated vulnerability and unconscious fear of abandonment drive him to such behavioural excesses.

Complete control is the misogynist's aim and Forward makes the point that while 'there are power struggles in all relationships . . . in the misogynistic relationship, negotiation and compromise are in short supply. Instead, the partnership is played out on a grim battlefield where he has to win and she has to lose . . . Of course, total control is an elusive thing . . . therefore, the misogynist's quest is bound to fail. As a result, he is frustrated and angry much of the time. Sometimes he is able to successfully mask his hostility. But at other times it will manifest itself as psychological abuse . . . the systematic persecution of one partner by another.'

The misogynist varies the tactics he may use to terrorize a woman into submission – he may shout at her or he may cut out on her; he may brutalize her sexually or psychologically: 'The misogynist has an extensive repertoire of scare tactics, insults, denigrating comments, and other intimidating behaviour designed to make his partner feel inadequate and helpless.' Because the misogynist is almost always an extremely intelligent and certainly artful individual, he manages to make the woman take the responsibility for his grossly unacceptable behaviour and place it firmly on her shoulders. Amy, whom we shall meet in Chapter 8, felt compelled to apologize to her misogynist, Gregory, after he stripped any vestige of value in her or the relationship over dinner on her birthday; he then took her home, made love to her, called her a whore and left. But with the tactical ingenuity of the misogynist he managed to make her feel responsible for his appalling behaviour, his gross insensitivity and the hurt he had caused her. As Forward explains:

> The misogynist's contention is that if he's behaving badly, it is only because he is responding to some crime of yours. Such men sincerely and convincingly argue that their outrageous behaviour is an understandable reaction to some terrible deficiency or provocation on your part. By doing this, the misogynist avoids having to consider the possibility that he has some serious shortcomings. By shifting the blame to you . . . he absolves himself of the discomfort of recognizing his role in the problem . . . Any criticism or questioning of him is immediately turned back on you as further proof of your inadequacies.

Denial becomes another of the misogynist's most effective weapons: in his attempt to paint an acceptable self-portrait – as much for himself as anyone else – he will blatantly deny certain incidents ever happened or rewrite history:

> What is so distressing about the use of denial as a tactic is that you are left with nothing to deal with. It creates a sense of desperate frustration. There is no way to resolve a problem with someone who denies the existence of certain events and who insists that what you know to be real never happened.

My late (first) husband – a Sun Aquarian with Mercury (his Ascendant ruler) square Uranus – displayed many of the aforementioned behaviour patterns of the misogynist: he proposed within three weeks of our meeting one April and the following August we were married; three months later, I had witnessed volte-face after U-turn and by Christmas he had made his first physical assault on me. He used every manoeuvre possible to cut down my armoury of friends, and although he had initially encouraged my interest in astrology – a consolation prize for refusing to let me continue my acting career – as soon as it became a serious commitment, he made pursuing it impossibly difficult – on one extraordinary occasion resorting to burning some of my text books and homework. He was also a man with a shadowy past – I never met a single member of his family and, even at his funeral, neither I nor his third ex-wife could trace any relatives. Dr Forward makes the point that the misogynist frequently plays the role of the tragic hero to enlist your support:

> This man has a distorted view of himself as honourable, hardworking, and noble. Unable to recognize how he orchestrates his own disasters, he sees the woman who is supporting him as the enemy. This man has had financial problems throughout his adult life . . . He is eager to explain that his difficulties are the result of what other people have done to him. His 'enemies list' may include his parents . . . a business partner who cheated or betrayed him, an ex-wife who 'took him to the cleaners', or a boss who fired him for no reason. It's only a matter of time before the misogynist's financial condition becomes his partner's fault.

The misogynist will again resort to denial to rewrite his past by simply editing people and events out of his life history; it takes a super-human effort on his part to substantiate his view of past reality, therefore the fewer people there are to stand testament to the real story the better, which means he has to move rather a lot. My late husband was forced to change countries three times in an attempt to escape creditors, ex-partners and his first ex-wife; sadly, in the end, his only escape was to have a massive coronary.

Then there's the sexual arena – perhaps the cold-bloodiest battlefield of all. Since the misogynist is self-evidently a man with a deep-seated hatred of women, this is the area that takes its greatest toll. While the self-expansive phase of erotic love will assure his sexual enthusiasm and tender loving care, as soon as eros has flown his more aggressive feelings start to emerge. Sometimes these are expressed by his increasing desire to brutalize the woman during sexual intercourse and make even greater demands on her availability; at others, they are expressed by a sexual withdrawal. Sometimes the switch from lover to hater occurs overnight; more usually there is a gradual lessening of care and consideration for the women – sex becomes a function of nature in which a woman's needs are an interference. And sometimes the misogynist's sexual 'machinery' packs up altogether: how can he make love to something that disgusts him on the one hand and terrifies him on the other? To him, it is of course the woman's fault that she no longer inspires the same erotic, loving response, thus he sets about destroying her desirability as a woman; if he cannot achieve or maintain an erection he accuses her of being too demanding, and if she recoils from his abrasive or brutal sexuality he tells her that she is frigid.

There is no denying that this is a particularly terrifying sort of man. He is dangerously attractive and his *modus operandi* – completely unconscious, of course – is lethal. His initial feelings and outpourings are entirely genuine, for he longs for relationship, he yearns for love, but when the Uranian switch is activated, he goes for the kill – as much because of a sense of betrayal of all the powers with which he invested his woman, as his repeated response to a deep-seated problem over women. The switch takes place at the moment eros departs (which I will discuss along with the animus-anima projection in the next chapter); at this point, he either leaves the relationship abruptly or, because he may well be married by this time, he begins the gradual process of the systematic destruction of the woman he 'loves'.

Clearly, this is not the action of a psychologically well man, nor, I hasten to say, is it the action of every Aquarian–Uranian man – although it is a theme to be aware of. The underlying roots of the misogynist's deep-seated aversion to women lie in his past – almost certainly a result of a childhood spent in a dysfunctional family.

The misogynist's cruel, tyrannical behaviour is, by and large, 'a cover-up for his tremendous anxiety about women. He is caught up in a conflict between his need for a woman's love and his deepest fears of her. This man needs to be emotionally taken care of, to be loved, and to feel safe. As adults we fulfil these yearnings through physical intimacy, emotional sharing and parenting. But the misogynist finds these yearnings terribly frightening. His normal needs to be close to a woman are mixed with fears that she can annihilate him emotionally. He harbours a hidden belief that if he loves a woman, she will then have the power to hurt him, to deprive him, to engulf him and to abandon him. Once he has invested her with these awesome and mythical powers, she becomes a fearful figure for him.'

The reasons why the misogynist fears women so much is because he is likely to have had a confused and deeply upsetting experience of mothering as a child, that is, either his mother or father became a tyrannical figure for him. If the father, the primary male role model, was a tyrant, the son would absorb his father's contempt for women and receive the message 'This is how you treat them.' But much also depends on the mother's behaviour as to how seriously debilitated her son's perception of women becomes. If the mother does not stand up to her tyrant husband and looks instead to her son to meet her emotional needs, she is denying her son his share of a mother's love and comfort; she is therefore not only depriving him of emotional nourishment at a time when he needs it most, but provoking a split in his unconscious about the male-female dyad and setting him up to feel overwhelmed by a woman's needs later on in life. The misogynist will here invariably perceive his mother as having the power to make insatiable demands on him and to frustrate his own needs in the process; and so this indelible childhood experience colours his perception of every woman he forms an attachment to. Every woman will become the devourer, the frustrator, the power-sucker. He, in consequence, faces an ever-present problem of impotence – whether in the sense of achieving financial solvency, worldly success or, in its most literal sense, in his sexuality.

On the other hand, in some cases the mother is herself a tyrant: it is she who abuses the misogynist's father and pours out a torrent of rage over him. If father does not assert himself and fails even to attempt to control the situation, the son will get the message 'This is what all women do to you and if Dad can't stand up to a woman, how the hell can I?' Mother and father both contribute to the embryonic misogynist's dilemma – whoever plays the tyrant – but if the father is strong and supportive for his son, the problem can be mitigated. Sadly, if the father is absent, or psychologically 'not at home', the boy will be effectively at the mercy of both his mother's and his own overpowering emotional needs and frustrations.

As far as the astrological portrait of the misogynist/tyrant/ Right Man is concerned, a strong Uranian or Saturnian theme is invariably present. I include Saturn because this planet is renowned for its ability to inspire criticism, coldness and cruelty; Uranus also has these same characteristics, but the 'whirlwind courtship' tactics, the Jekyll and Hyde 'switch', the tactical ingenuity and the behaviour 'flips' are entirely the province of Uranus. Men with hard aspects to Uranus from the personal planets have the potential for this behaviour, but it will not necessarily manifest as full blown 'misogynism' unless there are other factors, astrological and familial, to support it. Familial factors I have already discussed; in astrological terms, the misogynist is a particularly airy-Uranian character, that is to say he tends to have personal planets, especially the Sun, Mercury or Mars, or the Ascendant in Gemini, Libra and Aquarius, compounded by a Uranian factor – strong Uranus aspects to the personal planets or an angular Uranus. Air signs find extreme difficulty in relating to their feelings: they *have* feelings but they tend to feel threatened by emotion. So this combination of airy emotional vulnerability and the volatile, highly strung nature of Uranus makes a fine breeding ground for fear of women. Likewise, a tenth or fourth house placement of Uranus points to a potential tyrannical parent – and the Moon in hard aspect to Uranus connotes a Uranian experience of mother and/or mothering.[9] I would suggest that airy individuals with the Moon or Mercury–Uranus hard aspects incline to verbal and mental tyranny, while those airy men with hard contacts to the Sun or Mars from Uranus veer toward physical and sexual tyranny.

Certainly all individuals have Uranus somewhere in their charts, and to a certain extent, given the 'right' breeding ground, all men can and will respond to the tyrannical dimension of Uranus. I would also like to add, in case I am accused of taking a verbal 'swipe' at men, that Dr Forward's book was a Number 1 best-seller in the United States, and subsequently an international best-seller, which clearly demonstrates a huge demand for enlightenment on what seems to be a chronic problem. And while I have concentrated here on who and what the misogynist is, Dr Forward's book informs the reader how to cope with such a man; furthermore, since I have not covered the whole area of why certain women enter misogynistic relationships – what their 'pay-off' is likely to be and the underlying reason for their need to be exposed to such cruelty – I can only urge those interested to obtain a copy of her book.

It may be that in the feminist backlash towards centuries of male dominance, men are becoming increasingly adept at finding ways to cope with female oppression! However, as psychoanalyst Karen Horney comments, 'Man has never tired of fashioning expressions for the violent forces by which he feels himself drawn to the woman and, side by side, the dread that through her he might die or be undone.'[10] Men, in this modern high-tech age still feel the surges in the unconscious of the dark power of the lunar goddess.

Another Uranian dilemma that manifests similar patterns of behaviour as that of the misogynist is commitment-phobia – the inability to commit. But while misogynism is an exclusively male preserve, the commitment-phobic can be of either sex. However, since women are psychologically predisposed to gravitate toward monogamous, long-term relationships – certainly for the bearing and rearing of children – commitment-phobia is far more prevalent, and certainly more obvious, in males. Such sufferers almost always display a strong Uranian content in their charts: Uranus linked to the seventh or fifth house and, for the male, Sun, Mars or Mercury linked to Uranus, and for the female, Moon, Venus or Mercury in aspect to Uranus.

The commitment-phobic, like the misogynist, tends to embark on a relationship like a thunderflash, with all the attendant power and force of the storm of love. He often exits the relationship at equally break-neck speed. The commitment-phobic pulls out of the relationship as soon as commitment rears its Hydra's head, which is why, ironically, he so often pulls out when the relationship is at its best – when things are perfect and everything points to the requirement to commit. And this individual is terrified of forever-afterness. Steven Carter, the co-author of *Men Who Can't Love*, was inspired to research the material for the book when he recognized that he had a problem with commitment himself. Commenting on a commitment-phobic's behaviour, he says:

> His overall pattern falls into the 'pursuit/panic syndrome'. All this means is that the guy does a thousand degree pursuit until he feels that the woman's love and response leaves him no way out of the relationship – ever. The moment that happens, he begins to perceive the relationship as a trap. The trap provokes anxiety, if not total panic. Before the woman knows what is happening, the man is running from the relationship, running from her and running from love. [11]

The extraordinary factor about this process is that some men can go through all these stages in one night, while others may take a year. But the sequence is nevertheless the same.

When such an individual pulls out of a relationship, he, or she, needs a reason; like the misogynist, the reason can never lie at his feet, and so, like the misogynist, he will pick on some failing in the other, some drawback to the relationship to support his exit. However, sometimes the sense of panic is so crippling that the commitment-phobic has not the time to find or give an explanation before he vanishes; as if to bolster up the concept that the other party is beyond the pale of any explanation, he then refuses to answer any calls or respond to any letters. He may feel rather guilty about his sudden departure from a perfectly good relationship, but the guilt is not nearly as overpowering as the anxiety and panic provoked by the prospect of commitment.

Carter and Sokol outlined four or five basic stages to commitment-phobic relationships:

- *The Beginning*, which is typified by 'fearless pursuit';
- *The Middle*, where the first rumblings of panic appear: the commitment-phobic person changes the goal posts of the relationship;
- *The End*, which is characterized by moodiness and emotional and psychological withdrawal: he breaks arrangements, insists on more independence, avoids sex and refuses to discuss his change in behaviour;
- *The Bitter End*: he provokes the partner into leaving by his outrageous behaviour or he picks a fight; even more devastatingly, he 'totally disappears from your life, often in a way that is bizarre as well as destructive'.

Then there is Stage 5, *The Curtain Call*, when after a certain time span he returns – sometimes time and time and time again. However, the length of time spent back in the relationship becomes progressively shorter. Because the sufferer is *phobic* about commitment, like all individuals suffering from a phobia, once he is removed from the source of the anxiety, he returns to 'normal'. Distance is the antidote to his problem.

Indeed, the concept that his behaviour is the result of a phobia separates the commitment-phobic from the misogynist, although their *modus operandi* is extremely similar. The commitment-phobic is a prisoner of his fear; he does not necessarily have an underlying hatred of women: 'This is not a man who hates women, this is a man who wishes he could love women. But he is the victim of a fear – a fear that gives him only two choices: leave or fight.'[12] This difference is made absolutely clear by the 'confession' of one of Carter and Sokol's interviewees – 'a good-looking and genuinely likeable thirty-four-year-old plastic surgeon':

When I meet a woman I'm attracted to, I'm like the advertising executive who comes in with one thing to sell – me. But once I know I've made the sale, which usually happens the first evening, I'm off. I look at a woman I've just met, and instead of thinking about taking her to a movie, I'm worried about how I'll feel about her in ten years. I actually think things like, 'It may be fine now, but I'll get bored, and I won't want to be with her any more, and then there'll have to be a divorce, and what about the kids?' . . . You know, this doesn't work to my benefit either. I'm thirty-four years old. I haven't been out with a woman more than once in the last two years. I don't sleep with women on the first date. Your figure it out. I'm not happy this way, but the alternative seems to provoke so much anxiety. Ideally, my relationships should be like seasonal homes – you know, a winter relationship, a summer relationship . . . When I think of getting married, I worry that my life will be over. I don't want to lose my lifestyle, which in my case often turns out to be going home, watching television alone, and reheating an old slice of pizza. It's not terrific, but I feel the alternative would be like being stuck for all eternity within an airless room.

This 'confession' represents the classic Uranian dilemma: the individual 'hooked' by Uranus needs space at all costs; clip his wings and narrow down the field and he will fight or flee. But do not make the mistake of thinking that such a split individual is happy with his Uranian lot. At least not by the time he is in his thirties.

Commitment-phobics can and do display all the signs of someone caught within the paralysing and fearful grip of a phobia. An individual who is an arachnophobic only has to see a spider to be overcome by waves of fear: his heart rate increases, he over-breathes, he sweats, develops stomach pains and even faints. These same physical symptoms are experienced by an individual who fears commitment when the prospect of bonding 'eternally' looms in front of him. And fear of commitment may not just be linked to relationships – the commitment-phobic often faces the same panic where house purchase is concerned and future planning. Carter also made the important discovery that commitment-phobics invariably also suffered from claustrophobia.

As a hypnotherapist I have helped people to cope with certain phobias, and although fear of flying or fear of hospitals can be rationalized as an instinctive reaction to the association of these things with death or pain, in my experience there is almost always an initial event that triggers the phobia. Indeed, one of the techniques aimed at helping people overcome their phobias is to take them back to that initial experience, disassociate them from it, and then 'reframe' it. Likewise, I believe that there is almost always a root cause for the commitment-phobic's fear, and I would suggest that his inability to commit is based on a lack of trust and a lack of self-worth.

Some time ago, I was talking to a therapist friend of mine about men who, like the commitment-phobic, walk out on apparently ideal relationships. She too had come across several men in this category; in one or two of these cases, the men had not cut out when commitment came into view, but had left the relationship because it was too good. These men had been 'knocked sideways' by experiencing loving sex – not just good sex with the woman they loved, but the ecstatic, if not divine, sensation of sexual love. And instead of inspiring further growth in the relationship, it had terrified them so much that they felt compelled to leave it. My therapist friend considered that underlying these men's escape was a fundamental idea that they were not good enough to sustain such a relationship. She went on to explain that when she was younger, she also bowed out of perfectly good relationships. In her early twenties, she had been devastated by a man who broke off their engagement shortly before their wedding. After that experience, she 'took it out' on other men, and never allowed herself to 'get in too deep' – always ending the relationship when the man threatened to 'get too serious'. In her thirties, she met the ideal man: he was good-looking, established, interested in the same areas of life as herself; he took her to the most exciting places and openly adored her – the relationship was 'perfect'. So she stopped seeing him. At first she made excuses, then she pretended to have moved abroad. 'You see, I knew he was so wonderful that I couldn't possibly live up to him or his expectations of me. I knew what he saw in me wasn't the real me. I wasn't good enough for him. And I didn't want him to find out and then reject me. I couldn't bear that.'

My therapist friend, like Steven Carter, found herself in the position of being the physician who must heal herself. She realized that she was suffering from a deep-seated lack of her own self-worth. In this case, it was not so much the family background that had provided the fabric of her lack of self-esteem, but the appalling experience of losing the man she loved. At that time the message that was transmitted to her unconscious, and firmly took root there, was that if only she had been better, prettier, of more value, he would have wanted to marry her. And from then onwards, not only was she unable to trust another man, but she also lost trust in herself. I have emphasized more than once that trust forms the base of intimacy and without that in place the route to developing honest, loving and mutually fulfilling relationships is blocked.

My therapist friend provides a fine example of the woman who avoids commitment because she is frightened of being hurt: unlike the commitment-phobic, the prospect of forever-afterness does not cause her to break out in a cold sweat. Indeed, commitment-phobia is far less prevalent in the female since, as Carter and Sokol point out, 'even though a woman may fear commitment, she has many other fears, needs and instincts [primarily maternal] that are continually urging her to commit . . . Men, on the other hand, have no such dichotomous pushing and pulling within. They may have a strong sex drive, but once they have satisfied that drive, they are free to go, leaving women with the important work. And go they often do.'

However, I would suggest that women with commitment problems, invariably based on poor self-esteem and lack of trust, often work around this issue by committing themselves to men who will not be able to commit to them – this is the woman who constantly falls for married or 'unsuitable' men. This is certainly a pattern of behaviour to be observed with women who have Moon/Venus/Sun/Mars–Uranus hard aspects or Uranus linked to the seventh and eighth houses.

The legend of the Flying Dutchman provides us with a more mystical view of the Uranian dilemma. Wagner, who wrote both the libretto and the music for this first successful opera of his, was himself a highly Uranian character. [13] Apparently, he was inspired to write the opera after the ship he had boarded when fleeing his creditors in Riga was almost shipwrecked in a storm.

The Flying Dutchman *tells the tale of a ship's captain who angered Satan by daring to round the Cape of Good Hope (the edge of the world) – a deed for which he was condemned to sail the seas forever unless he could find a woman faithful to him until death. The Dutchman was only permitted to anchor every seventh year to search for her.*

The opera opens as the mysterious black ship of the Flying Dutchman pulls into the creek by the side of another ship. The Dutchman goes ashore reflecting that once again the seven-year cycle is complete. Soon Daland, the captain of the other ship, arrives on deck and commiserates with the Dutchman; he tells him that he has a beautiful daughter, Senta, who is of marriageable age. Sensing that this could be the woman who could save him, the Flying Dutchman offers his hand in marriage, much to the joy of Daland.

Meanwhile Senta is at home sharing her thoughts of love and marriage with her friends. She is haunted by the legend of the Flying Dutchman and keeps his portrait on the wall. Senta believes herself to be the woman who will break the curse on the Dutchman. However, she has a suitor, Erik, to whom she displays gross indifference. Erik has dreamed that he will lose her to a sinister stranger; somehow, his fears serve only to increase her desire to belong to the Flying Dutchman. Shortly after Erik has left, her father arrives with the Dutchman. On seeing each other Senta and the Dutchman fall immediately in love; she pledges herself to him until death and her father blesses their union.

The last act of the opera is set on Daland's ship. There is much rejoicing although the celebrations are interrupted by the ghostly chorus of the Dutchman's crew. Erik comes to Senta and reproaches her for being untrue to him; he reminds her of her past affection for him and the happy times they spent together. The Dutchman overhears and believes that he has lost his chance of salvation. He tries to board his dark ship, but Senta holds him back. He then tells her that not only is he damned until he finds a faithful woman, but any woman who joins him and then proves inconstant will herself be condemned to sail the seas until the end of time. To save her from eternal damnation, he boards his ship and departs. As the ship heads out toward the open sea, Senta climbs to the edge of the cliff and hurls herself into the water, proclaiming her constancy. With this, the Dutchman's ship disappears beneath the waves.

Moments later, as the sun rises, Senta and the Dutchman appear together, transfigured.

Although the tale has a Neptunian oceanic setting, the hero betrays his sky-god roots by being known as the Flying Dutchman; he has reaped the vengeance of Satan because he has flouted convention and dared to sail to the end of the Earth; furthermore, he is only permitted to land every seven years. Uranus, of course, is the non-conformist, free-wheeler of the zodiac to whom stability and permanency are deeply antithetical; and, as if to underline the link between Saturn and Uranus, Satan is angered because the Dutchman has overstepped his Saturnian limits; Uranus changes sign every seven years while Saturn also reveals a seven-year cycle.[14] Senta and the Dutchman fall instantly in love – they are struck by the Uranian thunderbolt of love. But, perhaps the strongest Uranian theme to emerge from this story is that of constancy; the Flying Dutchman is forced to wander the Earth, and his salvation lies in a seemingly impossible quest – for a woman who will remain faithful to him until death.

Although the Flying Dutchman is an essentially tragic character, in a sense, he is living the Uranian dream – he has no roots to place a stranglehold on his thirst for freedom and, like the archetypal sailor, he can have a different girl in every port. Yet he bemoans his fate. What might once have been a Uranian blessing is now a curse – he is fettered by his wanderlust, compelled to roam aimlessly from place to place and, surrounded only by men, he is cut off from relationship (removed from the feminine) so there is no chance to satisfy the deeper yearnings of the soul. Senta, like the Dutchman, is also cut off from relationship: she is indifferent to Erik because her heart is only available to the Dutchman – a man who, until he appears in the flesh, is merely a Ghostly Lover. (I will expand on the theme of the Ghostly Lover in the next chapter.) Thus, both characters are searching for something that seems humanly impossible – the impossible possibility. But, when they meet, they also meet their fate. It is their fate that they are bound to each other, but through love that they are transformed. The Dutchman must find a woman who is faithful to him until death. Senta knows that it is her fate to be that woman and that she, through her love, can break the curse on the Dutchman. But, ultimately, only through her death, her voluntary act of sacrifice, is the curse lifted and, in the process, they are both transfigured.

It was as I was pondering on this powerful theme that I had a chance encounter with a friend of mine. 'Rachel' had two disastrous marriages behind her – both to men who fell into the misogynist/commitment-phobic camp – and she was on the point of entering into a relationship with a man who had an appalling history with women – a man who bore all the hallmarks of a misogynist. 'Sean' – a 40-year-old Sun Aquarian with Uranus conjunct the Descendant – was only too aware of his problem and had been in therapy over it for some months. However, my friend wisely reasoned that no matter how much he talked about his problem and how much intellectual understanding he gained about it, the route to real change and resolution lay through the feelings. And while she knew that the therapist had helped other men with similar problems to reach the heart of the matter – break through the barrier of fear – thereby enabling them to form long-term relationships, both she and the therapist felt that Sean needed a different kind of catalyst to effect such a transformation. Rachel believed that the situation required a strong woman to 'take him through the fire'; she also believed that she was eminently placed to be that woman. Perhaps, it was, indeed, her fate. But the risk she was taking was with her own heart.

This dilemma mirrored precisely the relationship between Senta and the Dutchman. And for me, immersed in writing about the legend, of course, it was entirely synchronistic. Rachel is set apart from the majority of women who would enter into a relationship with Sean. She knows that his love is a curse and that she is potentially doomed to suffer from it. But, if she goes into this relationship in the full awareness of what she is taking on, might not this be the ultimate sacrifice demanded by the man who wants to love but cannot? And, through such an act of love, might he not be saved? If Rachel does indeed hurl herself off the cliff and into the stormy seas of love, she, most certainly, will be transformed through the joy and pain such a relationship can bring. But whether she can evoke such a change in Sean is another matter altogether. Having taken the plunge myself, and without effecting any transformation whatsoever in Damon, I may be forgiven, perhaps, for feeling somewhat dubious about the prospect of a successful outcome.

Leaving aside this almost literal depiction of the relationship between Senta and the Dutchman, their story also represents an allegory of the way we must sacrifice our unreal perceptions – those shadowy inner images based on our armoury of faulty beliefs – of men and women in order to transform our relationships. Only by truly trusting and committing ourselves totally to loving an other can we find a haven from our separateness. By running away from relationship – as a mistaken form of self-protection – we experience an even deeper pain – the agony of isolation. We seal ourselves not only from the love of another but from our own capacity to love.

This is all too often the apparent fate of Uranian individuals. The compulsion toward unfettered experience and the repulsion for any obligations or ties denies them the union and respite from the emotional wildernesss that they inwardly crave. At the same time, the Uranian senses, like Senta, deep within his soul, that there is something greater than the mundanity of human love – a love limited by the Saturnian narrowness of earthly passions. And he is determined to seek it. Sometimes, as we shall see later, the Uranian desire for the extraordinary, the out-of-this-world, can lead to some exceedingly bizarre and hair-raising experiences.

When Uranus is linked to relationships – by its position in the seventh or eighth house, its rulership of these houses or strong angles to the Sun or Mars (for women) and Moon or Venus (for men) – the individual is brought into contact with this unusual and extraordinary force through the partner. In this way, it is the partner who displays some, or all of the Uranian characteristics that I have discussed so far. Relationships in this case are never straightforward; they are volatile, exciting sometimes, but rarely stable and often short-lived. This is particularly true of Uranus conjunct an angle in the Composite chart or closely aspecting one of the personal planets.

One of the most common themes to emerge with Uranus in regard to relationships is tendency toward romantic triangles. As the Uranian Mr Wilde noted, 'In married life three is company and two none.'[15] In one sense, where the misogynist is concerned, the impulse toward extra-marital affairs is yet another route to unconsciously punish and humiliate his wife and at the same time escape her over-controlling, all-powerful clutches. As soon as he finds another woman, the whole procedure begins again; the new beloved is seen as the route to his salvation, she is invested with all the powers formerly allotted to his wife. The Uranian misogynist basically wants to keep his wife, since she represents his primary source of maternal nourishment, yet the 'other woman' also feeds his excessive need for love and comfort; in this way affairs represent a sort of never-ending quest to make up for what he missed as a child. However, the pattern of leaving the 'dragon' of a wife for the goddess of the other woman is inevitably doomed – the other woman soon develops all the 'warts' of the wife. To the misogynist it is as if he, like the Flying Dutchman, is cursed – all the women he chooses are dragons. Until he realizes that it is his underlying hatred of women that causes this, he will repeat the pattern unceasingly. The commitment-phobic needs affairs because they provide him with the illusion that he is still free to explore alternatives and distract him from the terror of deep emotional bonding: affairs effectively serve to keep his panic level down.

No one, of course, is immune to a triangular relationship – whether or not there is a Uranian link to partnerships in the natal chart – but the aroma of forbidden fruit, the intoxicating allure of dangerous waters, often coincides with a transit of Uranus to the Ascendant or Descendant, the seventh house ruler or the Moon, Venus or Mars. A triangle comprises of the 'beloved' who is committed to someone else, the 'interloper' and the 'cuckold'. Leaving aside the fact that some partnerships are dead and there is every good reason for the 'beloved' to look elsewhere and the 'interloper' to enter into relationship with him or her, there can be a number of different underlying impulses behind the triangle. One is the increased level of desire that is promoted by the fact that the beloved and the interloper cannot always be with each other – another stands in the way. For the interloper this adds a sense of competition and, for the beloved and the interloper, the exquisite agony of separation becomes a powerful aphrodisiac. In contrast to this 'rivalrous triangle' there is the 'split-object' triangle; here the underlying reasons tend to relate to issues we have covered through the misogynist and the commitment-phobic; here the 'beloved' experiences a tension laced with guilt – guilt over his disloyalty to his spouse and guilt for not being able to cement the relationship with the 'interloper'. Sometimes these triangular relationships continue for years: Victor Hugo, although married, maintained a life-long liaison with the actress Juliette Drouet – a relationship that bore all the hallmarks of Uranus with constant separations and reconciliations – but more often than not, like all things Uranian, they have a limited life span.

A triangle of Uranian proportions evolved between the scientist Sir William Crookes and the medium Florence Cook. In 1874, the 17-year-old Eastender, Florence Cook, turned up on the doorstep of William Crookes. She wanted him, she said, to investigate her powers of mediumship. Crookes had just finished investigating the medium Daniel Dunglas Home and had found his gift very persuasive, attesting to it in writing. During his investigation of Home, Florrie had been earning quite a reputation for herself, getting the sack from a school in East Ham where she had been an assistant teacher because the spirits that followed her around made her rather conspicuous. Shortly after leaving this job, her séances became the talk of the area – the spirits had a tendency to throw her into the air and rip all her clothes off. There was often standing room only. She then became a rich old man's private medium, but her employ was abruptly ended after an unpleasant incident when one of her spirits – the full-form materialization of 'Katie King' – was grabbed during a séance and the entranced Florrie was found to be very dishevelled. It was at this point that she arrived on Crookes' doorstep.

Crookes took to her immediately, inviting her to stay at his Camden Home. His wife, pregnant with their tenth child, was rarely to be seen.

It was here, in a specially set up room in William's house, that Katie King made further appearances. Katie would walk around arm-in arm with Crookes and also with Florrie. But after three months of this odd threesome, Katie declared that she must return to the spirit world; an announcement that curiously coincided with Florrie's declaration that she had been secretly married for some months. The investigation came to an abrupt end and Crookes never contacted nor even saw Florrie again.

There have been many opinions on the nature of this relationship: some consider Florrie to have been a superb con-artist who sexually fascinated the cerebral Crookes; others, that she had a genuine gift and that Crookes in a fit of pique over her 'infidelity' refused to acknowledge her contribution to his scientific research of the paranormal. However, Zoë, whom we shall meet in a moment, sees the affair rather differently. In a past life regression where she 'became' Florence Cook, it transpired that Crookes fell head over heels in love with her. Florrie believed she was a fraud, but she clearly had genuine mediumistic ability: Katie King manifested before Crookes and Florrie on many occasions, and when she didn't, Florrie felt obliged to fake her. Crookes found out about this and simultaneously ended the affair and the investigation. Florrie never really got over his rejection of her – ending her days in Monmouthshire, drinking heavily and seducing tradesmen. Crookes felt betrayed and hurt by Florrie on all fronts. And it may be that some unfinished business has spilled over into a current life.

'Zoë' is a bright, attractive, zany – and certainly controversial – writer and broadcaster. She is also a talented medium and healer. Her career has brought her much success, if not a degree of fame, and she has a coterie of loyal friends and admirers. What she does not have is a husband, 2.4 children and a home of her own. In fact, her romantic life is in a constant state of flux. Relationships for Zoë have see-sawed from the desultory to the disastrous – one inappropriate marriage to a politician and series of affairs with a disarray of unsuitable and unreliable men. But nothing and no one compares to the apocalypse that was 'Keith'.

Zoë first met Keith in 1980 – shortly before the break up of her marriage. At the time, although she was impressed by his 'unfussy'

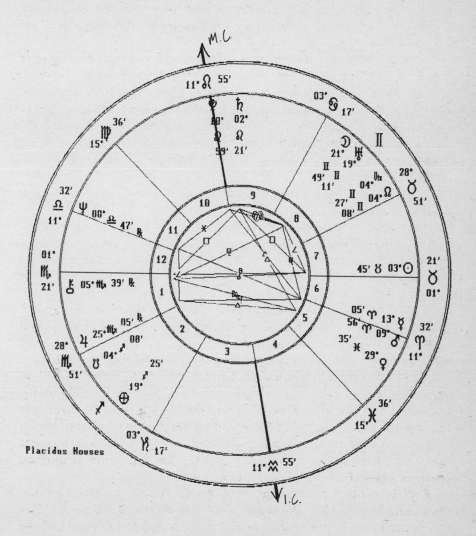

Figure 4: Zoë

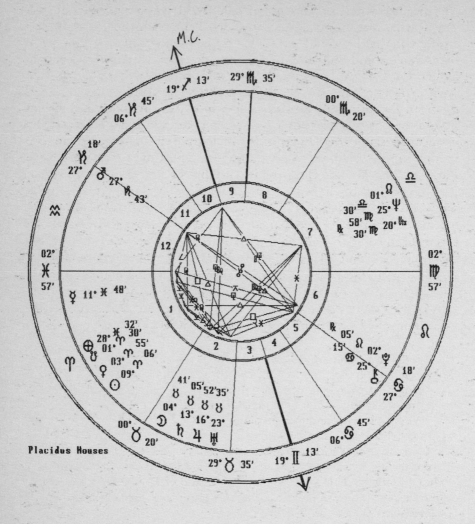

Figure 5: Keith

approach to astronomy, which made a rather dense subject eminently accessible to one and all, she was in no way romantically drawn to him. Eight years later, on Bonfire Night, she met him again, and this time the sparks really flew. Within 24 hours, Keith was to declare that he was madly in love with her – she was his destiny, and his wife, Bernice, an inevitable casualty of that fate. Three weeks later, Keith changed his mind: he wouldn't be seeing Zoë again. By mid-December, he was on the phone trumpeting his love for Zoë. On 29 December, it was all over:

'Bernice needs me.' In the April of 1989, Keith was back yet again with Zoë – at least in principle: he informed her that his love was just as strong and that he would leave Bernice; he then went home (some 200 miles away from London and Zoë) and wrote her a series of passionate letters. On 23 July, he wrote to Zoë, informing her that she was 'the devil incarnate' and that there was to be no further contact between them. In January 1990, Keith was once more back in touch and visited Zoë on one or two occasions. But after a scene in early February, he yet again disappeared. In April he apologized and announced to Zoë that he simply could not live without her: 'This time I really will leave Bernice.' And he did. He told his wife that he was going to live with Zoë; he packed his bags and set off for London. An hour down the motorway, he was taken seriously ill and had to be driven home – to his mother's. But he telephoned Zoë, assuring her of his love. He arranged to come to London for her birthday on 24 April, but on the day itself, he changed his mind three times – on the last occasion, at 7p.m., explaining that it was 'impossible'. At midnight, there was a knock on Zoë's door. She opened it to find Keith standing on the step, arrayed in a dinner-jacket with a bottle of Moët clutched in his hand. What happened next is best left to Zoë to describe:

> I went to kiss him and he stepped back.
> 'Don't touch me!'
> 'Why have you come, then?'
> 'I'm not sure . . . I'm going back to Bernice.'
> 'Why have you brought the champagne?'
> 'Well, I had to bring something.'
> So I hit him with the champagne bottle. He was so completely unreachable, I went wild . . . After all, what kind of man travels 200 miles with a bottle of champagne festooned with a pink bow to tell a woman he's supposed to be in love with that he's going back precisely where he came from . . . and on her birthday!

Predictably, in Keith's case, the affair did not end there. A month later, he phoned a mutual friend telling her that he missed Zoë 'quite dreadfully'. He then wrote her another epistle:

> A while ago you said to me that more than anything else you wanted me to come to you because I wanted you, overriding all other considerations. Well, darling, although all those other considerations are still fighting in me every inch of the way, that has to be where I'm at . . . I really thought on that dreadful night of your birthday that that was the end of Us. I even told myself (and others) totally emphatically that you had to be evil,

and although no one else knows it, I could scarcely believe it when less than 24 hours later all the old yearnings were beginning again. Whatever my responsibilities to the rest of the world, and whatever the rest of the world may think of me for it, so help me, I am still irrepressibly, uncontainably in love with you. So help me God . . . So, darling, please accept this letter as a State of the Soul address. Whenever we meet I simply want to fall into your arms at the earliest opportunity (despite the 'heroic' resistance last time) . . . Early in this letter I spoke about mending fences, but the imagery was wrong. What I really long for is the day when there will be absolutely no fences between us ever again. Know that I adore you – *almost* helplessly . . . Ever, Keith

That was the last Zoë ever heard from him – at least at the time of writing in March 1991. He never answered her letters – and, of course, she couldn't phone him. The nearest he came to explaining his inexplicable behaviour was in conversation to a mutual friend when he implied that he had been exposed to some revelation about Zoë but, of course, he wouldn't say what it was. Zoë did run into him at a conference in the October of 1990 but he cut her dead.

Zoë came to see me shortly after that. She was, understandably, in a state of some distress, although with her wry sense of humour, she constantly focused on the funny side of it all. The sorry tale, recounted as it is here, has, admittedly, an amusing edge to it, but the experience of it for Zoë was deeply upsetting and Keith's schizophrenic behaviour was baffling to say the least. Here was a man with whom she had fallen madly in love, a man who had promised her everything she had always yearned for, yet who had not only failed to deliver his promises but driven her into the ground – ultimately declaring that the only reason he had 'tangled' with her was because she had bewitched him.

Keith, of course, had behaved like a text-book commitment-phobic. He had wooed Zoë with the intensity of a man possessed but ducked and dived when commitment came into view to the extent that, on the occasion of his leaving Bernice for Zoë, the overwhelming prospect of forever-afterness had provoked his psyche into making him seriously ill. Apparently, poorly as he was, it was only when he saw the words, 'Jesus is for life not just for Christmas' on the back window of a car that he took the next motorway exit. With all the skill of the commitment-phobic, he kept Zoë – an intelligent and hardly gullible woman – 'on the hook' by his spontaneous, grand gestures of love for her and his Oscar-winning performance as a man wrestling with his conscience against overwhelming odds – the love of Zoë.

But even if he could not commit himself to Zoë, he had managed to commit himself to marriage to Bernice for 25 years; he had a large house and two children and was an astonishing success, with all the attendant financial rewards. Thus, if we look a little deeper into Keith's life, we find more than just a hint, not of the commitment-phobic, but of the misogynist.

Keith was an only child with a precocious intellect. He was the 'apple' of his parent's eyes, and ultimately rendered them ecstatic by gaining a scholarship to Cambridge. On leaving university he spent a short time managing an electric retailers before joining a local newspaper. He worked his way up to become a journalist, while at the same time pursuing his real passion – astronomy. His first book on dark stars became an international best-seller and he never looked back. But astronomy was not his only passion – in the Sixties he became a Catholic convert and he is, to this day, evangelical about the faith.

But if his outer life is a hymn to success, like all emotionally immature men, Keith's inner life is in chaos. He maintained to Zoë that he had married Bernice because he knew he would. She had sent in a written application for the job as his secretary; he took one look at the letter and knew that he would marry her. But right from the start, his mother began to cause trouble and she eventually forced him to break off the engagement. He did, but was so distressed by Bernice's despair that he married her. However, from that point, he clearly emotionally and psychologically withdrew from the marriage, taking refuge in his writing and his religion. Bernice went from being an attractive, sophisticated economics graduate to a dumpy and depressed housewife. Keith continually complained to Zoë about Bernice's inadequacies and the way she suffocated him with demands for him to be ever more successful; he admitted he loathed her and longed to be free of her. He even maintained that their daughters hated her. It also rankled him, he told Zoë, that Bernice was forever begging him to move away from Chester, preferably abroad, when she knew he would never move too far from his parents. He told Zoë that, for some strange and clearly embittered reason, Bernice always referred to him and his family as 'the package'.

Keith, like many men, particularly Englishmen, secretly despises women because he doesn't understand them and he's very frightened of what he cannot understand. At the same time, he is drawn, like a magnet, to a woman's 'breast'. As an only son of a strong, dominant and over-possessive mother and a weak and retiring father, he cannot separate himself – either psychologically or physically – from his parents, especially his mother. According to Zoë, when his mother informed her by phone that Keith was too ill to drive to London, she used the rather telling expression, 'I'm keeping him in for a few days'!

Inwardly, Keith is seething at this possession; he cannot free himself from his mother, nor his internal perception of women. Like the archetypal misogynist, he perceives women as devourers and aims to destroy them before they can get to him. The result of this, in Keith's case, is that he conducts his cold war on women with Bernice while replenishing his emotional vacuum with another woman. Yet, because the hatred and fear is so deep, he is constantly repelled from making his romantic advances anything other than a brief skirmish on the edge of the main battle zone. The affair serves to humiliate his wife and also the other woman – both are to blame for his turmoil and their hysterical outbursts justify his behaviour. Coupled with this is all his underlying guilt about sex and infidelity, which is reinforced by the religion he has taken up. His constant perception of Zoë as 'evil' and 'possessed' stands testament to this internal dilemma. It also explains why he was only able to make love to Zoë once during the entire span of their relationship.

Certainly Uranus is a very prominent figure in this affair. At the time Keith and Zoë fell in love, Uranus was squaring Keith's Venus, ultimately making its way to his Sun (and Zoë's Mars) by the end of 1990. Radically, Keith has a Mercury–Uranus quintile and a Sun–Uranus semi-square but, more significantly, Uranus is involved in a stellium with the Moon, Saturn and Jupiter in Taurus. Mars in the Saturn-ruled sign of Capricorn in opposition to Pluto certainly adds to the tyrant-misogynist potential in his chart. However, I would add that Keith does not have the chart of someone unable to commit: the Uranian content in the chart is counterbalanced by Mars in Capricorn, the Mercury–Saturn sextile and the Sun at the mid-point of Mercury–Saturn – all of which point to an individual with integrity and staying power, albeit one with a ruthless and cruel streak. I suspect that the extraordinary to-ing and fro-ing in the affair with Zoë was triggered by the transit of Uranus to his Sun and Venus, which brought out the inherent pattern of pursuit/panic–fight or flee behaviour of the misogynist. Also, I must add that Keith's Moon–Pluto square is redolent with the theme of 'mother obsession', and is clearly a major contributory factor to his deep-seated emotional conflict and his fear and hatred of the feminine, especially the dark feminine (see Chapter 8).

This much I explained to Zoë, which helped her to recognize that it was not any fault in her that prompted Keith's behaviour. I was also able to reassure her that he had every good astrological reason to adore her, since they had some classic synastric links. Keith's Moon in Taurus – a primary indicator not only of the feminine in general but mother and 'wife' in particular – was precisely conjunct Zoë's Sun and her Descendant while her Mars – a primary indicator of the masculine

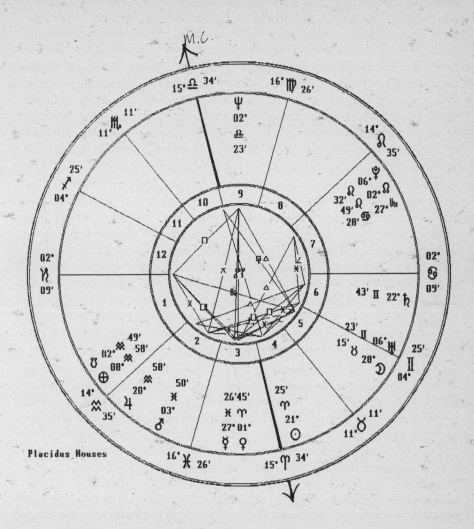

Figure 6: The Composite

and the experience sought in men – is precisely conjunct his Sun. Most significantly Zoë's Moon–Uranus conjunction in Gemini 'sits' exactly on Keith's IC – in other words, her feminine soul touches the roots of his being. This powerful contact is also likely to be 'responsible' for triggering such a Uranian response in Keith. I might also add that the Moon/Mars/Pluto configuration in Keith's chart that intersects with Zoë's Sun/Saturn–Pluto/Ascendant formation acts as a powerful anchor between them and more than hints at a deep-seated, unconscious, power struggle – one, perhaps, that has its roots in other times, other lives. The composite chart is also not without power and influence: the Sun in the fourth house indicates the potential to be 'at home' with each other – both in the psychological sense and in the way of four-square walls. And the Sun is beautifully placed at the mid-point of Saturn and Jupiter, investing the relationship with staying power. Uranus by no means dominates the picture: 'he' is placed in a relatively innocuous position in the sixth house, although I would suggest that this positioning places a heavy emphasis on duties and obligations to each other of the karmic variety. The Moon's wide conjunction to Uranus certainly gives a flavour of the unusual and the volatile.

However, major synastric contacts are no indicator of longevity; they merely point to the 'dialogue' of the relationship which, in Zoë and Keith's case, is certainly 'throbbing with life'. It may be, of course, that this relationship will end happily ever after but, with the pattern it has already, taken combined with Keith's psychological problems and Zoë's own emotional conflicts, the prognosis is not good. Nevertheless, the synastry underlines the fact that the interaction between them was neither lightweight nor unproductive.

Apart from a strong physical attraction between Zoë and Keith, there was a mutual interest in the paranormal. Although Keith was a scientist, he was fascinated by such phenomena as remote viewing, telekinesis and telepathy; yet because he feared ridicule by the scientific fraternity, publicly he maintained a critical stance to it all. Thus, Zoë with her powers of mediumship and familiarity with all things occult was a source of all the mystery he craved. But this was a double-edged sword: she was, to Keith, the personification of the dark side of the feminine that both fascinated him and repelled him, so that, when he was in one of his anti-Zoë phases, she became the embodiment of all that was evil and dark – all that his revered religion abominated. Poor Zoë – if it wasn't Bernice who stood between her and Keith, it was God and the Virgin Mary; although, in reality, it was Keith's tortured psyche. He was at war with the feminine on every front.

Zoë knew about the regression work I was doing and wondered if taking her back to a past life might shed some light on the Keith situation. She was familiar with hypnotic states and went instantly to another time and place. Suddenly I was no longer talking to Zoë but to Florence Cook. Florrie had a lot to say, not just about Sir William, but about Daniel Dunglas Home. She spoke about Daniel's arrogant behaviour toward her; how he thought he was not just a great medium, but the only one of any note. Florrie thought otherwise. She knew that her spirit, Katie King, had revealed to Sir William the existence of life after death, while Daniel's materializations only ever ran to a disembodied arm or leg. But, as far as Zoë was concerned, the most revealing aspect to this past life recall was that the present-day Keith was none other than D.D. Home.

My attitude to these past life recalls is not whether they are genuine in the literal sense, but what psychological and therapeutic value they have. For Zoë, the understanding that Keith's ambivalence toward her was, in part, a memory of an old 'professional' jealousy resolved some of the confusion. Florrie also revealed that the greatest conflict Keith was experiencing was that of a denial of his psychic abilities in favour of his scientific objectivity, a conflict that was also bound up in his obsession with Catholicism – a religion antithetical to mediumship. As Zoë saw it, in denying her, Keith was also denying his real calling. And this concerned her almost more than the loss of him, his love and their future together.

Zoë consulted me for hypnotherapy for some weeks after this initial regression. With a Moon–Uranus conjunction in Gemini in the eighth house of emotional and sexual exchange, she had much 'work' to do on developing trust and intimacy in relationships. With Pluto conjuncting the Midheaven and Uranus (with its conjunction to the Moon) ruling the fourth house, her relationship with her mother has been fraught with conflicts and, with a close Sun–Saturn square, father was no 'picnic' either. Zoë had been adopted at birth, and even though her parents had loved her and cared for her as if she had been their own flesh and blood, she always felt like an alien in her family. Like Keith, she was an academic 'high flier' and read English and philosophy at university. Also like Keith, she was extremely religious, becoming a Mormon in 1961 which she pursued with 'fanatical, door-stepping missionary zeal'. But her childhood experiences of seeing UFOs and assorted ghosts and poltergeists eventually propelled her into working with the paranormal, which, in turn, made her sceptical about the creeds of the orthodox religions.

In a typically Moon–Uranus way, she craved the extraordinary in life and love – and clearly got it with Keith – but in her Taurean heart, she longed for the security of married life, complete with 2.4 children. In therapy, we worked on building up the levels of trust in herself and her self-esteem, and gradually, she not only came through the most painful stage of bereavement over Keith, but regained her optimism about the future. As a result, there have been some major shifts in her perception about herself which in turn will make their presence felt in any future relationship. Perhaps the brief flirtation with divinity that she experienced with Keith will one day lead to a truly divine and lasting encounter. And if and when Keith does return, she will have the wisdom to send him back to 'mother' immediately.

I also have Zoë to thank for introducing me to the strange and fascinating world of Whitley Strieber, whose divine encounter I have chosen to keep until last.

Whitley Strieber, the author of *Communion* and *Transformation*,[16] must be the quintessential Uranian. He has written two international best-sellers on his encounters with aliens and his subsequent spiritual awakening through the trauma of these experiences. I was intrigued to find the chapter headings in *Transformation* included such Uranian concepts as 'Extreme Strangeness', 'The Storm Gathers', 'Lightning', 'The Terror of the Real', 'The Jolt of the True' and 'The Razor's Edge'. Strieber is, as far as I know, the only individual to go into print and survive blanket ridicule about an encounter with an alien of the romantic kind. Indeed, I think his experience with the 'White Angel' is both touching and beautiful. And, of course, eminently Uranian:

> The bedroom light was flipped on and a small being dressed in white came walking quickly across the room . . . I remember nothing at all of the size or facial features of this person, being, visitor, or whatever it was. All I do remember is an impression of unusual whiteness and light blue eyes . . . The being sat down on the bedside. She seemed almost angelic to me, so pure and full of knowledge. As she bent close to me I felt all the tension go out of my muscles. The sensation was exactly as if they had turned to oatmeal . . . The being looked into my eyes and said, 'I want to talk to you about your death.'[17] When we made eye contact I saw only blueness – the blue of heaven. It was like entering another world . . . The being moved its arm slightly, a gesture that I recall with absolute vividness because of the impact it had on me. I will never forget the next moment. Superficially it didn't seem like much: the edge of the white sleeve touched the middle and forefingers of my left hand, which had been lying along the outside of the quilt. This touch was so incredibly soft that it filled me with a peace unlike any I had ever felt before. In that instant it seemed to me that all the rich hours of childhood . . . the joys of a thousand perfect mornings combined together to offer me a kind of sustenance that I did not know I needed, but once felt seemed essential.
>   That sleeve was like an edge of heaven.

In these words, Strieber captures an experience of the divine. For him, the touch of an alien magically transmits the extraordinary feelings of bliss – Uranus, in the form of a white angel, had awakened him to the divine. And this is perhaps Uranus's most crucial function – to awaken us to the divine within ourselves.

Uranus has always seemed to have had more to do with the mind than the heart – the awakening to truth of which Uranus is so eminently capable, by implication, connotes an intellectual leap rather than an emotional one. It is possible, however, that we astrologers have rather missed the point with Uranus by perceiving this planet as having dominion over the mind – not in the Mercurial way of mental dexterity and logic, but in the more expanded sense of intuition, telepathy and visionary genius. To a large extent, the concept that Uranus is the higher resonance of Mercury has reinforced the notion that Uranus is above all a 'mental' planet. But, following the natural planetary sequence – Uranus as the higher resonance of the Sun, Neptune as the higher octave of the Moon and so on – we are brought fairly and squarely back to the association of Uranus with the heart centre of our solar system, the sun. Not only this, but Uranus is the only planet that, like the sun, gives off ultra-violet light. [18] And there is, indeed, a fiery quality about Uranus: after all, electricity creates light, energy and heat. Astrologically, the Sun is the ruling 'planet' of Leo and the fifth house of the horoscope; Leo and the Sun are synonymous with affairs of the heart – from the heart as a physical organ to the heart as the psychological centre of love. Uranus, therefore must be a higher resonance of the heart. We can begin to make more sense of this if we take into consideration the fifth house of the horoscope and its association with creativity and love affairs; the eleventh house, as its polar opposite, takes creativity onto another level altogether – a more transcendent, expansive plane – an Aquarian/Uranian all-embracing love of the Higher Self. Ethel Person also provides us with a connection between the Sun and Uranus in her description of the symbiosis of love and the imagination:

> Love is an act of the imagination. For some of us, it will be the great creative triumph of our lives. In its very nature as an act of the imagination lies the power for both good and ill, for it can indeed exploit the lover's illusions or delusions, but alternately can lead the lover to transcending truths. [19]

The importance of the imagination and idealization of the beloved in the process of falling in love cannot be underestimated. More importantly, one of the most potent phenomena of falling in love (which I discuss at length in the following chapter) is the sense of the expanded self. Falling in love is a creative act: we endow the beloved with all the magical powers of having generated this marvellous feeling in ourselves – and forget that it is we who have tapped our own creative force. Love is the most immediate way of accessing the truly remarkable gifts of the Higher Self – because we love, we are filled with the 'incredible lightness of being', we feel super-human. When we are struck by the *coup de foudre*, the thunderbolt, we are awakened to the power of love with all its transformative and restorative properties.

It may seem strange, in a chapter where the male of the species has been taken to task for failing to love, that it is this same planet which is synonymous with so much upheaval and heartache that is the one that holds the key to unlocking, or rather awakening, the heart. It may be, however, that this difficulty men are experiencing with opening and trusting their hearts to women – for misogynism and commitment-phobia seem pandemic – represents an evolutionary thrust, a bizarre transitional stage, toward a new kind of loving between men and women and a new kind of human relationship – one that transcends the sexual antagonism of male and female and brings to an end the battle of the sexes. I am also reminded here of my friend who used the phrase 'taking him through the fire' in connection with helping a man to burn through the barrier of his fears and perceptions of the feminine. Maybe this, then, is the ultimate power of Uranus: to initiate us into the mysteries of the heart and so revolutionize our capacity to love and, in turn, our relationships.

Whatever the larger view of Uranian potential, of one thing we can be absolutely sure: with a foundation of trust and self-value, we can receive the Uranian awakening to the divinity of the expanded self. And once we have tapped this, it is only a matter of time and greater consciousness before we can have the all-embracing love of the Higher Self as a permanent fixture in our lives.

> Oh we've got to trust
> one another again
> in some essentials.
>
> Not the narrow little
> bargaining trust
> that says: I'm for you
> if you'll be for me –
>
> But a bigger trust,
> a trust of the sun
> that does not bother about moth and rust,
> and we see it shining in one another.

Oh don't you trust me,
don't burden me
with your life and affairs; don't thrust me
into your cares.

But I think you may trust
the sun in me
that glows with just
as much glow as you see
in me, and no more.

But if it warms
your heart's quick core
why then trust it, it forms
one faithfulness more.

And be, oh be
a sun to me,
not a weary insistent
personality

but a sun that shines
and goes dark, but shines
again and entwines
with the sunshine in me

till we both of us
are more glorious
and more sunny.

'TRUST', D.H. LAWRENCE (*Selected Poems*, Penguin, 1954)

Appendix

1) Liz Greene, *Relating* (Coventure, 1977).
2) Close aspects infer any aspect that is within 2–3° of exactitude – with the exception of the semi-sextile, sesqui-quadrate, semi-square, quintile or bi-quintile, which require 1° closeness of orb.
3) Penny Thornton, *Romancing the Stars* (The Aquarian Press, 1988).
4) Colin Wilson, *Mysteries* (Granada, 1978).
5) *Romancing the Stars*, op.cit.
6) Dr Susan Forward and Joan Torres, *Men Who Hate Women and the Women Who Love Them* (Bantam, 1989).
7) This, and all subsequent quotes about the misogynist taken from *Men Who Hate Women and the Women Who Love Them*.

8) See Chapter 7 for a full discussion on eros.

9) The Moon in hard aspect to Uranus is frequently found in charts of individuals whose mother is volatile or constantly 'coming or going'.

10) As quoted by Dr Forward in *Men Who Hate Women and the Women Who Love Them*.

11) Steven Carter and Julia Sokol, *Men Who Can't Love* (Bantam, 1989).

12) This, and all subsequent quotes about commitment-phobia taken from *Men Who Can't Love*.

13) Uranus in Scorpio conjunct the Ascendant; Moon in Aquarius and Mars in Aquarius.

14) Saturn's 29-year cycle divides approximately into four seven-year periods and yields two squares, one opposition and the conjunction to its original position.

15) Oscar Wilde, *The Importance of Being Earnest*. Act I.

16) Whitley Strieber, *Transformation: The Breakthrough* (Arrow, 1989).

17) See Chapter 8, pp.199–200.

18) *National Geographic* magazine, Vol 170, August 1986: Voyager II spacecraft discovery.

19) Ethel Spector Person, *Love and Fateful Encounters: The Power of Romantic Passion* (Bloomsbury, 1989).

7

Neptune: The Enchantment

IMAGINE YOURSELF ALONE IN A FOREST. THE MOON IS A PALE DISTANT crescent glimpsed from time to time between the branches of the trees above; dawn is some hours away, but already frost is forming on the ground and edging the fern with a sparkling crust. A little way ahead, the tendrils of mist that have draped themselves across your path, like an intermittent carpet, have formed themselves into a white veil. As you move into this veil, all sense of reality is suddenly suspended; sounds become distorted, shapes and forms are barely distinguishable. A fallen tree trunk becomes a lurking predator, a dangling frond, the caress of an unseen hand; danger is announced in every snap of a twig and each screech of an owl. You can but feel your way ahead relying on your intuition to guide you through. Your mounting sense of disorientation throws you into panic – should you go back, continue on, or remain where you are until the dawn breaks or the mist disappears? You have never felt so alone, so vulnerable, so afraid. Somehow you are drawn on until you reach the bank of a lake. As you peer into the water, you see a strange, even grotesque, form staring back at you. So great is your discomposure that you lose hold on reality and fall into unconsciousness.

Almost at once a numinous figure appears at your side. Taking you to the water's edge once more, you gaze at a reflection that is now filled with light and beauty. Your numinous guide waves his hand and instantly, there, before you, is the heaven you have always imagined. You can see it, hear it and feel it – nothing on Earth can match its radiance. Sweet and melodious sounds are all about you, the landscape is bathed in all the colours of the spectrum and the scent of frangipani and hibiscus fills the air. Your guide waves his other hand and there beside you is the lover you have known only in your dreams: this is your soul mate, you are told, now you are one. In that moment you are filled with an ecstasy that knows no bounds: love is within you and around you. You merge into your soul mate and simultaneously become one with all that is. You have not just touched divinity, you are divine. 'This is reality,' you say, 'the world I have left behind is illusion.'

On waking, the mist has gone and the morning sun is warm and pleasant. The birds are singing and here and there a squirrel can be seen darting from branch to branch. As you clear the sleep 'dust' from your eyes you begin to recall the events of the night before. You go towards the water, wondering who will be there among the ripples, but all that beams back at you is your familiar reflection. There is no hint of the danger you felt some hours before, but gone too is the heaven that you had known. 'Was it a dream?' you ask yourself. 'Yet it seemed so real . . .' Plunging your hand into the water, the chill sends a shiver through your body. 'Ah, this is real,' you say, 'the other must have been a dream.' Although, just for a moment in the spreading ripples flecked with the sun's dazzle, you can't be sure . . .

You have just fallen under the spell of Neptune.

Neptune is a planet synonymous with the divine. We have already encountered his realm in Chapter 4 through the veil of Isis – the veil of *maya*, illusion. Esther Harding says of this veil, '[It] is the ever-changing form of nature whose beauty and tragedy veil the spirit from our eyes. This perpetual interplay in the manifest world . . . seems to have such an absolute reality that we do not question it. Yet in moments of insight, induced, perhaps by pain and suffering or great joy, we may suddenly realise that this which makes up the obvious form of the world, is not true, the real . . .' Until we have experienced a truly transcendental state, we tend to believe that the world we inhabit – the world filled with motor cars, televisions and supermarkets – is the real world; only in moments of revelation or in an altered state when we may in full consciousness enter another reality do we know with absolute certainty, 'Ah, *this* is real.'

So it is that in astrology Neptune is considered on the one hand the great deceiver and on the other the illuminator, the planetary archetype who opens the doors of perception and allows us to experience the ecstasy of the spirit, whether through music, art, poetry or literature, or through revelation or love, yet who betrays us because we cannot sustain the reality he proffers. He tantalizes us, then makes us doubt what we have perceived and reject it in favour of the material world. But what he has revealed is just enough to make us long to recapture that unearthly experience, to escape once more to that heavenly plane.

Sometimes, though, we can only do this by taking drugs and becoming hopelessly addicted to them or by rejecting reality completely and becoming insane.

The lower resonance of Neptune is not, by and large, a beatific experience. When we resonate with the underside of Neptune we are prone to sheer escapism, dependency – often through drug or alcohol addiction – deception or treachery. Who has not, during a Neptune transit, undergone a loss or betrayal of some sort; who has not experienced some erosion of faith or had their perceptions shaken to the very roots?

Delusion and illusion are two of the most bitter of Neptune's poisons. In the watery deeps of Neptune, we suffer; we identify with the suffering of others. Individuals with Neptune strongly featured in their charts invariably become the social workers, healers and helpers of the world, the ministers – God's earthly representatives – and the 'mopper-uppers' of life's flotsam and jetsam. They care, they empathize with the poor, the needy, the neglected and the unwanted; they are the ones most frequently called upon to make a sacrifice or to become a martyr to a cause that may or may not be worthy.

The Neptunians dance to a different drummer: they are the poets, artists and dreamers of this world, the diviners and the sooth-sayers. They have been touched by the numinous but are so often crucified or rejected for their visions or fail to marry their divine perception with the dross of everyday life – the real world. Neptunians so easily become life's derelicts, life's misfits and life's misunderstood geniuses. Under Neptune they seek to escape from reality by whatever means available, sometimes through art and ecstatic encounters, sometimes through lies, drugs or madness.

It is only now, as the new consciousness emerges, that we can more assuredly access the higher resonance of Neptune without endangering our health or our sanity. I have already discussed the properties of the higher resonance of Neptune in Chapter 3; here I shall focus on Neptune's role in our quest for the inner marriage. What themes does this archetype yield? And what dangers, what wonders, what enchantment may we find through his portals?

Neptune is synonymous with romance, both in its 'smaller' sense as flights of fancy and in its larger sense as romantic love. Romance – the love of eros with its sexual component as opposed to the 'brotherly' love of agape – has always existed, but the ideal of romantic love came into being in the Middle Ages around the time of the Crusades; it first emerged in the tale of *Tristan and Iseult* – a story we will 'dip' into later in the book. Romantic love, or 'courtly love', was a distinctly Neptunian affair with specific characteristics:

> First, the knight and his lady were never to be involved sexually with each other. Theirs was an idealised, spiritualised relationship, designed to lift them above the level of physical grossness, to cultivate refined feeling and spirituality. The second requirement of courtly love was that they not be married to each other. In fact, the lady was usually married to another nobleman. The knight-errant adored her, served her, and made her a focus of his spiritual aspiration and idealism, but he could not have an intimate relationship with her. To do so would be to treat her as an ordinary mortal woman and courtly love required that he treat her as a divinity, as a symbol of the eternal feminine and of his feminine soul. The third requirement was that the courtly lovers keep themselves aflame with passion, that they suffer intense desire for each other, yet strive to spiritualise their desire by seeing each other as symbols of the divine archetypal world and by never reducing their passion to the ordinariness of sex or marriage.[1]

It is thus quite easy to see how this model of perfect love has served to confuse so many men across the ages. On the one hand, a woman should be 'worshipped' and placed on a pedestal; she should be 'a hostess in the drawing room, a mother in the nursery and a . . .' – the old adage goes on to say, 'a whore in the bedroom', and this, of course, is where the trouble lies, since many men with the archetype of romantic love rooted firmly in their unconscious simply cannot marry their sexual desires to a woman they have chosen to worship 'from afar'. How can they love a woman yet lust for her at the same time? In these men's unconscious the two are mutually exclusive. This phenomena has come to be known as 'the whore-madonna complex' and it is an entirely Neptunian quandary. On the one hand, and in its 'higher' manifestation, Neptune connotes the divinely untouchable, the unknowable. Its planetary glyph of the three-forked trident represents, among other themes, the trinity – Father, Son and Holy Ghost. Mary, the mother of Christ – *la mère* (mother), *la mer* (the sea)[2] – is yet another Neptunian archetype. The Virgin Mary does not conceive her divine Son in the way of all other mortals – such a conception is not sullied by sexual intercourse, but, in keeping with divine untouchability, she experiences an Immaculate Conception. Indeed, the most famous romances of all must surely be those about King Arthur and his Knights of the Round Table. Here, chivalry, courage and the love of fair lady were intricately interwoven with the mysterious quest for the Holy Grail – a perfect melding of Neptunian courtly love and Christianity.[3]

Yet, on the other hand, in its 'lower' expression, Neptune is synonymous with pornography, dissipation and prostitution; the fallen woman as opposed to the Blessed Virgin. Even the word 'passion', most usually associated with physical love, also serves to describe the suffering of Christ and in the Christian calendar we celebrate Passion Sunday. Thus, with all this confusion between love and sex, the sacred and the profane, it is no surprise that many individuals who experience a Neptunian calling simply give up the idea of sex altogether and become celibate.

Neptune is almost certainly an archetypal figure I have met time and time again in my divine and not so divine encounters: I have, in the past, all too often been drawn to those who are the personification of Neptune – artists, actors, dreamers and sensitives – and also those who subsequently turn out to be con-men, alcoholics and emotional psychopaths. But I have to confess a great liking for Neptune. Even with all the subsequent disillusionment, the sacrifices and the betrayals, the illumination and the ecstatic heights have been worth the pain and suffering – although, perhaps at the time, I would have been hard pressed to admit it. Neptune is without doubt the most mystical figure we must encounter on our way to the wedding.

Hans Christian Anderson's tale of *The Little Mermaid* is to my mind the quintessence of Neptune and unveils the archetypal process at work in our quest for union:

The Little Mermaid was the youngest of six princesses. Her father, the Sea King, was a widower whose old mother kept house for him. As each princess reached the age of 15, she was allowed to come up out of the sea 'and sit in the moonlight on the reef and watch the great ships sail by'. [4] *All the sisters looked forward to this privilege but none longed for it as much as the youngest. Eventually her turn came. On the night of her fifteenth birthday, she swam up to the surface. A large ship had anchored and as she watched the comings and goings of the sailors she saw in their midst a young and handsome prince. She remained on the reef much of the night unable to take her eyes off the prince. Then, in the early hours of the morning a great storm arose, engulfing the ship, which sank beneath the water, taking 'her' prince to the bottom of the sea. Realizing that her human prince would drown, she held his head above the waves until the dawn and let the seas carry them toward an island. There she left him sleeping on the beach while she hid behind some rocks. Eventually, a young maiden emerged from a temple and spying the sleeping prince on the sand, she knelt by his side and gently brought him back to consciousness.*

Night after night, the Little Mermaid went back to the island, but she never saw her prince again.

After some time, one of her sisters discovered that the prince had been returned to his kingdom. She took her little sister to the shores of this kingdom so that she could once again gaze upon the prince. But gazing at him from afar was not enough; the Little Mermaid wanted to know him and stay beside him always.

The longing became so great that she went to her grandmother to ask if there was a way that she could become human. Her grandmother was horrified. She explained that while they, as creatures of the sea, lived for 300 years, human beings had a much shorter span of life; and while, when life was ended, sea creatures were turned into foam upon the waves, humans went to the heavenly kingdom. 'A human being has an immortal soul . . . [that] rises through the clear sky up to the host of shining stars.' The only way that a mermaid could gain an immortal soul was if a human being was able to love her more than anything else on Earth and married her, 'then his soul would flow into your body, and you, too, would receive your share in the happiness of mankind.'

The Little Mermaid resolved to have her prince – whatever the cost. She made a perilous journey to the witch of the sea who exacted a heavy price: first, that while her fish's tail would dissolve and in its place would emerge two 'human stumps', every step she took on them would feel as if she were walking upon swords; second, that the witch would cut out the Little Mermaid's tongue so that she could never use her beautiful voice again. And before she left, the witch warned her that should her prince pledge his troth to another, the morning after the marriage, she would lose her chance for an immortal soul and be turned into foam upon the water.

The little mermaid believed the sacrifice was worth it and, swimming up to the shores of the prince's kingdom, she swallowed the witch's potion. Sure enough, her tail vanished, and two pretty legs appeared in its place.

The prince, on finding the Little Mermaid, was captivated by her beauty and her grace – she moved like no earthly dancer. He spent his waking hours with her, sometimes telling her that she reminded him of a beautiful maiden from a temple who had rescued him after he had been shipwrecked. Of course, because she was dumb, the Little Mermaid could not tell him that it was she who had really saved his life, not the maiden from the temple.

In the fullness of time, on the orders of his father, the prince was sent across the seas to meet a prospective bride. 'I must see the beautiful princess though I can never love her! She is not like the lovely maiden of the temple, whom you resemble. If I should ever chose a bride, then it would be you.' But when the prince met the princess, he discovered that she was none other than the young maiden from the holy temple with whom he fell in love after the shipwreck.

He pledged his troth to her and they married. That night, the Little Mermaid's sisters swim up to the surface of the water and, handing her a knife, told her that before the sun rose she must plunge the weapon into the prince's heart. 'When the warm blood spurts over your feet, they will grow together into a fishtail, and you will become a mermaid once more . . . Make haste! Either you or he must die before the sun is up.'

But the Little Mermaid could not bring herself to harm her prince. Instead, she threw the knife into the sea and plunged, dying, into the waters. As she began to feel her *body melting into foam, she saw above the water the Daughters of the Air. They had come to take her into their midst: 'When we have striven for three hundred years to do all the good we can, we receive an immortal soul . . . You, poor little mermaid, have striven, like us, with all your heart. You have suffered and endured, you have raised yourself to the spirit world of air and . . . you will be able to gain your immortal soul.'*

Unseen, the Little Mermaid watched the prince and his beautiful bride searching for her; she then kissed the bride on the brow, smiled lovingly at the prince and soared up into the heavens.

In this story, Hans Christian Anderson has included almost every possible Neptunian theme. His story is set right in the midst of Neptune's underwater realm, symbolically the great depths of the unconscious; his Little Mermaid – half fish, half woman – is the quintessential Neptunian figure – a creature of the depths, of instinct, of the great feminine. Her fish's tail anchors her in the unconscious and the instinctive, though she can rise from the depths to access the upper world, the conscious world. But for all her human attributes, she is fundamentally a creature of the sea: only through enormous sacrifice and the love of a human being can she gain her immortal soul. Symbolically, only by sacrificing the ego, by rising out of the instinctive world and becoming conscious, can she find her divinity, her divine Self.

Not only does Anderson set his archetypal tale in Neptune's realm, but the text is saturated with Neptunian symbolism. The Little Mermaid, the maiden and the grandmother/witch represent the three phases of the moon, waxing, full and waning, which, in turn, is implicit in the trident symbol of Neptune. The Little Mermaid's father, the Sea King, is a widower who, like his Grail mystery counterpart, the Fisher King,[5] evokes Neptunian images of loss, loneliness and suffering, themes which repeat throughout the story. And, perhaps, most important of all, there is the Neptunian theme of divine love – a love that soars beyond the ordinary, a love that touches the soul.

To become human, the Little Mermaid undergoes intense physical and emotional suffering: when she loses her fish's tail, she severs her links with the underwater world and every step thereafter is taken in extreme agony; she also sacrifices her voice and, ultimately, her prince. Metaphorically, to grow in consciousness, we, like her, must suffer the pain of awareness and of real feeling, we must lose our attachment to our primitive instincts and be released from the dark power of the unconscious. The Little Mermaid rises up through the oceanic world of the instinctual and the unconscious to become human, to become conscious. Only then can she acquire a soul: only by making conscious what is unconscious can the true, divine Self be found. This concept is reinforced by the point that only through marriage to a human can the Little Mermaid gain immortality: only by a marriage between the unconscious and the conscious can the divine process occur. Furthermore, should she fail in her task, she will dissolve into the sea itself – allegorically, if we fail to consciously integrate the shadows that lurk in the depths of our unconscious we shall suffer fragmentation.

The Little Mermaid sacrifices everything she holds dear for the love of her human prince, yet he betrays her – not consciously, not knowingly – by binding himself to another. Both the prince and the mermaid, each in his and her own way, experience unrequited love – yet another Neptunian phenomena – although both of them ultimately achieve their heart's desire. And for the Little Mermaid her love is not only unrequited, but she is ultimately rejected in true Neptunian fashion. Also, it is a demonstration of sheer Neptunian convolution that the prince cannot know who really saved his life and to whom he is truly bound because the Little Mermaid cannot speak – and, of course, she cannot speak because her tongue was the sacrifice demanded for his love. But it is in the suffering that she herself is saved – she proves herself worthy of an immortal soul because she shows herself capable of loving another more than herself, more than life itself. Even when she is given the opportunity to save herself, she cannot kill the prince she loves above all else.

The Little Mermaid is a supremely Neptunian tale of epic proportions that portrays how, through suffering, sacrifice and love, divinity is found; it is also a profound allegory of the way we, as individuals, through sacrificing the ego may be redeemed from our bondage to the ego and our primitive instinctual depths.

In many ways, the Little Mermaid's prince represents her Ghostly Lover: he is an unobtainable love who both blocks the way to the inner marriage, yet who also leads to a divine union. The Ghostly Lover is a phenomena of the psyche familiar to all women – he is an aspect of the animus, the 'masculine soul':

The Ghostly Lover, in his psychological or subjective aspect, is a living reality to every woman. He holds his power and exerts his lure because he is a psychological entity, part of that conglomerate of autonomous, or relatively autonomous, factors which make up her psyche. As he is part of her so she is bound to him; she must find him and consciously assimilate him if she is not to suffer the pain and distress of disintegration. For he is her soul mate, her 'other half', the invisible companion who accompanies her throughout life.[6]

The Ghostly Lover is almost always perceived as a destructive aspect of the animus, because such an unreal and unrealizable image obstructs the way to a real-life relationship. It is as though the ghost of this idealized image constantly stands between a woman and her ability to truly relate to a man. Yet, at the same time, it is through the love that is inspired by such a powerful psychic image that our divinity can be glimpsed; but we must recognize it and claim it as our own. Another way in which the Ghostly Lover gains a divine bearing is within Christianity itself, when a nun dedicates her life to her Divine Lover, takes the veil and becomes a Bride of Christ, perhaps the ultimate Neptunian personification of the Ghostly Lover.

While for some women the Ghostly Lover represents the memory of a lover who once existed, in most cases this psychic image is a self-created fantasy figure. As such, the dream lover can never be matched in real life and therefore causes untold disappointments and frustrations for a woman. Certainly this is a theme common to all strongly Neptunian individuals, especially those women with an angular Neptune, hard[7] contacts between Neptune and the Sun and Mars, or Neptune linked to the seventh house of relationships. Time and time again in my astrological work I come up against Neptunian women whose romantic, over-idealized concept of men and relationships causes them unfulfilment in love. Sometimes the man with whom they are 'in love' turns out never to have so much as kissed them, sometimes the man in question is so out of reach as to live on the opposite side of the world. Almost always, at the root of this unrealizable love is a father problem.

In the story of the Little Mermaid, we are told that her father was a widower. We can infer that he is 'lost' in some way, because it is to her grandmother and her sisters that the mermaid goes for advice and support. The Neptunian woman, especially she who has Sun or Mars linked to Neptune, or this planet associated with the fourth house, has never come to grips with her father: he is either impossibly wonderful, or completely hopeless. He may have been absent, either psychologically or physically, or he may have been an alcoholic, a womaniser, or a failure. Thus, to compensate for this lack, the daughter has had to rely on her inner world to create an acceptable version of father. Consequently, this image may be so powerfully constructed that it overwhelms her perception of men in later life. In a way, this image which develops into the Ghostly Lover, serves two purposes – it protects the woman from the hurt of her father-loss and arms her against any potential future hurt from a man. But, cut off from reality, she still, nevertheless, suffers: either because she never enters fully into a relationship with a man, thus experiencing sexual and emotional disappointment; or because the men with whom she becomes involved fail her in some way, perhaps by being unfaithful or through becoming alcoholic, or by manifesting some 'condition' that draws them away and causes her emotional pain.

While Esther Harding is one of a body of psychologists who considers the Ghostly Lover to form a destructive aspect of the animus, and therefore represents a major psychic issue for women to integrate, Linda Leonard believes that the Ghostly Lover is 'a part of the psychic reality of *all men and women*, the one who promises us divinity, an experience of infinity, of magical union with the sublime'.[8] And I am inclined to go along with her.

The ballet *Giselle*, most particularly Act II, is a classic rendition of the theme of the Ghostly Lover:

Giselle is a beautiful young peasant girl who loves to dance, but because she has a weak heart, she is constantly urged to rest. Her mother – a widow – warns her that if she doesn't look after herself she will die and, like all young girls who die before their wedding day, she will be transformed into a Wili. The Wilis are a band of spirits who haunt the forests after sunset; they seek out men who have become lost in the woods and force them to dance to their deaths. The only way a man can be saved is if he continues to dance until the sun rises.

Unbeknown to Giselle and all the villagers, her suitor, Albrecht, is none other than a prince. However, Hilarian, a woodsman, who has designs on Giselle himself, stumbles upon the truth of Albrecht's origins when he finds his royal robes concealed in the forest.

One day, a royal hunting party descends upon the village. Giselle and her mother are called upon to serve the princess and her party. The princess is drawn to Giselle and asks her about her life. Giselle tells her that she is soon to be married and the princess shares her happiness by revealing that she too is betrothed. Thus the stage is set for its inevitable denouement. A short while later, Hilarian confronts Giselle with the evidence that Albrecht is a prince. Just as Albrecht is about to explain himself, the princess emerges from her 'rest' in Giselle's cottage. She immediately recognizes Albrecht as her betrothed and goes towards him, while Albrecht kneels before her and kisses her extended hand. Giselle cannot take in what has happened; she loses her mind and dies in her mother's arms.

Act II is set in a clearing in the forest. As the sun sets, a ghostly image briefly darts between the trees. When darkness descends completely, the fragile white forms of the Wilis emerge. Each one is dressed like a bride, with a wedding veil covering her face. But when the veils are removed, each beautiful face is tinged with evil. At the command of their queen, Giselle emerges from her grave and joins their number.

At the sound of an approaching figure, the Wilis disappear. Albrecht enters the clearing, carrying a bunch of white lilies. He lays them on Giselle's grave and weeps. Consumed by grief, at first he fails to notice Giselle as she wafts around him, but eventually he sees her; he expresses his love for her and his despair at what he has lost. Their tender reunion is cut short by the return of the Wilis, who now intend to dance Albrecht to his death. Giselle intervenes, supporting his weary body throughout the night until, as he falls senseless to the ground, the dawn breaks. As the Wilis fade into the sun's early morning light, Giselle and Albrecht embrace for the last time.

Like the Little Mermaid, Giselle is the personification of Neptune. Our heroine is delicate in health, she loves to dance, is betrayed, falls insane and dies – she then gains a certain immortality. But unlike *The Little Mermaid*, this story is more concerned with the *man's* divine awakening. At first, Albrecht is a 'bit of a lad'; after all he has become engaged to two women, has resorted to masquerade and in the process been forced to tell a series of lies, or at least some serious half-truths. Only when Giselle dies does the full realization of what he has inspired assault him. He is awakened. And as he makes the journey into the forest at night – in the certain knowledge that he will be lured to his death by the Wilis – he is bent on repentance. But his Ghostly Lover rescues him – Giselle, through her love for him, both dies for him and saves him. And Albrecht, through his experience of divine union, is transformed and released.

Albrecht represents the man who is led by his instincts and held in the grip of his unconscious; he plays at loving, but his heart is not engaged. As a result, his romantic life plays havoc with him – he may, like Albrecht, end up betraying two, or more, women to whom he has bound himself. Then, through a powerful outer experience, he is compelled to journey into the darkness and confront the shadows of the feminine haunting his unconscious. Amidst the fearful chaos of the dark power of the feminine, he faces psychological death. But he is saved: he unites with his Ghostly Lover and is subsequently released from 'her' power. He can go out into the light and in full consciousness enter into a real relationship.

Unlike the spirits of the air in *The Little Mermaid*, the Wilis are by no means benign creatures. They are bent on revenge – revenge on all men – because they were denied marriage. In this way, the Wilis personify the destructive part of a man's anima, his 'feminine soul', the part that is ignored and therefore unintegrated, the part that is denied marriage. To a certain extent the feminine counterpart of the Ghostly Lover is the Siren. I stress 'to a certain extent' because of the universality of the Ghostly Lover, and because the Siren, unlike the Ghostly Lover, has more devastating properties.

The Sirens of Greek mythology were half-women, half-fish who, with their enchanting voices, lured sailors to their deaths – just as the Wilis lured men to their death through the dance. The Little Mermaid is, of course, half-woman, half-fish herself and therefore she is symbolically linked to the Sirens; in the same way, Giselle, although not exactly jilted and therefore not filled with such animosity toward all men, nevertheless becomes a Wili. The implication here is that while the destructive part of a man's anima has the capacity to 'kill' his chances of a real relationship with a woman, within this dark aspect of his feminine soul is the potential to awaken his heart and lead him to a true union with a woman.

'Edward', one of the individuals who took part in the regression project for my last book, graphically demonstrated this potential when, under hypnosis, he actually gave voice to his anima: 'I am mostly kept in a different place and I'm not allowed out very often. So I get *very very* angry . . . I am a crude, primitive, shadowy creature, but full of absolute beauty if I could be properly released and integrated.'

All men, of course, have an anima – and a destructive aspect to that anima. But the man who falls victim to the Ghostly Lover, or the Siren, is often one with a strong Neptunian link to his Moon, Venus or seventh or tenth house. Such a man is likely to have re-invented his mother – restructured her image internally – to compensate for any inadequacy or failing on her part. His mother may have been missing in the literal or psychological sense or he may have perceived that she was one of life's victims and that she suffered a lot. On the other hand, mother to the man 'hooked' by Neptune may have been a truly magical woman – so perfect that no other woman could possibly live up to her. However, this is rare; more often than not such a man experiences a sense of loss about his mother which then haunts his later relationships with women. He is invariably let down by women, betrayed by them or suffers loss through them. He may wander from woman to woman in search of the elusive lover so firmly rooted in his psyche, finding her only briefly when his projection of her image overpowers a real woman. When the projection fades – as it must – he is devastated by what he finds: he may be so angry that what he thought was 'it' has gone that he blames the woman and feels intense anger toward her. Since he has not integrated this part of his psyche it draws him like a magnet. Only when he confronts the reasons underlying his enthralment by the Ghostly Lover can he be released from its power.

While the Ghostly Lover tends to deny relationship for men and women because the inner image constantly obfuscates the reality of a lover, the Siren, for a man, denies relationship because she poisons his perception about women. Since he refuses to acknowledge she-who-lives-within, she exacts a murderous revenge. Although I do not want to be accused of holding a blatantly sexist attitude toward the destructive elements of the animus and the anima, I would suggest that the man faces a greater threat from the destructive aspect of his anima than the female does from her animus. A woman is far more a creature of her emotions; she tends to find herself through relationship – therefore she is much more inclined to explore her emotional 'territory', take responsibility for it and meet any difficulties and any projections. A man, on the other hand, tends to find himself through his role in life and, since he invariably considers his emotions secondary to his achievements, he has much more difficulty in accepting any 'blame' for his failure in relationships and is far less likely to look within for a solution. If we return to the fairy-tale world for a moment, we might be forgiven for assuming that it would be preferable for a man to cover his eyes and block his ears so that he could sail by the Sirens without being lured by their enchantment; likewise, a great deal of trouble would surely be averted if a man were to avoid entering the forest at night, thereby escaping a dance with death? Of course, many men do evade such a deathly confrontation time and time again, but the lure remains. And only by meeting the dark power of the anima – not by avoiding it or becoming blind to it – can a man rid himself of his unconscious projections and fears, find his heart and enter a real relationship.

To a certain degree we have wandered away from an important issue: that it is the power of love that ultimately delivers the individual from the clutches of the Ghostly Lover, and love that dissolves the destructive aspect of the anima and the animus. No amount of intellectual reasoning can release a man or woman from the power of the unconscious: such a process demands the co-operation of the unconscious and involves *feeling*. A therapist can aid the process by allowing the individual to access his unconscious through hypnosis and through the imagery evoked in dreams and visualizations; in this way, feelings are triggered and the way made open for resolution. Indeed, like the homoeopath who treats a patient by giving him a distillation of the same compound that caused the condition, Neptunian phenomena need to be addressed by Neptunian techniques in order to be resolved.

In Massenet's opera, Manon, *set in eighteenth-century France, the heroine, Manon Lescaut, is a beautiful and successful courtesan. At the beginning of the opera, she is on her way to a convent, but her beauty attracts a young but impoverished aristocrat,*

Des Grieux; inevitably, she never reaches the convent but goes to Paris instead. But although Des Grieux is in love with her and they are happy together, Manon yearns for wealth and jewels. Ultimately, her desire for riches outweighs her feelings for Des Grieux and she agrees to be 'patronised' by an elderly nobleman. In the process, she betrays Des Grieux, who subsequently takes holy orders.

Some time later, Manon visits Des Grieux in the seminary and, despite his anger toward her, he cannot resist her. He and Manon run away together. However, since Des Grieux has no money, the couple are soon reduced to poverty. In desperation, Manon persuades him to gamble at cards. Des Grieux wins a fortune but is accused of cheating. Although he is defended by his father, Manon is taken to prison and condemned as a common prostitute.

In the final act of the opera, Manon, desperately ill from consumption, is waiting to be deported. Des Grieux comes to rescue her but she is too weak to run away. She begs Des Grieux's forgiveness for all the wrongs she has done him and, as he tenderly kisses her, she dies in his arms.

I don't know whether Massenet was familiar with astrology, but the themes and text of the opera are a veritable hymn to Neptune – convents, holy orders, prostitution, downfall and double-dealing are just some of the Neptunian themes not already covered in this chapter. Manon, herself, is a typical anima figure to men – in other words she is the type of woman who has an innate, but usually entirely unconscious, ability to reflect a man's anima: decorative, beguiling but capricious, self-seeking and treacherous. That is, until her heart opens fully to Des Grieux at the very end, Manon typifies the destructive fascination of the Siren; she is aloof and cold yet every man who falls under her spell believes he can capture her heart. In one aria, Des Grieux confesses that he will do anything for Manon in spite of her passion for pleasure; he calls her 'my enigmatic sphinx'. The Siren, in common with all anima-women, is so irresistible because she allows men to see precisely what they want in her – she is all women to all men.

The Neptunian woman – she with a Neptune–Ascendant link, Neptune in the fifth house or her Moon or Venus in hard aspect to Neptune – is a ripe candidate for the anima-woman. Marilyn Monroe – Neptune conjunct the Ascendant, Moon opposition Neptune and Venus trine Neptune – was perhaps the ultimate anima-woman: in her personal life, she reflected each of her husband's or lover's anima projections and in the process lost any sight of her own identity; likewise, she became an ideal woman for millions of men across the world – she embodied an archetype of feminine desirability common to virtually all men. Her Neptunian male counterpart is the *Beau Idéal* – a man who personifies all the archetypally desirable male qualities. Men who succumb to the *Beau Idéal* syndrome are invariably those with a strong Neptune – Neptune conjunct the Ascendant, Neptune in the fifth house or the Sun or Mars linked to Neptune. Film stars who have that certain 'something', that charisma, are almost always anima-women or 'animus-men'; they become Ghostly Lovers to millions! And while there is nothing innately wrong in becoming an ideal figure for thousands of men and women, if the individual in question cannot find his or her real self within the projection, serious psychological damage, and certainly a disastrous love life, is the result. Like the anima-woman who loses sight of herself within her admirers' projections, the *Beau Idéal* is invariably drowning under the Neptunian chimera of the role thrust upon him. Whether a man or woman consciously or unconsciously allows himself or herself to beam back the archetypal qualities of the anima or animus, unless they begin to know themselves and find a way to express who they truly are, they will be forever struggling for survival in psychological quicksand, posing as much danger to themselves as those who try to enter a relationship with them.

While this is one of the downfalls of such Neptunian identification with the anima and animus, there is, of course, a higher, more positive dimension. When a woman assumes all the divine qualities of the anima for a man, she can put him in touch with his highest aspirations as well as opening his heart; she can become his muse, his *Femme Inspiratrice* – and vice versa. If a woman becomes the *Femme Inspiratrice* for a man, he will tend to put her on a pedestal, even consider her divinely wise; he will find through her his slumbering creativity and become inspired to scale previously unassailable heights of achievement. Likewise, a man who assumes all the poetic, heroic and romantic aspects of the animus for a woman can inspire her to tap her own creative power – put her in touch with her own soul. Sometimes the individual who has invoked such a response is not worthy of the projection – but sometimes he or she is.

> Certain women are . . . particularly well fitted for this role of *femme inspiratrice* on account of their own contact with the deeper things within them. Such a woman can lead a man whom she loves into touch with the hidden truths of life because of the reality of her own experience . . . Such a woman is in a different category from one who is nothing but anima, for she gives of herself and is not playing a role in which her unconscious motive is to hold the man.[9]

Manon, for instance, is an example of the kind of woman who is, indeed, playing a role to ensnare men, yet to Des Grieux, she becomes his muse and, because of his love, she is in turn awakened to her own deeper nature. Des Grieux sees her inner radiance even when Manon is only aware of her manufactured appeal, but through his love, she finds that radiance for herself.

> There is . . . [a] way in which a woman may be redeemed from the bondage of instinct and of the ego, namely through a worked out relationship with a man. If the woman falls in love with the man who has projected his anima on to her, she is no longer aloof and indifferent. The projection of her animus is caught by him. She, as well as he, is under an inner obligation to get in touch with her soul. [10]

So far, we can see that a Neptune influence in the birth chart leads to many potential experiences – delusion, sacrifice, loss, betrayal, even infamy and madness. Yet also contained within this same archetype is the potential to be divinely blessed, both in the sense of genius, especially artistic genius, and through the capacity to know love of the highest order.

Individuals who have Neptune linked to the seventh house or in close contact to the personal planets and angles are, in a sense, in the front line of such experiences, although, I must continue to stress that Neptune is a theme we all respond to in some way. As self-awareness increases in tandem with the capacity to love, the higher attributes of this particular planetary consciousness can be met. In earlier chapters, I have discussed the concept of the trans-Saturnian planets representing the higher octaves of the personal planets – Uranus becomes the higher octave of the Sun, Pluto the higher resonance of Mercury, and Persephone the higher dimension of Venus. Neptune acts as the higher octave of the Moon – a relationship which on the physical level is reflected in the way the moon's gravitational pull causes the tides in the ocean, and on the symbolic level by the trident glyph of Neptune, which represents the three phases of the Moon. Neptune elevates and expands the lunar principles of instinct and emotion: through Neptune we transcend the immature feelings of the small self and experience the expanded love of the Higher Self – we no longer demand love and seek to be loved, we comprehend that love flows through us – infinitely and eternally.

And so we finally come to the ultimate Neptunian goal – soul contact. The individual in the thrall of Neptune, like the Little Mermaid, seeks to find his soul. He may already believe that he has one, although he has not touched it, but when he connects with another in that entirely Neptunian, blissful state of in-loveness, his soul is animated; he experiences at long last that sense of 'coming home' that sense of utter completeness. He has found his 'other half', his soul's complement, his soul mate. Plato's observation that man was originally androgynous but then divided into male and female by the gods has spawned a common belief that somewhere, 'out there', our soul mate exists. But his great insight was that love is a restoration, not just a longing to be reunited with the missing half, but the yearning to connect with a greater self. Of course, when one falls in love, the experience is not of finding your own soul, but of meeting its twin in another. And while the experience can be explained in terms of the mutual exchange of anima-animus projections, whatever the 'nuts and bolts' of the process, the actual experience is quite literally out of this world, utterly magical. Indeed, the real world looks quite different – one's perception has changed entirely: pain disappears, appetites are lost, commitments forgotten; all that exists for the lovers, all, that is, that has meaning, is each other. In this state all things are possible; the individual not only sees the other as divine but suddenly develops a sense of his own divinity.

This state of in-loveness is eros by another name:

> Eros is the nearest thing to love the undeveloped spirit can experience. It lifts the soul out of sluggishness . . . It causes the soul to surge . . . When this force comes upon the most undeveloped people they become able to surpass themselves . . . Eros gives the soul a foretaste of unity and teaches the fearful psyche the longing for it. The more strongly one has experienced eros, the less contentment will the soul find in the pseudo-security of separateness. [11]

When eros strikes, a couple sense in each other their missing halves and they yearn to achieve complete union, absolute merger – the supreme Neptunian experience of each dissolving into the other and becoming one. This may not, of course, be possible in physical terms, but it can be experienced psychologically in moments of deep intimacy. Ethel Person calls these moments 'epiphanies': [12]

> But although the lovers may strive for complete merger (what we might then describe as fusion) . . . if they are lucky enough to enjoy a *passionate* love, their feelings of union will be interspersed with ecstatic moments of merger. These magical moments are experienced as epiphanies. [13]

While 'epiphanies' can be experienced simply in a spell-binding moment of 'togetherness' – a shared look, even – more often than not, such magic is encountered in rapturous states during sexual intercourse.

This state of in-loveness is much maligned – almost always, I suspect, by those who have never experienced it, or by those who have been disenchanted by its disappearance. The point is that the ability to fall in love places certain demands on the individual. To fall in love, one must be prepared to give oneself over to another person, to surrender one's ego and to submit to a force that is patently not under one's control. Anyone whose ego boundaries are set like cement will need the equivalent of a psycho-spiritual bulldozer to soar to such Neptunian heights. But it is possible for all – we all have Neptune in our charts, the archetypal force exists within us all. And no matter how brief the experience, it is the nearest most of us mortals may ever come to touching the divine.

There is, of course, a distinction to be made between infatuation and falling in love: infatuation can produce the same physical phenomena but it carries none of the higher dimensions of soul contact, none of the numinous qualities and certainly no 'epiphanies'.

Almost all psychologists would suggest that when two people fall in love there is inevitably an element of animus and anima projection at work. And sometimes, when the projection fades, the love that seemed so eternal also evaporates. I am not going to argue with this. But I do consider that there is something greater at work when two people fall in love, something infinitely more mystical. Somehow, by denoting the experience as a psychological phenomenon and breaking down its component parts into the projection of her animus and his anima, eros is de-mystified. Such explanations may satisfy the rationalist, but they detract from the transcendence of the experience and somehow devalue it. Ethel Person seems to be coming close to a happier marriage between the psychology of love and the magic of love when she says of 'epiphanies':

> At such times, there is, if not a loss of ego boundaries, at least a permeability of ego boundaries. During those moments, the lovers experience a sense of timelessness, bliss, and transcendence. Their intermittent experience of merger is completely unlike the obliteration of the sense of self that one sees in psychotic states and which leads to terror. Rather, the self is preserved, the spirit exalted.[14]

Eros is the divine aspect of love; as such it can be present in platonic relationships. Indeed, on more than one occasion, when the composite chart[15] has revealed a strong Neptunian theme – perhaps an angular Neptune, or a hard aspect, particularly the conjunction, between the Moon and Neptune or Venus/Mars–Neptune – the relationship may never be consummated. Yet, if it is consummated, the potential is there for all the Neptunian ecstasies. However, eros is at its most powerful when it is combined with the sexual force. Sex without eros has a certain crudeness; sex with eros lifts the experience into an altogether different place.

However the function of eros is to act as a bridge to true partnership; as such it has a limited life-span. [16] And herein lies the problem and the reason why so many people believe that in-loveness is an inferior aspect of love and certainly an unreliable marker for long-term relationships. When eros disappears – sometimes as rapidly as it struck – the couple, not always at the same moment, will experience a distinct vacuum, the relationship will seem to have lost its sparkle. This is the moment when the projection of the anima or animus fades to reveal the living person hidden behind the image. If the other person bears no hallmark of the attributes of the anima or animus and is, indeed, a deeply inappropriate partner, then the relationship should, and must, be terminated, because to struggle on with a hopelessly incompatible partner is doomed to failure in the long-term. But if the partner 'fits' the projection and is, indeed, lovable and highly compatible, then the transition to a deeper bond should be forthcoming. When this does not happen, it will be because the person who has 'fallen out of love' invariably lacks the emotional maturity to move on to a deeper bonding. This is why this phenomena is so common among teenagers and people under 30, effectively those who have not reached the maturity engendered by the Saturn Return. [17] If a person over 30 continues to fall in and out of love with monotonous regularity then there is almost certainly a major psychological problem underlying his or her emotional immaturity; such a person may or may not be ignorant of the deeper meaning of eros but pursues the experience like an addict in search of a 'fix'. Commenting on such individuals, Eva Pierrakos makes the rather sobering point, 'They look for one subject after another, emotionally too ignorant to understand the deep meaning of eros. They are unwilling to learn pure love and simply use the erotic force for their pleasure and when it is worn out they hunt elsewhere. This is an abuse [karmic and sexual] and cannot continue without ill effects.' [18]

Since we all have Neptune in our charts, every single one of us has the capacity to attract eros, then to abuse it, or to allow it to lead us into a deeper experience of love. Eros provides us with a unique sense of merger and union and while for most of us this experience is sought in relationship with another human being, the greatest merger of all must surely be the union with the Godhead. Origen maintained that the greatest goal of Christianity was nothing less than the 'transformation of man into Oneness'. Likewise, in most of the Eastern religions the ultimate aim of the disciple is to unite with the Guru. A small proportion of men and women devote themselves to this Neptunian path since they are developed enough – divinely blessed – to experience the mystical oneness through a purely spiritual encounter. Such souls are in a very different category to most of us: they have effectively risen above human desires and seek an intimacy beyond anything another human being could provide.

All of us, though, can and should seek wholeness, at-one-ness with the Self, which means following the path of individuation and meeting with the archetypal figures in the landscape of the psyche. Only then, when we have integrated these images, can we successfully relate to an Other. Jung talked of the *mysterium coniunctionis*, the mystic marriage, in regard to the constellation of the anima and animus in a relationship, maintaining that every genuine encounter of two human beings must be conceived of as a *mysterium coniunctionis*. And here, once again, we find a marriage between the magical and psychological: 'The living mystery of life is always hidden between Two, and it is the true mystery which cannot be betrayed by words and depleted by arguments.'[19] Eros is a divine part of that mystery. When it strikes two people who have the emotional maturity and wisdom to grasp its deeper implication, they can use the erotic force to lead them into the mystery of each other and themselves. In this way, eros does not have to disappear; if the desire to explore each other's unfathomable depths is maintained, the ability to pierce the infinite layers of the soul becomes an act of reciprocity so that love deepens and the bond strengthens. As each one reveals more of himself to the other, growth in the relationship is assured and the spark of eros will be kept alive.

> Two developed souls can fulfil one another by revealing themselves, by searching the depths of each other's soul . . . Then the life-spark is maintained so that the relationship can never stagnate and degenerate into a dead end . . . In this way . . . you not only maintain eros . . . but you also transform it into true love.[20]

It is not through love that the desire for union is engendered, but through the desire for union that love, true love, is born.

A soul relationship is what we seek in Neptune's mystical realm and while we may meet another soul with whom we resonate perfectly, the soul we really touch is our own. In a sense, there is no such thing as a soul mate; only the meeting of two beautifully attuned souls who can reveal and reflect the light of each other's soul. Indeed, I once heard somebody say that if it were possible to meet your soul mate the effect of such a mirror image would be disastrous – similar to electronic feedback on a cosmic scale. Certainly, whenever we meet and form a relationship with someone who touches our soul, we are never the same, and that person will forever find a place in our heart. And sometimes, that's very painful.

Caroline Cossey is a name that has flashed across Britain's newspaper headlines periodically over the past two years. She was once known as Tula, and before that as Barry. Caroline is a trans-sexual; more than that, she is a woman. Caroline is not a client of mine, she is a friend and, in keeping with her 'up front' persona, she did not want to hide behind a pseudonym. Indeed, she has just published a book about her life[21] which is equally as honest about herself – and, indeed uncomfortably so about some of the people to whom she has been linked.

Caroline is a beautiful, elegant and feminine woman; there is not the slightest hint of someone playing a role, nor the merest suggestion of a 'man in drag', and this has nothing to do with the outer dressing, with successful surgery or with any contrived behaviour, but with the inner woman. She, of course, has always been the same person, the same soul, but there was a time when the outer and the inner were in such conflict that she despaired of ever finding equilibrium.

Caroline comes from a close-knit Norfolk family and although she received much love and affection at home, her childhood was unhappy. Caroline, then Barry, did not seem to fit in: 'he' preferred the company of girls and absolutely detested boyish pursuits. He was bullied at school and therefore was never able to do justice to his natural intelligence.

With Mars in Capricorn in the fourth house of the horoscope, it is no surprise that Barry suffered under his father's strict regime; indeed, he was very frightened of him. Of course, his father could not understand why the son he loved was such a wimp, and he tried to instil some 'fibre' into him. (Later, however, when he came to understand the nature of his son's problem, he was entirely loving and supportive.) At the age of 13, though, it became clear that Barry's problem was more than just a psychological one: he suffered dizzy spells, fainting fits and hot flushes. The doctor diagnosed a hormonal problem; Barry was chromosomally 'all at sea' with three 'X's and one 'Y'!

By the time he was 17, Barry had taken the first steps to becoming the woman he knew he was. Although the hormone treatment gave Caroline, as he became, more than just the illusion of being a woman, actual surgery to remove any vestige of his manhood did not occur until

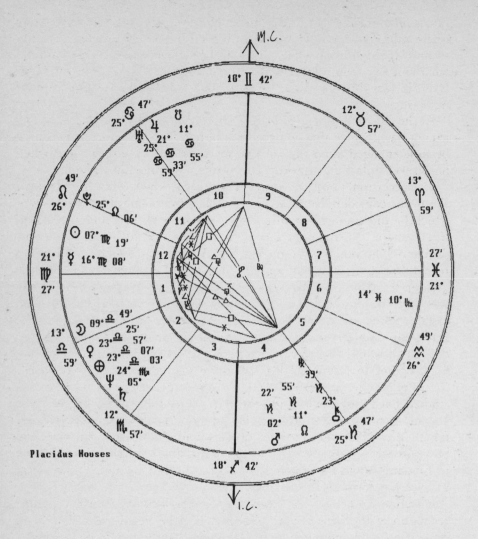

Figure 7: Caroline Cossey

the age of 21 – at the entirely appropriate astrological time, as transiting Pluto conjuncted the Moon in Libra. Pluto's transformative properties quite literally brought a death to one dimension of his being and gave birth to a 'new' woman – and an extremely Venusian one at that.

Even before the operation, Caroline was working as a (female) dancer – mainly in cabarets and shows, all over the world. Attractive as she was, she kept men at bay. At no time had she felt comfortable with the 'gay scene' and preferred to bide her time until she could enter into a relationship fully as a woman. However, she did succumb to one relationship, with an older man who tried in vain to persuade her not to have the operation. The attitude of her lover concerned Caroline: what kind of a man wants a half-man, half-woman, she questioned? Her lover, in fact, just loved her for who she was. But the relationship did not last.

At the age of 29 – again entirely appropriately as far as the astrology is concerned, since this was the year of her Saturn Return – Caroline became engaged to an Italian. But she broke off the engagement when he proved unfaithful. Shortly afterwards, she met Elias Fattal.

It was certainly not love at first sight, according to Caroline. In fact, she never considered him as a potential husband until he proposed – which he did some 18 months later. Although by this time, she loved Elias very much, his offer of marriage presented her with two major problems: she would have to convert to Judaism and she would have to reveal that she was legally a man. The second problem was by far the greater, but Elias took the news with aplomb. He loved her for who she was; indeed, he was determined to put his weight behind her decision to take her case – to be allowed to marry legally as a woman – to the European Commission of Human Rights in Strasbourg. However, he thought it would be prudent not to tell his parents, since the fact that he was going to marry a Gentile was quite enough for them to stomach.

In the two years that followed, Caroline converted to Judaism; she studied hard and passed the required exams and, in the process, she became very committed to her new religion. The wedding day was set for 21 May 1989 and, a matter of days beforehand, she won her legal battle in Strasbourg. It was now just a question of time before the law in England would be changed, giving her both the right to marry and to have her birth certificate altered.

Caroline and Elias's wedding was a stylish affair with a huge reception at the Savoy. The following day, the newly-weds flew of to Acapulco for their honeymoon: it was the happiest time of her life.

A day or so before they left Acapulco, Elias and Caroline made a snap decision to go to Jamaica. They returned to England on Sunday 11 June and went straight to Caroline's flat. There, they were met by the stunned faces of Caroline's mother and sister: silently, they handed over the Sunday newspapers. In the uniquely graphic and overblown style of tabloid journalism, their marriage was declared a travesty: Caroline emerged from the print as 'gay' gold-digger and Elias as dubious, to say the least. Emotionally drained and exhausted from the flight, Caroline elected to stay behind while Elias went off to explain things to his parents. It was virtually the last time she was to see him.

Elias's family closed ranks. For legal reasons Caroline was prevented from ever speaking to Elias again. Elias's brother became the family's spokesman and he informed her icily that she must get a lawyer immediately: the marriage was to be annulled.

Caroline was in shock and, like many individuals, and certainly many Virgos, in such a psychological state, she sealed herself off from the horror of it all by becoming extremely pragmatic. It was clear that Elias had been advised to declare that he was entirely ignorant of Caroline's gender status. This would not only protect the family's name but assure a speedy annulment. There was effectively little she could do. The press were constantly at her door and if the assault on her personality wasn't enough, her car's petrol pipe was severed – apparently a mistaken attempt to interfere with the brakes. Luckily, no physical harm came to her, although she had to have police protection for some months afterwards.

Her one meeting with Elias came a few weeks after the return from honeymoon. Seeing the man she loved stony-faced and surrounded by his family and sundry legal advisors must have emphasized the unbridgeable gap between them. Caroline ran out of the office and Elias followed her. Once on their own he said to her, 'I'm so sorry. You know I love you and I'll always love you. But you've got to understand our relationship is doomed. If you love me, let me go.'

And she did.

I met Caroline in the early February of 1991, some 18 months later, and although she appeared outwardly to have weathered the storm it was clear that emotionally and psychologically she was far from over it. For her, 1990 had been a difficult year, made even worse by the British Government's appeal in April against the Strasbourg Commission's 1989 ruling; an appeal that was to prove successful in the High Court on 27 September 1990. Caroline lost her case to be legally considered a woman by one vote. Sadly, this not only made it impossible for her to seek any legal redress where her marriage to Elias was concerned, but also set a precedent for any other trans-sexual hoping to have a marriage recognized in law.

As I mulled over the astrology of the situation, I was a little disappointed to discover that there were so few exact pointers to the extraordinary events of the May and June of 1989. The most striking transits, involving Uranus, Neptune and Saturn, had occurred some six months earlier and repeated themselves in the October of that year. Nevertheless, the themes were right, even if they missed the precise date marker and, perhaps, more pertinently, it was not until the October of 1989, when the transiting Neptune–Saturn conjunction squared her

Moon and transiting Uranus conjoined her Mars that the full weight of what had happened descended upon her. Significantly, the presence of these powerful outer-planet transits in October were augmented by the simultaneous passage of the Sun, Mercury and Mars in Libra and Jupiter's station at 10 degrees of Cancer.

Caroline has a radical conjunction of Neptune and Saturn, so that the repetition, by transit, of this difficult combination on her Moon – her instinctual, feeling centre, her emotional roots and the seat of her femininity – was bound to signify a major life transition. The combined effect of Saturn's depressing realism and Neptune's illusion in a radical chart is confusing; by transit it evokes the theme of a night sea crossing, the dark night of the soul. Anyone born between November 1951 and September 1954 has this conjunction to contend with: while the goal of this conjunction is to bring Neptunian dreams into Saturnian reality, the counter effect is to crush hope and inspiration. When this transit repeated between October 1988 and December 1990, this entire generation would have been challenged to face the reality of their inner world; few may have perceived it in such terms, most would have experienced only loss and severe difficulties, whether in the emotional, financial or material sense. Certainly if this duo contacted any radical personal planet, the effect would be to test that aspect of the individual and hopefully to awaken him or her to any illusions about 'himself', to attend to the ground work and lay the Saturnian foundations for future dreams.

For Caroline, this conjunction signalled another period in her life when the powerful Neptunian theme in her horoscope was to be played once more. The Neptune–Pisces theme emerges time and time again in Caroline's chart: her Sun and her Ascendant ruler, Mercury, are both in the Neptunian twelfth house and Neptune rules her seventh house of relationships; but most dominant of all is her Venus–Neptune conjunction, which is separating from the Moon and applying to a conjunction of Saturn. While Neptune's exact conjunction to Venus has inspired Caroline to seek her womanhood, Saturn, although crystalizing those aims, has always made the way difficult and frustrating for her, and has exacted a heavy personal cost. Although Caroline has been blessed with great beauty, a loving family and a life of colour and excitement, she has nevertheless experienced suffering, sacrifice and betrayal on a grand Neptunian scale. Like the Little Mermaid who gladly lost her tail, Caroline also joyfully gave up part of her anatomy in order to become a real woman. To begin with, this was an outer, physical, process; later it would become an inner quest. In a sense, fate, or nature, has betrayed her by condemning her to a life as a woman in a man's body and even though this act of God has been righted, in the eyes of the legal system, at least, she still has to suffer the iniquity of being considered a man. There was betrayal too at the final High Court hearing, since many of the politicians who had previously backed her cause suddenly became invisible – presumably either through pressure from the Fattals or through the fear of what such a notorious association might do to their image. She has also been crucified by the Press – admittedly in common with thousands of other well-known individuals. But, as far as Caroline is concerned, the biggest betrayal of all has been Elias. Nothing can compare to the devastation he has wreaked in her life.

Whatever gender Caroline may have been born, with a Venus–Neptune conjunction she was destined to experience some confusion over the feminine aspect of her being; as a man, she would clearly have been in line for some problems with her anima. While Neptune's presence so close to Venus has certainly synchronized with her natural grace and photogenic looks, it has also brought her some extraordinary romantic experiences and an encounter with the divine – it's not everybody who has to change their faith for the person they love, but a Venus–Neptune conjunction definitely increases the odds. As it is, Caroline's conversion to Judaism is one of the most positive aspects to have emerged from her relationship with Elias, and she has found much solace in her new religion and received endless emotional and spiritual support from her local rabbi.

There is also something else that is beautiful to have emerged out of this betrayal and suffering, although I don't believe Caroline recognizes it yet. In effect, the loss of the man she loved – and still loves – and his subsequent betrayal has provided the wound the personality needed to inspire the inner journey – Persephone's journey. For Caroline, like Ishtar, has embarked on a quest to find the lost treasure within. When I last saw her, she talked about a conflict she was experiencing in that intellectually she felt that she should be 'throwing' herself into life, forging new relationships and psychologically moving away from Elias; yet there was an equally strong instinct to go to ground, find her roots. In this way, she is responding to the call of the heroine's journey. She needs to retreat to the deeps of the dark side of the moon, to contact her essence as a woman. When she emerges, whatever vestiges of doubt she may hold about the nature of her womanhood will surely have been resolved.

Caroline's story still leaves many issues unresolved, however, and it will take some time via the hypnotherapeutic route to probe for any answers that may lie in her psyche. Clearly there is a huge karmic legacy behind Caroline's extraordinary fate and, if and when any memories of a past life reveal themselves, it may be that in the process of therapeutic release her life will subsequently become less of a battleground and that ultimately she may find equilibrium with a kindred soul.

Neptune, as an archetypal theme, exists for us all. As our levels of consciousness increase, so does our ability to resonate more fully with this outer planet. We can no longer consider Neptune only as a collective theme; his influence reaches to each and every one of us. And while we may have our share of sacrifices to make, of betrayals to bear and illusions to conquer, so too can we expect the most profound experience in love. Some of us may be 'light' enough to move beyond the need and desire for human intimacy, finding ourselves at one with the divine within – seeking nothing more, nothing less than spiritual ecstasy. Yet others of us may contact our divine Self and still continue to need the reciprocity of human relationship. There are no absolutes with Neptune. The divine has no limits. And when we touch souls and enter into that numinous space where we become one with an Other, we can be sure that we have truly experienced Neptune. We have been enchanted, we are blessed and we are enriched.

Appendix

1) Robert A. Johnson, *The Psychology of Romantic Love* (Arkana, 1983).
2) By using the same word for apparently unrelated concepts, the French language expresses the connection between 'mother' and 'the sea' as symbols of the great feminine; astrologically, the Moon represents the mother and Neptune, the sea.
3) See Chapter 2.
4) All quotes taken from *Hans Anderson's Fairy Tales* (Heirloom Library).
5) See Chapter 2.
6) M. Esther Harding, *The Way of All Women* (Rider, 1983).
7) Hard aspects include the conjunction (0 – 10°), the square (90° +/- 8°), the opposition (180° +/- 8°), the quincunx (150° +/- 4°).
8) Linda Schierse Leonard, *On the Way to the Wedding* (Shambhala, 1986).
9) *The Way of All Women*, op. cit.
10) Ibid.
11) Eva Pierrakos, *The Pathwork of Self-Transformation* (Bantam, 1990).
12) Epiphany in the Christian calendar celebrates the manifestation of Christ to the Magi. How perceptive and divinely in tune of Ms Person to provide such a quintessentially Neptunian name for such a magical moment!
13) Ethel Spector Person, *Love and Fateful Encounters: The Power of Romantic Passion* (Bloomsbury, 1989).
14) Ibid.

15) The composite chart is a horoscope derived from the mid-points of pairs of planets produced from two natal charts: i.e. the half-way point in the zodiac between his Sun and her Sun, his Moon and her Moon and so on.

16) The life span of eros lasts, on average, three months, although, if and when the transition is made to a deeper bonding, eros can be retrieved time and time again over the years. This three month period no doubt has some connection with the chemical effect of opiates released by the brain when an individual falls in love which have a life span of roughly three months.

17) Saturn takes approximately 29 years to orbit the sun, or circle the birth chart and return to its natal position. This Saturn Return can be perceived as the astrological 'coming of age'. It coincides with a time when the individual wants to make his mark in life and lay the foundations of his future, based on experiences and understandings gained in earlier youth. After the Saturn Return, the individual should have acquired the emotional maturity to make emotional, financial and professional commitments.

18) *Love and Fateful Encounters*, op. cit.

19) Letter, 12 August 1960, as quoted in *C.G. Jung: Word and Image*, ed. Aniela Jaffé (Princeton University Press, 1979).

20) *The Pathwork of Self-Transformation*, op. cit.

21) Caroline Cossey, *My Story* (Faber and Faber, 1991).

8

Pluto: Liebestod

*I*T WAS A PERFECT PASSING AWAY FOR BOTH OF THEM AND AT THE same time an intolerable accession into being.[1]

Liebestod, love in death, is the quintessential Plutonic theme. On the face of it, love and death seem antithetical – while love is synonymous with life, with celebration and a beginning, death marks an ending, a sadness and a darkness – yet they are inextricably bonded. Writers and artists – those instinctively at one with the archetypal world – have used this theme to give us some of the greatest love poems and stories of all time – epic soaring tales of love like *Romeo and Juliet*, *Tristan and Iseult* and *The Flying Dutchman*, where only through death can the lovers become one, only death transforms their earthly love into that which is eternal and transcendent. The rich, and all too often underrated, language of astrology has long revealed that love and death are potent and destined bed-fellows: the eighth house of the horoscope, ruled by Pluto/Scorpio, governs the areas of sex and death which, until we start to explore the reasons for such connections, seem entirely unrelated and odd.

Death is the only true inevitability in life. It is what each man fears most in his heart, yet, if we understand the mystics, death is ecstasy. And so, somewhere, deep within our souls is that yearning to enter that bliss – a bliss remembered, perhaps, or an archetypal longing. In life, we experience a death of consciousness when we fall into sleep; we also experience a death when we surrender to the passion of the heart; in the delicious moment of orgasm we know *la petit mort*, the little death, and both the ecstasy of that moment and the existential *tristesse* that all too often follows it – as if we have yet again been denied love's ultimate destiny, entry to the eternal bliss of the spirit. Pluto is death and transfiguration, and while we can glimpse our divinity through passionate communion, only in death can unity with the soul be restored absolutely. But we are nonetheless transformed by love; it is the greatest catalyst of transformation available to the individual. Beyond the boundaries of the ego, when we have sensed merger in epiphanic moments, we are transported to the gates of heaven. To enter, finally, only through death.

Pluto is a profoundly sexuo-spiritual planet in the largest sense of the word – in Pluto we do not find the animal coupling, conquering spirit of Mars, but the creative, all-consuming passion of a dark and mysterious force – a force which threatens to destroy us every bit as much as it promises us a profound emergence into being. It is this extraordinary mix of life and death, love and death, that fascinates and magnetizes us to Pluto's dark, Underworld realm. Pluto compels us to sink into the depths of our being and the further we 'dig', the higher we can ultimately soar; just as the higher the skyscraper, the deeper the foundations. In the bowels of our being, like the molten, fiery core of the Earth itself, rests the nucleus of our creativity which, when tapped, releases a power of atomic proportions.

And so it is when we reach Pluto's realm in the small self we risk being 'nuked' by its awesome power; we cower helplessly as Pluto majestically sweeps us along with the collective momentum of human destiny; we yield any vestige of personal control and stand by while he carries away our treasures, strips us of our assets and destroys our very foundations. Yet, in the Higher Self, we may meet that power and allow Pluto to transform our life, and to restore our soul. What, in the small self, might be obliterated and eliminated, in the expanded Higher Self is replenished and augmented.

Of all the planets, Pluto, the outpost of the solar system, must surely be beyond the personal grasp of any individual. Yet Pluto's themes have a real presence in our lives. It is as if Pluto's very distance from Earth underlines the remote way in which we relate to his themes. Sex, death, power and all that is 'dark' and taboo occupy a vital place in all our lives; they are all issues that we cannot handle easily and therefore such things tend to overwhelm us. We all have Pluto in our charts – passion, sex, power and death are something we are more than touched by – thus it is time we stopped heaping the responsibility of Pluto on the shoulders of the collective and met him face to face in our own lives. Whether or not we have Pluto in a prominent place in our natal charts, his planetary presence is there somewhere, and even if we studiously avoid the issues he represents, when he transits a personal planet or strategic angle, we must confront his issues, bring our darkness up to the light, or risk being destroyed by it.

Along with sex, death, power and the taboo, Pluto connotes compulsion, magnetism and possession. In this way, Pluto is synonymous with the Demon Lover:

> On our journey to the wedding we may confront the frightening figure of the Demon Lover who halts our progress by possessing us. The state of possession can be experienced in many different ways – for example, through obsessive jealousy, any form of addiction, being a perpetual willing victim, feeding off the blood of others, or offering up one's own lifeblood or creativity to another. Whenever we come under the power of the Demon Lover, we experience a loss of soul. [2]

In Bram Stoker's *Dracula* we are presented with one Plutonic image after another – here Pluto's themes of darkness, sex, and love and death abound throughout.

The story is set in Transylvania in the remote Carpathian Mountains – the haunt of werewolves, witches, vampires et al. Dracula himself is a count – an archetypal prince of darkness – tall and gaunt, deathly pale with haunting, black eyes. He invites a London solicitor, Jonathan Harker, to his castle to oversee a business transaction. Harker is somewhat unnerved to find that he is a virtual prisoner in this ghostly castle and mystified that he can never find his host during the day. To ease his fear and keep boredom at bay, he keeps a journal detailing all the extraordinary goings on in the castle.

Back home in England, his fiancée, Mina, a fair-haired, innocent beauty, is beset with her own kind of strangeness. Her friend, Lucy, is not well and has taken to visiting the grounds of an old abbey after dark. One night, Mina finds her lying white-clad on a tomb with a dark, shadowy figure bending over her. By the time Mina reaches her, the figure has disappeared; Lucy, eyes transfixed, has two tiny marks on her neck. From that night, Lucy's strength rapidly fails until she dies. At her funeral, however, her colour seems to have returned and she looks younger and even more beautiful. Later, as Mina lovingly packs away her friend's possessions, she comes across Lucy's diary in which she has recorded her nightly visitations by a black bat.

These strange events are compounded when, some time later, there are reports of children being abducted at night by a beautiful lady. Mina and her family are forced to accept the incredible, that Lucy is now a vampire. And so they enlist the help of a Dutch metaphysician and doctor, Van Helsing. On his suggestion, they open Lucy's coffin and find her sweetness of expression and bloom have vanished, and in their place glitters a voluptuous wantonness.

In the meantime, Harker has returned to England with Dracula, who subsequently mysteriously disappears. Reunited with Mina, he joins Van Helsing in a plan to eliminate Dracula. Thanks to Harker's meticulously detailed diary they are able to arm themselves with facts about vampires:

● *They only flourish on the blood of the living.*

● *They throw no shadow nor any reflection in a mirror.*

● *A vampire can come in mist and on moonlight rays.*

● *He or she can become so small as to come from anything and into anything.*

● *Vampires can see in the dark.*

But . . . .

● *A vampire cannot enter unbidden.*

● *His power decreases in the light.*

● *He can transform himself only at certain times – at noon, sunrise and sunset.*

The men now involve themselves wholeheartedly in the quest for Dracula, but in the process they fail to notice that Mina is becoming increasingly lethargic and deathly pale. When they do notice, it is almost too late. She is already under the power of Dracula; under hypnosis, Mina is able to tell them of Dracula's whereabouts, for now, only his death can save her. The final pages of the book are given over to the journey back to Transylvania; each day, Mina becomes less and less like her sweet self and more and more the vampire. But, ultimately, good triumphs over evil: Dracula is found in 'a great square chest'; the men decapitate him and plunge a silver dagger through his heart. As his body crumbles into dust, Mina is restored to her former beauty with no trace of the vampire about her.

The extremes of Pluto are in full array in this story – the darkness of Dracula set against the fair beauty of the young women, the purity of Mina (a curious but entirely coincidental anagram of *anima*) and the seductiveness of the vampire. We are also told in the vampire 'checklist' that 'he can become so small as to come out of anything and into anything': mythological Pluto, of course, had a magic helmet which made him invisible, and the size of the planet Pluto poses a great mystery to scientists since it appears to be tiny yet incredibly dense – the main hypothesis is that Pluto is covered by ice thereby reflecting the sun and rendering the planet itself invisible. Inasmuch as the sun diminishes the size of Pluto, in the light, the vampire's power is similarly reduced. But, perhaps the most compelling theme in *Dracula*, and, indeed, in vampire mythology generally, is that terrifying, evil and deathly as vampires may be, they evoke an incredible longing in the victim, offering a potent cocktail of sexual pleasure laced with fear – and once bitten, there can be no going back:

There was something about them [three beautiful women] that made me uneasy, some longing and at the same time some deadly fear. I felt in my heart a wicked, burning desire that they would kiss me with those red lips . . . The [fair] girl went on her knees, and bent over me . . . There was a deliberate voluptuousness which was both thrilling and repulsive and as she arched her neck she actually licked her lips like an animal, till I could see in the moonlight the moisture shining on the scarlet lips and on the red tongue as it lapped the sharp white teeth . . . Then the skin of my throat began to tingle as one's flesh does when the hand that is to tickle it approaches nearer – nearer. I could feel the soft, shivering touch of the lips on the supersensitive skin of my throat, and the hard dents of two sharp teeth, just touching and pausing there. I closed my eyes in a languorous ecstasy and waited – waited with a beating heart.[3]

Dracula is the essence of evil's awesome attraction. He invites us to unimaginable pleasures. He offers us sensual immortality. We admire him and are horrified by our admiration of this elegant symbol of temptation.[4]

This Plutonic combination of sexuality and power spiced with death and evil extends a fascination to us all: it is almost irresistible. But this is without question the 'inferior' function, the 'Lake of Fire', of Pluto and we all fall prey to it in some form at some time of our lives. Pluto-as-Dracula can enter our lives surreptitiously 'on a moonlight ray'; he has an advantage over us, he can see in the darkness, through our darkness; in effect, he *is* our darkness. But he cannot enter unbidden; we must let him in. Sometimes Pluto-as-Dracula enters our lives as jealousy or obsession, compulsions or addictions. Usually, we have no idea the hold he has over us until we are powerless to stop the course we are embarked upon – a course bent on self-destruction. Pluto-as-Dracula can steal in under the cover of dark as anger in disguise, and unresolved emotions and fears we have buried, feelings which have festered, are released as toxins which invade the body and threaten to take our life away: we get cancer, we get AIDS, diseases that attack our immune system. AIDS is a quintessentially Plutonic sex-linked syndrome – in the secret silence of the inner-body world, cell upon cell is destroyed by a dark disease that never announces its deathly intention until it has drained our life's blood.

In the area of relationships, Pluto eats away at our need to love and be loved; when we fall prey to the inferior pull of Pluto, we become obsessed with a love object. Wanting to own it, we fear that if we don't possess it absolutely, we may die; in effect the reverse is true – bound up in our obsession, we drive away the thing we love. Sometimes, we even 'kill' the thing we love, rather than let it leave us. *Fatal Attraction* – one of the most successful movies of the 1980s – was based entirely on a woman's obsession for a man with whom she had had the equivalent of a 'one night stand' – a passion that inspired a murderous violence. *Last Tango in Paris* revealed another aspect of Plutonic obsession; in this case the love object was a young woman to whom her older lover was hopelessly addicted; his descent into self-destruction was mirrored by his abuse of her, which at the same time emphasized his increasing dependence on her.

The Demon Lover that possesses our psyche may also emerge as an addiction to a substance, like alcohol or narcotics, to gambling or shopaholicism and, most appositely, in sex-addiction; or the Demon Lover can erupt in a behaviour pattern. He is anything, in effect, that eats away at our power and drains our creativity.

But there is also a Demon Lover who we may meet in our relationships. It is probably true to say that within every woman lurks a secret, or unconscious, perverse longing for an encounter with the Prince of Darkness – a man who, with his power, can hold her and possess her, like no earthly man; likewise, in every man there is a deep-seated fascination for the Dark Lady who, with her erotic aura, promises to release his power and reveal to him the secrets of his soul. Sometimes the longing is so great for these dark, all-powerful figures that we enter into a relationship with someone who personifies them, but until we can sift the wheat of our projection from the chaff of their reality, we are instead led away from the riches of relationship and into the Plutonic Tartarus[5] of a power-sucking encounter.

While a Demon Lover or a Dark Lady may lurk within all our psyches, it is especially those with Pluto linked to the seventh or fifth house or women with Sun/Mars – Pluto hard aspects or men with similar angles from Pluto to the Moon or Venus, who find such figures to relate to in their intimate encounters. Likewise, it is these Plutonic souls who fall prey to fatal attractions and all-or-nothing relationships. I have also found that Pluto conjunct an angle in the composite chart or forming hard aspects to the personal planets indicates a passionate, all-or-nothing relationship or one beset with constant power-struggles – sometimes played out with physical or sexual brutality, or more often in psychological warfare.

Possession can take a variety of forms, as we have seen, but of all the possessions, that by mother can wreak the most havoc – especially in men's lives. In an article in *The Times* (30 March 1991), it was claimed that 60 per cent of the Japanese males attending a Tokyo marriage counselling clinic were suffering from 'no-touch-syndrome' – an extreme fear of sex which manifested in an inability to even touch or kiss their wives since such gestures might effect a prelude to love-making. These men, almost all members of Japan's elite bureaucratic, business and academic circles, had fathers who had been married to the corporation and were thus rarely at home; in consequence their mothers had 'compensated for their sexual and emotional frustration through excessive care and pampering of their only child'. I don't know whether all these men had a Pluto factor to account for their mother-fixation in their charts, but Japan, with its obsessive, kamikaze attitude to life is certainly a quintessentially Plutonic nation. Men with Moon–Pluto aspects – particularly the hard angles – or Pluto linked to the tenth house are prime candidates for the devouring mother syndrome – as to a certain extent are those with hard Venus–Pluto contacts or Pluto linked to the fifth or seventh house. From birth, these men have either been over-protected by mother, subsumed by her being or been so devastated by her abandonment or cruelty that they cannot claw their way out of the dark cavern of her influence. To a large extent, the devouring mother comes from the same stable as the mother-as-tyrant already discussed in the chapter on Uranus. Little boys who have been swamped by their mother or cut off from her have tremendous emotional needs, which become overwhelming by the time they reach adulthood. The Moon–Pluto, Venus–Pluto man's emotional needs resemble the bottomless pit – and if there were a bottom, there would surely be a monster there with cavernous, ever-open jaws. These men are bound to their mother by a Plutonic mix of love and hate – they want their mothers and want to be the only 'thing' she loves, yet they hate them for making them so vulnerable. Such men either avoid making emotional and sexual commitments to women (as in the case of the commitment-phobic or by becoming homosexual) or beat women into the ground, like the misogynist. Women with similar Plutonic contact to their Moon, Venus or tenth house are also 'sitting targets' for the devouring mother syndrome. Subconsciously, these women sense that mother has eaten away their power and thus, as adults, they either enter relationships with men who reinforce this subjugation or they become like their mothers and seek absolute power and control over their men. Women with Pluto linked by hard aspect to their Moon or Venus are invariably the Dark Ladies of the zodiac.

Possession is a supremely Plutonic theme, but as we can see, it is almost entirely destructive. Behind the urge to possess is the will to power. Individuals who want to possess another crave power over him or her. And the other side of that coin is surrender; for, inasmuch as one partner wishes to dominate and hold the other, so must the other submit and 'lie down and die' for him. History, and certainly literary history, is full of couples who have followed this Plutonic path – Trilby whose sinister mentor, Svengali, used hypnosis to control her and her exquisite voice; Professor Higgins who reshaped Eliza Dolittle. In real life, Picasso's possessive love for Françoise Gilot was so intense that he wanted her to live with him secretly and dress in black with a veil over her face. More recently we have the example of the successful composer Andrew Lloyd Webber who plucked an unremarkable dancer from the insignificance of the chorus line and made her his wife and a star. His final act before he moved on to a new protégé, and a new wife, was to create the role of Christine for her in *The Phantom of the Opera* – a tale which tells of the obsessive love of a man forced, through his grotesque appearance, to live in the bowels of the Opera House. Through this obsessive love, the phantom makes Christine into a great singer; yet this same love almost destroys her as well as himself.

These larger-than-life relationships are built on the interplay between surrender and domination. And while little Trilby was clearly a victim of Svengali's domination, Eliza Dolittle positively blossomed under Higgins' choreographic power. Yet the fine line between the 'making' or 'breaking' of a love object is all too easily crossed. Somewhere within us all are the seeds of our own destruction and there is, as we have seen, a certain sweetness and terrible longing for the kiss of Dracula; but surrender needs its helpmate, domination. And make no mistake, for every seed of self-destruction within each of us, there is also one of power. This deathly dance is played out religiously on the battlefield of our relationships. Power and love, like love and death, are inextricably linked and belong to the realm of Pluto.

The balance of power strikes at the heart of every relationship. It is a supremely Plutonic matter and since we all have Pluto in our charts none of us is immune to power struggles both within ourselves and within our relationships. In earlier chapters I have discussed the struggle that many men seem to be engaged in where women are concerned and that women are clearly on the receiving end of men's anger and aggression. Since misogynism and commitment-phobia seem to be pandemic, it would appear that a collective impulse is underlying this behavioural trend. The biggest development in society to have occurred in the last 30 years is the rise of woman-power. This began at the turn of the century with the Suffragette movement and by the Sixties, feminism was the radical new flavour of the era in the Western world. Then the Eighties spawned a new type of woman – not the die-hard feminist who rejected male values but a woman who espoused men's values and endeavoured to 'beat men at their own game'. But women's rise to power in the 'market place' has come at a cost; we have needed our shoulder pads to cushion us against the male backlash and the side-effects of 'superwoman-itis'.

Power struggles in the work arena are only the tip of this gigantic Plutonic iceberg, for it is in the intimacy of the bedroom and close personal relationships that this power-shift is taking its greatest toll. In *Successful Women, Angry Men,* Bebe Campbell discusses the problems of the two-career couple and how, at the seat of the difficulties, rests the man's feeling that he is losing his power – and therefore the upper hand in the relationship – by the woman gaining hers. At a deep-seated level, men are utterly unhappy with this new arrangement; it is not simply that they have become attached to their bread-winner/hunter stereotype, the roots of this unease go far deeper than that: it is as if men are reacting to an ingrained sense of *displacement* – a fundamental wrong of nature. Men not only resent women taking over their territory, but recognize that this power-gain is at the expense of the woman's home-making and nurturing abilities. Women also sense this, and in an effort to compensate for any failure in their strictly feminine roles, they attempt to do it all. The results are predictable: women are burning themselves out with the effort and no one is truly happy. The Catch 22 becomes, of course, that for entirely economic reasons, two people in a relationship *need* to work and there is no way that the clock can be put back so that the symbiosis of domesticity and career can function as it once did. The only way is forward to something very different. But I will come to this later. Ideally, men need to throw their hat into the domestic ring as well as women, but because they feel so threatened and deeply unhappy about the state of power-play instead of participating in the home they dig their heels in and refuse to co-operate.

I tend to think that misogynists and commitment-phobic men are also affected by this current shift in the balance of power, even though their behaviour may have its origins in personal emotional history. The tendency for the misogynist to 'put down' the woman he 'loves' is the classic response of someone who feels extremely threatened by her and her abilities. Bebe Campbell cites many case-histories where the men act towards their women in exactly the same way as the misogynist:

> The second stage of backlash is an outpouring of rage from men who cease expressing their dissatisfaction in vague criticism and become blatantly hostile . . . this period reflects the deep-seated anger that has festered while men watch their superwomen move even further away from them . . . As male hostility escalates, husbands begin to sabotage their wives' careers in an effort to minimise and even destroy the vehicle of

her independence . . . Implicit in this hostility is the male's attempt to regain power he feels he's lost by virtue of his wife's professional status and accompanying independence.[6]

In the Plutonic depths of the unconscious men fear that they will be abandoned by their women. From babyhood, most men have been nurtured by women and conditioned to believe that this nurture is central to their outer success. On top of this, men must contend with another fear – that other men will consider them unmanly if they do not dominate their wives, financially or otherwise. Thus, a great many men are in a psychological fix, and they tend to handle it by finding more and more ways to assert their dominance – which invariably means less and less consideration and support for their wives. But at this stage, the ball is very much in the woman's court. She must recognize that her man's actions and lack of support are indicative of his terrifying fear that she doesn't need him any more; to resolve the problem she can either make him her career or prepare for a 'war to the death':

> Stage III backlash is women striking back. Those who haven't thrown in the towel fight to avoid being dominated by husbands and to maintain equality in their marriages. Stage III is ushered in when women go from blithely thinking of themselves as equal to feeling harassed, to attempting to be super-women, to considering themselves the martyred victims of burnout. They acknowledge their rage and turn it on their husbands . . . As backlash escalates, more and more women reject the role of wife.[7]

Ultimately, there is nowhere else to go but out of the marriage completely. And this is indeed, the route many couples take. But there is another path. Women also find it difficult to surrender their domestic power and often sabotage their men's attempts to help with the home and the children; they too need to accept a power-share on their territory, to give men 'permission to move away from the masculine imperative'. Women must recognize that they cannot have their cake and eat a man's too. We cannot demand protection from our men if we have bulldozed our way to the front line. It may be that women have moved too far too soon with the acquisition of power and the heady sense of freedom it has given them; now, it is time to look at what the force and speed of this development has meant in psychological terms. Perhaps we must simply wait for men to catch up – grow out of their fear of abandonment and see a woman's power as an enhancement to a relationship rather than a threat. Women, for their part, must wield their new-found weapons with grace. With the issue of power out of the unconscious and firmly in the open, the way to dissolve the defensive walls that have grown up in the process is to surrender power. This demands a two-fold declaration of peace; a two-fold surrender.

Ethel Person makes the point that in a relationship, 'Love is most likely to evolve and be sustained when both lovers are sovereign.' To illustrate this point, she uses Chaucer's story of The Wife of Bath from his *Canterbury Tales*:

> A young knight in Arthur's court is sentenced to die because he has raped a girl. Arthur's Queen commutes the death sentence on one condition: that within twelve months the knight must tell the Queen what it is that women most desire. The knight travels the country and receives diverse replies: women want riches, clothes, love and many other things. But no two people agree on a single answer. Near the end of the year, fearing for his life, he happens upon an old hag. She promises to answer the question on condition that he do her bidding when his life is again his own. He agrees and gives the hag's answer to the Queen: women want sovereignty. The women gathered at the court – wives, widows and maids – all agree, and the knight's life is spared. The hag then asserts her claim to the knight and orders him to marry her. Although, loathing the old woman, he feels obliged to comply. She, however, notices his distaste for her and gives him two alternatives: she will be faithful and loving, while as an old hag, or, if he prefers, young and beautiful, but he will have to take his chances regarding her fidelity. And how does the knight choose? Very wisely, in light of what he has just learned about what women really want: he leaves the choice to her. Granted her sovereignty, the hag responds generously; she transforms herself into a woman both beautiful and faithful. Thus he learns by his own experience the meaning of that 'sovereinetee' that women desire above all things. And she, transformed by the trust he puts in her and the unconditional freedom of choice he allows her, becomes that which he had wanted her to be – but does so of her own free will.[8]

Power is in essence a masculine function while surrender is essentially feminine, but on the way to the wedding both the masculine and feminine components of the psyche must be developed: women must be able to wield their power without rejecting the value of surrender and men must learn that by surrendering control they do not become weaker. To possess and control, to brutalize and show aggression is to have no power at all. One is merely paving the way for one's own destruction.

Surrender and transformation are two of the issues at the heart of the fairy story of Beauty and the Beast:

Once upon a time, there lived a beautiful maiden called Beauty. She was the youngest of 12 children – six boys and six girls – and the favourite of her father. When Beauty was 15, the family was struck by disaster. All her father's ships were lost at sea and their house was burnt to the ground: from great wealth, the family went to extreme poverty and was forced to live from hand to mouth in a small cottage in the forest. One day, news arrived that one of Beauty's father's long-lost ships had anchored. Jubilant at the prospect of recovering some of his wealth, he set off for the port, asking all the children what they most wanted: Beauty asked for a rose.

But her father's joy was short-lived. When he arrived at the port he discovered that his last remaining ship has been stripped of all its riches, and had no alternative but to return home empty-handed. On the journey, he was beset by storms, snow and ice, and in the process he lost his way. Eventually he found himself on a small path that led to a beautiful sunny garden surrounded by a hedge of roses. Remembering his promise to Beauty, he picked a rose. As soon as he did so, a hideous beast leapt up from behind the hedge and threatened him with his life. Beauty's father begged the Beast's forgiveness, and the Beast agreed to save his life provided one of his daughters would consent of her own free will to come and live with him in his palace.

When he arrived home, the father told his children all that had happened. The boys offered to kill the Beast, while the girls blamed Beauty for wanting the rose in the first place. With a heavy heart Beauty consented to go and live with the Beast. When she arrived, he was delighted – especially when she told him that she had come to him willingly – and allowed her father to take home all the riches he could carry.

That night Beauty had a dream. In her dream, a handsome prince came to her and told her that she would be rewarded for all that she had suffered. He also told her that she must not be deceived by appearances and added that he hoped that she would find him no matter how he was disguised. 'Be as true-hearted as you are beautiful, and do not desert me from my cruel misery.'[9]

Beauty was happy at the palace, although she felt like a prisoner. On the first day, she began to explore all the rooms: one was filled with mirrors and jewels, another with paintings – many of them of the prince – yet others were filled with musical instruments and hundreds of books. Towards the end of the day, Beauty found her way to a room where there was a table laid out for supper. The Beast joined her and asked her if she would marry him. Beauty told him she was happy but that she could not marry him. That night, in her dreams, the prince returned and rebuked her gently for being so unkind. He reminded her not to be deceived by appearances and to trust her heart. Beauty's next day was spent exploring more of the wonderful palace with its store of treasures, and again in the evening the Beast joined her for supper. He seemed even kinder than before and asked her for a second time if she would be his wife; but, once again, Beauty refused.

As the days went by, despite the pleasure she found in the Beast's company and the palace, Beauty began to miss her family. At her request, the Beast agreed to let her visit her home but urged her to return to him soon or else he would die. He gave her a ring, saying that when she was ready to return to him, all she had to do was turn the ring and speak his name. The night before she went home, she dreamt of the prince, who asked her if she were not leaving him to his death.

Once home, Beauty asked her father the meaning of her dreams, and he suggested that the dream prince might want her to marry the Beast. Beauty thought he could be right, but she was in love with the prince and not the Beast.

After two months at home, Beauty became bored and her restlessness was increased by the absence of any dreams of her prince. Then one night, she had a dream that the Beast was dying in a cave. Upon waking, she twisted his ring and instantly was back at his palace. She searched for him everywhere but he was nowhere to be found; even at supper, he failed to appear. Beauty was now consumed by worry; she went out of the palace and into the grounds. Soon she came across a path shaded by tall cypress trees and recognized it from her dream. The path led to a cave and there, crouched in the dark, was the Beast. Upon seeing him her heart was filled with relief and she rushed to hold him in her arms: 'Oh dear Beast . . . I never knew how much I loved you until now.' The Beast, raising his head, looked into Beauty's eyes. 'Can you really love such an ugly creature as I am?' [10]

That night, at the supper table, he asked her to marry him, and this time Beauty said yes. Suddenly the room was filled with a blaze of light and there before her, instead of the beast, was the handsome prince of her dreams.

The fairy-tale world of Beauty and the Beast is the realm of Pluto. Here is a palace which, like Pluto's Underworld kingdom, is full of riches, yet such treasures belong to a fearsome beast. In other words, the treasure of our creative power which lies within our depths can only be made available to us when we have dealt with our darkness. Throughout the story we are presented with Plutonic images of extremes: light and dark, wealth and poverty, summer and winter, beauty and ugliness. At the beginning of the story, Beauty's rich and worldly father is reduced to poverty – in true Plutonic fashion he is stripped of his assets and suffers a massive loss of status; his destruction is virtually complete when he is threatened with death by the Beast and the price he must pay for his life is almost too high – his beloved daughter, Beauty. Then Beauty finds her way to the cave where the Beast lies dying marked by an avenue of cypresses – trees associated with death. And when, ultimately, she declares her love for the Beast, he is, in the nature of Pluto, utterly transformed.

The Beast who must be transformed into the beautiful creature that he truly is represents the most powerful psychic process of all and one that must be undergone by both men and women if they are to become whole. In this fairy story, the Beast personifies the primitive, brutish and fearsome aspect of the animus. Many men despise the Beast within themselves and do their best to hide him away in a dark place; but like anything that is hated and hidden away from the light of consciousness, he becomes highly dangerous and entirely destructive. Men who suppress their beastliness, while at the same time fearing it, are in danger of becoming consumed by its power: their inner, angry Beast either emerges in an overly aggressive, totally uncontrolled way, or it erupts as an icy blast, freezing their creativity and sometimes devouring the 'maiden' of their ability to love. For in failing to deal with the Beast a man is unable to relate wholly to his feminine side – in effect, the psyche is out of balance. The inability to integrate primal energy hampers a man's ability to relate to the feminine and to truly love; wearing the mask of the Beast, a man is cut off from his own beauty of heart. Primal energy and beauty of heart are opposite ends of the same pole and for an individual to be whole, the polarity must be brought into balance. The Beast inside must be addressed, if he is to be integrated, and by connecting with the Beast, the way to the beauty of heart is released.

Women, of course, also have their inner Beast, which is sometimes so terrifying and unacceptable it can only be perceived through the mirror of the men with whom they enter into relationship. A woman's Beast represents her primal masculine power and her sexuality, which can seem antithetical to her feminine spirit of gentleness and acquiescence:

> Women have not been allowed to have their own Beast, because men have been so entranced by the collective image of beauty. They want a woman who is young and pure so they can project the beauty of soul on her. This saves them (men) from the labour of love that soul work requires. The woman who accepts this projection is also saved from facing her inner beast, with its anger, possessiveness and power. But, at the same time, she misses discovering the magical rooms in the Beast's palace, the rooms of creativity. [11]

Some women, unfortunately, identify too strongly with the animus, perhaps because of upbringing or through the pressures and demands of a career in a predominantly man's world – journalism and the media, in particular, seem to be a bastion for the animus-dominated woman. Such women have a strident, aggressive quality that overshadows their feminine spirit; since they are out of touch with their anima, they cannot allow her to 'subdue' the Beast and so what they may gain on the career front is almost always at the cost of fulfilment in a relationship.

While the Demon Lover sucks our life's blood, our creativity, the Beast, with his rooms full of treasures, offers it to us; while the Demon Lover takes our soul, through the Beast we find it. Pluto, the King of the Underworld of the unconscious always presents us with two paths: one that leads to destruction and another that leads to transformation; one that leads to death, the other to rebirth. Astrological Pluto rules the regenerative and procreative organs of the body, and by association he is synonymous with the creative power of the dark side of the animus, so that when we are out of touch with this dark creative force, we are removed from the very core of our power – our power source:

> When we fear the Beast, when we are afraid of the vitality of the life force . . . when we are afraid of that great unity of life and death which the Beast's being vibrates, we frequently try to put it behind bars . . . [thus] its beauty is imprisoned, its great life energy encased and numbed. [12]

To free this powerful beauty and in the process free our heart, we must, like Beauty, conquer our fear and, with a love born of courage, embrace the ugliness in the dark core of the psyche and so release the prince within. For the Beast to be transformed, he must be loved for what he is. But before he can be loved, he must be found, and while the route to his summer palace can be reached by accident, or by the hand of fate, the way to his riches demands a journey of awareness. Beauty must come willingly to meet the Beast (just as Dracula must be invited in) and ultimately she must of her heart accept his hand in marriage. To do so without consciousness is to invite 'death'. The Beast within us, the darkness in the psyche, is ultimately the stuff of our enrichment; just as that which emerges from the bowels of our being engenders growth. While Beauty is still deceived by appearances and unable to love the Beast, she may but wander through the palace of riches; only when her heart is open – and this has involved some questioning and isolation on her part – is she ready to love the Beast and become his wife, thereby earning the right to own the treasures that are his. Only once the barrier of fear is dissolved and the dark power of the animus is recognized for the creative source that it is can we, in full consciousness, lay claim to its creative power:

> Deep in the forest dwells a beast so terrifying that many maidens fear to make the journey through the forest on the way to the wedding. And the Beast, who is longing for a bride of beauty to transform him is afraid that no maiden will dare to brave him. The Beast wears a veil of ugliness and anger which conceals his inner beauty, and the maiden who will wed

him must be able to see through that veil to the mystery of him, herself, and of their relationship.[13]

Only when a woman can love the Beast inside herself will she open the doorway to her own creative power; likewise, only when a man can connect with the Beast inside himself can he free his feminine soul, his inner creative muse.

Women must embrace the Beast within themselves if they are, in turn, to be able to accept a man in his entirety. Likewise, a man must address his inner Beast if he is to avoid hurting or destroying a woman. For a woman, connecting to her Beast allows for a finer balance within her feminine self – she becomes a whole woman, free to express her sexuality and assert herself without brutalizing or tarnishing her femininity. As *Beauty and the Beast* reveals, it is the power of the feminine that transforms the Beast. Linda Leonard makes the poignant observation, 'Often men need to hear from a woman that their Beast is beautiful. But this requires that they are also open to hear it.' So, sometimes this journey to transform the Beast can be undertaken in the context of an intimate relationship. But, as Leonard reminds us, even if the woman accepts the man and loves him in his entirety, if he is unable to address his own Beast, he will be unaffected by the gift of transformation that she offers them both.

Essentially, this is what Senta offers the Flying Dutchman: he, like the Beast, is enchanted and only the love of a woman – the power of the feminine – can break the spell. The Dutchman and the Beast are both in search of their feminine soul and, when Senta and Beauty give of themselves freely and unequivocally, the men are transformed:

> What is really at issue for the man is to relate to his own soul. As in the story, the Beast has to let Beauty leave to see if she will come back of her own free will. This means giving up control, allowing his vulnerability to show . . . It means assuming a receptive role, allowing the feminine in himself to be . . . All she asks for is a rose, the symbol of spiritual love. For a man to find his inner rose means being more gentle to himself, letting go of the controlling demands he makes on himself, and accepting himself both as Beast and Prince. There is a paradox here for the man: he has to be able to let the soul go to have it come back to him. This may mean letting go of a soul-image projection on a woman and of his attempt to possess her.[14]

The marriage between the masculine and the feminine, the animus and the anima, demands a sacrifice on both parts; it demands a recognition of the value of each so that both may be sovereign. Surrendering control has been a constant theme in this chapter and, in essence, this is the key to releasing Pluto's transformative power. The single rose is not just an emblem of spiritual love but a symbol of completion, of wholeness. The rose is taken from the Beast's garden and given to Beauty so that she may embark on the journey that will lead to wholeness. The Beast faces death if Beauty cannot love him for who he is, and when Beauty, through her love, saves him from the clutches of death, he is transformed: love triumphs in the face of death. In the same spirit, Senta's act of love breaks the spell on the Dutchman and in death they are both transformed: love in death, *Liebestod.*

And so we move on to the transformative nature of passionate love – a love that threatens to destroy every bit as much as it promises to transform. The legend of *Tristan and Iseult* is to my mind the most powerful story of passionate love encompassing all shades of Plutonic experience. The story is set at the time of the Holy Crusades and was the first of a genre of romances based on the themes of chivalry and courtly love:

Tristan was the noble nephew of King Mark of Cornwall. In those days, Ireland was a kingdom that wielded considerable power and influence such that the Irish King was able to demand that Cornwall sent 300 of its maidens and 300 of its youths every four years to serve as slaves in Ireland. King Mark had refused to comply with this levy and, in response, the Irish King ordered his brother-in-law, the giant, Morholt, together with a small army, to go to Cornwall to sort matters out. But the Irish had not counted on the bravery of Tristan, who slew the mighty Morholt, breaking a piece of his own sword in the process – a splinter of which remained embedded in Morholt's head. Tristan, although victorious, was himself wounded by the poisoned barb on Morholt's sword. Daily he grew weaker, but no one in Cornwall could heal him, since only Morholt's sister, a sorceress and the Queen of Ireland, had the antidote. And so, Tristan's 'heart told him to go to sea and seek there either healing or death'. [15]

For six days, Tristan drifted in his little boat, until on the seventh he was borne ashore on the rocky coast of Ireland. There, some fishermen carried him to Iseult the Fair, the daughter of the Queen of Ireland and the niece of the slaughtered Morholt. 'Of all the women in the world, she alone could heal him. But of all the women in the world, it was she who most wished him dead.'

Iseult the Fair tended the mysterious stranger for many days. Tristan became well and returned to Cornwall, never revealing his identity. During his absence, simmering jealousy over Tristan had reached boiling point and a party of barons had approached the King to air their concern over the future of the kingdom. Tristan was not the rightful heir, they asserted, and so Mark agreed to marry and produce a son. Within a short while of this decision, two swallows flew in to the castle and dropped a long, golden hair onto Mark's outstretched hand. He thus declared that he would have none other for his bride than the lady of the golden hair. But as soon as Tristan touched the hair, he knew it was Iseult's.

Seizing the opportunity to vindicate himself in the eyes of his enemies, Tristan volunteered to find the lady of the golden hair — knowing full well of the danger that awaited him in Ireland, since he would have to reveal himself as the murderer of Iseult's royal uncle, Morholt. But fate played into Tristan's hand. Upon reaching Ireland he found the country in utter disarray due to the ravages of a dragon. Tristan immediately slew the dragon and was hailed as Ireland's saviour. However, he had been gravely wounded by the dragon so once again it fell to Iseult to draw him back from the claws of death. It was while she was tending him one day that Iseult took it upon herself to clean Tristan's sword; as she did so, she noticed its broken edge. Trembling, she fetched the splinter of steel that she had lovingly kept since her uncle's death and matched it to the sword. Realizing that Tristan was none other than Morholt's murderer, she flew at him with a dagger. But Tristan stilled her hand, showing her the golden hair he had kept sewn in his coat of arms. Iseult stared deeply into his eyes for some long minutes, then kissed him on the lips.

Iseult, of course, believed that Tristan had kept her hair close to his heart because he loved her, so that when, for his reward for slaying the dragon, he asked for her hand in marriage not to himself but King Mark she was angry, considering herself the victim of a hoax and betrayed by Tristan in no uncertain terms. So, before Tristan journeyed back to Cornwall, taking her with him, she made a potion of death which she poured into a jug of wine. At the same time, unbeknown to Iseult, her sorceress mother had prepared a love potion, also in some wine, which she had placed in the care of Iseult's maid, Brangien, telling her to offer it to King Mark and Iseult on their wedding night: the power of this potion, she added, would last but three years. As soon as the ship had left the shores of Ireland, Iseult sent Brangien to fetch the pitcher of wine so that Tristan and she might drink of its deathly sweetness, but Brangien accidentally brought them the wine of love instead. Hours later she returned to find them gazing spellbound into each other's eyes. 'Stay and return if you can . . . But oh! that path has no returning. For already Love and his strength drag you on and now henceforth forever never shall your know joy without pain again . . . for . . . in that cup, you have drunk not love alone, but love and death mixed together.'

Iseult duly married King Mark although, on the wedding night, she sent Brangien in her place, having magically transformed her into her own likeness. From then on, Tristan and Iseult met nightly in an orchard, but their love was obvious to one and all and their trysts were soon discovered by Tristan's enemies at court. Eventually, Mark learned the terrible truth of their betrayal for himself and ordered them to be burned at the stake, but they escaped and hid in the forest. After three years of exile, their hideaway was revealed to the King, who determined to kill them, but when he found them asleep in each other's arms, a look of pure innocence on their faces, he could not bring himself to strike them. Instead, he left behind his sword and ring as tokens of reconciliation and forgiveness.

Upon waking and finding the signs of Mark's compassion, Tristan and Iseult felt compelled to return. But before they did, Iseult gave Tristan a green jasper ring as a token of her unending love. Back at court, Iseult and Tristan were still unable to put aside their passion for each other; they continued to meet under the cover of darkness and took their fill of love. But they were, at the same time, consumed with guilt over their feelings and the betrayal it had engendered. Thus, there seemed to be no other solution but for Tristan to leave Cornwall. 'Apart the lovers could neither live nor die, for it was life and death together.'

In France, Tristan tried to make a new life for himself. He met another Iseult – Iseult of the White Hands – and married her. But on the wedding night, as he prepared to bed his beautiful bride, the green jasper ring fell clattering to the floor, and Tristan was overwhelmed by the realization that by marrying another he had betrayed Iseult the Fair. 'Now I know that without Iseult the Fair, I can neither live nor die and the life I lead is a living death.'

Tristan returned to Cornwall disguised as a beggar; he found Iseult and showed her the green jasper ring, whereupon she fell exultantly into his arms. For three nights they remained together and on the third, their passion still not spent, Tristan told her that he sensed death was at hand. 'My death is near, and far from you my death will come of desire.' 'O friend,' she said, 'fold your arms round me close and strain me so that our hearts may break and our souls go free at last . . .'

A mere few months later, Tristan was wounded in battle. As he hovered at the edge of death, he sent for his faithful friend, the knight, Kaherdin, and asked him to fetch Iseult the Fair. 'Show her [the green jasper ring] and tell her if she does not come I die; say she must *come* for we drank our death together and to remember the oath I swore to serve a single love, for I have kept that oath.' *He made one further request of Kaherdin, that if he were to return with Iseult he was to display a white sail, but if she refused, a black one. Unbeknown to the two men, Iseult of the White Hands overheard his impassioned plea.*

Tristan's strength faded by the day until, too weak to wait on the cliffs and watch for Kaherdin's ship, he was forced to take to his bed. But, each day, he asked his wife if she could see the boat and each day she replied that she could not. Eventually a ship bearing a white sail loomed across the horizon. When she saw that the ship must bear Iseult the Fair, Iseult of the White Hands was overcome by bitterness, for Tristan had never loved her as she longed to be loved, and so she took her revenge, telling Tristan that Kaherdin's ship carried a black sail. Tristan turned to the wall, saying that he could keep his life no longer; he called Iseult's name four times and died.

Too late to save her beloved's life, Iseult the Fair drew to the bedside. 'She moved the body and lay down by Tristan . . . She kissed his mouth and his face, and clasped him closely; and so gave up her soul and died beside him . . .'

'When word came to King Mark, he crossed the sea and brought them home to Cornwall and made them each a fine tomb, to the left and right of a chantry. One

night a briar bush sprang from Tristan's tomb. Strong were its branches, green its leaves, and fragrant its flowers. Quickly it climbed over the chantry and descended to root close by Iseult's tomb. And for many lives of men it endured, strong and lovely and fragrant.'

Robert Johnson, who has woven his book, *The Psychology of Romantic Love*, around the theme of Tristan and Iseult, perceives this story as an allegory of the human psyche with Tristan as the main protagonist:

> The dilemma of the myth, and the source of all the conflicts, confusions and sufferings, is one simple demand: Tristan demands the right to possess Iseult for himself. She who should be Queen for a whole kingdom is stolen away by an individual. Ego usurps that which belongs to the self.

From this single act, not only do Tristan and Iseult suffer but the whole of the kingdom of the self is torn apart. If only Tristan were able to leave Iseult in her proper place, if only he were able to withdraw the projection of the anima instead of forcing her to be externalized and embodied in the flesh of a woman, if only he would allow her to fulfil her role as the *Femme Inspiratrice* from within, all would be well, his fate would not be the tragedy that it becomes, the psyche would be whole and an outer union, free from betrayal and suffering, possible. His inability to let go of Iseult blinds him to the reality of a flesh and blood marriage to Iseult of the White Hands, and because she, like the anima figures we have met in the Wilis and the Sirens, has not been properly wed, she takes her fatal revenge. Iseult the Fair portrays the same internal drama from the feminine aspect. She cannot make a full marriage to King Mark because she is bound to Tristan, her masculine soul.

Robert Johnson draws our attention to the repetition and significance of the numbers three and four throughout this story: the love potion whose power lasts three years, Tristan and Iseult's final three nights together, Tristan's calling of Iseult's name four times before he dies, and so on. When Tristan and Iseult escape burning at the stake, they remain in the forest for three years before King Mark finds them and leaves his signs of reconciliation, thus it is at the beginning of the fourth year that they feel compelled to leave the forest. And it is in the fourth year that Iseult returns to her marriage and Tristan journeys to find Iseult of the White Hands. The number four, like the single rose, is the number of completion, of wholeness: when Tristan and Iseult leave the forest, they emerge from the enthralment with the animus and anima. Like all men and women, they must each claim their masculine and feminine soul for their own without attaching it to another human source; in this way they can come out of the forest and into real relationship. In the process of individuation, a man and woman find their wholeness, they find their individuality, which leaves them free for a relationship unsullied by the projections of their inner images. When we fall out of love, when we emerge from that intense period of in-loveness (which, as I discussed in the previous chapter, seems to take the magical period of three months) we should be ready to form a bond with the real person behind the projection. When we fail to do this, provided our lover is 'fit' to love, we are not just emotionally immature, but we are not whole within ourselves:

> No man can be fully an individual unless he is fully related, and this capacity for genuine relatedness grows in proportion as he becomes a complete individual. These two aspects of life are yoked together by a deep and ancient bond, for they are really two sides of the same archetype, two faces of the same reality.

But we have dealt long and hard with issues of the anima and animus during the latter portion of this book and I would like to move into deeper Plutonic waters – into the steamy passionate climbs of passionate love itself.

The love in death theme that began this chapter dominates the Tristan and Iseult story. Beset by grief, betrayal and suffering, they long for death; and in death they do, indeed, find union and, as if to emphasize the link between the earthly and divine, after their death, the spirit of their love takes root in the fragrant briar bush that grows around their tombs. Robert Johnson interprets the couple's quest for union in death as an allegory of the death of the ego, yet he also reminds us that in Tristan's day – circa the twelfth century – the symbol of death was taken literally:

> They believed that they would only find the world of soul and spirit by dying, by leaving this physical body. Yet in one way they were wiser than we: They were more conscious of, and more direct about, what they sought in romantic love. The Cathars and troubadours flatly stated that they were seeking the transformation, that they were seeking it through passionate love and through death. Death because it released them from the slavery of the flesh. Passion, because, in its otherworldly intensity, in both its ecstasy and its suffering, they saw a foretaste of the divine world. Romantic love was for them an initiation. The passion of love was thought to spiritualise the elect in anticipation of the final passion.

Robert Johnson goes on to say that we, in the West, have inherited these beliefs, although we do not consciously recognize that we are in search of this transformation, and it is this that propels us into passionate encounters:

> Unconsciously, impulsively, like men and women possessed, we seek it in passion, falling in love, delivering ourselves over to a power that envelopes us and possesses us. It is ecstasy, it is suffering, it is a kind of death, but most of all it is a taste of what used to be sought in the after life: transfiguration. It is death and rebirth . . .

Tristan and Iseult do not behave very well: they heap betrayal on betrayal, they risk everything for love – life, honour, integrity and reputation – and, in the process they also ruin other people's lives. Passion does this to people: it clouds reason; it is a form of madness. 'We link love to madness and call it divine.'[16] But Tristan and Iseult are driven to these excesses because they have drunk the magic potion, the Neptunian elixir of love that possesses them and offers them a taste of the divine; yet this wine is laced with a bitter poison – a poison that invites death.

Plutonic individuals never do anything by half; individuals with Pluto conjunct an angle, or Pluto linked by hard aspect to the personal planets, pit themselves against life's vicissitudes. They love and hate with an intensity that, in their language, makes 'compromise' a four-letter word. But Pluto waits to be invited into all our lives, and while we may bar the window against his entry, the bolts will only hold firm for so long; when Pluto transits a strategic point in our charts, especially our Ascendant, Descendant, Sun, Moon, Venus or Mars, we may 'feel the tingle . . . and in the ecstasy and anxiety of anticipation, wait and wait with beating heart'. When Pluto with his powers of death and transformation beats at our window, we are compelled to let him in. And often the way he comes in is through a passionate and compelling encounter.

But why love and death? What is it about passion that invokes the desire for death, or if not the desire for it, the sudden awakening to the vulnerability of one's mortality? Lovers who are in the grips of a passionate love feel that their love will make them or break them; the extraordinary power and intensity of the feelings and sensations aroused by their passion engender the possibility that they might in some way 'die' from it. When the Plutonic ingredient of sexual passion is added to the Neptunian touching of souls, a great slumbering, molten mass of yearnings and feelings is aroused:

> In the uproar of sexual ecstasy, the particular woman or man can become a symbol . . . of ancient terrors exceeding the individual person . . . the

ecstasies of sexuality in awakening the primeval, archetypal powers can bring forth the ancient terrors of the Sirens . . . of the Demon Lover, as well as the bliss of Beauty and the Beast. [17]

While the overpowering sensations of passionate love invoke the prospect of death, when lovers are so consumed by their need for each other, their longing to merge so completely seems only possible through death. In the light of reason, when one is removed from the fiery furnace of passionate love, such ideas seem ridiculous; but when such a love is evoked between two people all the archetypal yearnings and primal needs erupt like a volcano and extend no ear to reason.

When we fall in love, our ego boundaries may shatter with the impact, but what we *feel* is transformed. When we, like Tristan and Iseult, drink the wine and fall under Neptune's enchantment, we invoke the death of old patterns and values and the birth of a new and better self. As 'Gregory', whose story is told later in this chapter, wrote to 'Amy' at the beginning of their love affair, 'We sense that something far greater is being stirred – patterns and old relationships that we may have intimated, but certainly never made conscious. Who knows what they are? I both welcome and fear them. In some way we will experience a death before we realize, or step into, what is being born.'

Tristan and Iseult, like Romeo and Juliet, are not lovers from afar; their sexual relationship is the medium through which all their deepest soul yearnings are expressed. Sexual love, when it is combined with the sense of soul contact, is, without question, the most potent route to transcendency, which is why tantric sex is the quintessential Plutonic experience. The release of the kundalini energy in sexuo-spiritual intercourse is the most profound experience of all, and lovers who actualize this are, indeed, transformed. Such a spiritual event changes the individual completely, for he, or she, has undergone a death – neither a physical death, nor an egoic death, for it has nothing to do with the withdrawal of the animus-anima projections or the integration of these archetypes – but a psychic death from which a new being slowly emerges. The love in death theme that has dominated this chapter can be seen to work on all levels – predominantly psychological and yet, somehow more than this.

Whitely Strieber described two vivid experiences where sex and death were sensed as one and the same thing: the first involved the White Angel, which I have already covered in Chapter 6, the second concerned a 'long grey hand of a visitor that pointed to a box two feet square on the floor. For some reason this image had the effect of causing an explosive sexual reaction in me. My whole body was jolted by what I can only describe as a blast of pure sexual feeling.'[18]

This experience provoked Strieber into remembering a poem he had written some 20 years before:

> I will go when I must
> to the sentence of my box
> where I will seek the love
> behind life's black truth.[19]

The significance of the box combined with the extraordinary physical excitement evoked by its presence caused Strieber to pose the question: 'Is death really a secret ecstasy?'

The comprehension that death is an ecstasy and that Pluto offers us this ecstasy through love and death is, to my mind, rooted deeply within our being. When we fall in love, the flood gates of the psyche are opened and we are plunged into contact with these fundamental knowings – they infiltrate our language of love and the way in which we perceive and relate to the beloved. Passionate love, Plutonic love, is a great and glorious creature; it is both mystical and mad; it rockets us to the canopy of the stars and plunges us to the dark depths of despair, yet in that inky Plutonic blackness, we find enrichment for our soul:

> Although love is illusory in its insistence that possession of the beloved will magically lead to eternal bliss, love is in fact magical . . . By virtue of the real relationship it engenders, the exultation it creates, and the changes in the self that it facilitates, love is vindicated as change-agent and creative endeavour.[20]

A myth like *Tristan and Iseult* is a wonderful allegory of the inner world of the psyche, but this is not all it is. *Tristan and Iseult* tells of the extraordinary power of passionate love itself. Passionate love is *always* a transformative experience: it puts us in touch with the very roots of our being yet at the same time it exalts the soul. Whether we go on to build a long-term relationship from its rapturous overture or whether we are torn apart by its very nature, we are *always* changed because of it. When we feel with such intensity, we are no longer cut off from life; we are alive in a way that makes us realize just how grey and unlived a life can be. But passion is not an end in itself, but a beginning. If we, *in full consciousness*, understand that the path we have been offered does not have its end in the beloved but in something beyond the beloved, then we draw nearer to comprehending what the Cathars knew in their hearts – that passion is an initiation. Undertaken correctly, the Plutonic path through ecstasy and suffering leads to the divine process of self-transformation.

It was as I was contemplating the transformatory ashes of my own Plutonic encounter that Amy came into my consulting room. It was during the summer of 1990 and I was in the midst of several writing commitments and so had suspended any consultancy work. But when Amy phoned in such a distraught state, I felt compelled to see her. We had barely sat down when she thrust a crumpled piece of paper into my hands. I could see from the way the pen had scoured the paper that whoever had written it wanted to put his point across in no uncertain terms.

'I can't be more specific than this,' it ran, 'don't call, don't write . . . it is not for us to be together in any shape or form – in this lifetime, at least. Gregory.'

'So, tell me about it,' I urged Amy.

I met Gregory in the October of 1989. I know it sounds like a bad romantic novel, but the moment I saw him, I knew we were destined for each other. It was like the thunderbolt . . . there was this thump in my solar plexus. We had joined a group involved with Earth mysteries; one of the members was a medium and she had singled out six of us as key figures in a sort of quest to re-establish Gnostic ideas. It was heady stuff, especially when she disclosed that we had all known each other across many lifetimes – Gregory and I having the strongest connections of all. I expect it was what we wanted to hear, because within a matter of weeks we were in the throes of a passionate affair. Both of us had been in love before, but somehow the aura of mysticism and destiny made our love seem incredibly special – it seemed almost holy. We weren't just two ordinary mortals subject to human passions, but two old souls allowed at last to consummate a union that had spanned many lifetimes. We felt brought together for some great purpose. I know it seems mad to say this, but this is what we felt . . . it was so powerful.

Amy went on to explain that just after Christmas Gregory left his wife, Anne. It was a turning point, but at that time it seemed too early to make any large-scale plans for the future since there were not only huge complications on Amy's side – a husband and two little girls – but she was also about to leave England to play Gwendoline in a production of *The Importance of Being Earnest* that was to tour South Africa, and it seemed too unkind to tell her husband, John, that she was in love with another man and then leave him all on his own for six weeks to contemplate the end of his marriage.

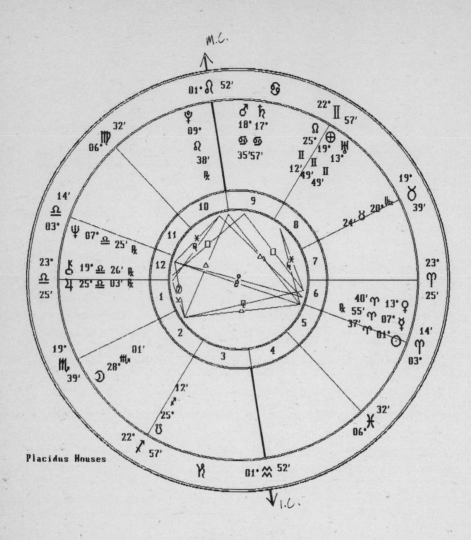

Figure 8: Amy

As the days drew nearer for Amy's departure, the prospect of being separated for six weeks appalled her and Gregory, so they decided that he should go as well – it would, at the very least, give them time together to know whether what they had was worth all the upheaval and sacrifice involved in leaving their marriages for each other.

It was the most magical experience two people could ever have dreamed of. Our love was new and we were learning, or maybe re-learning,

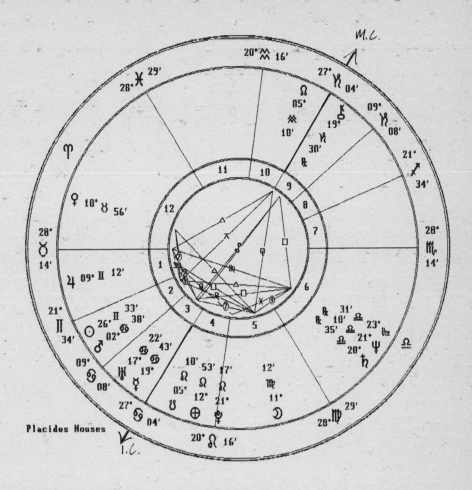

Figure 9: Gregory

everything about each other – and against the background of a beautiful and fascinating country. It was the perfect honeymoon! Although I was on stage most nights and it was an exhausting tour professionally, being together was paramount. We did the most romantic things, trekked up Table Mountain, had moonlight swims in the Indian Ocean. But at the same time we were forging a powerful professional union. We worked on a screenplay together and took the first steps to forming our own production company. We discussed marriage, children, where we might base ourselves . . . You know, all the things you do plan when you know you want to be with that person forever.

Returning to England was a daunting prospect, but Amy was convinced that, even with all the hurdles that awaited them, their love was strong enough to pull them through. She was wrong. Within a month, the alliance that had once seemed so glittering and impregnable was in total disarray.

As soon as Amy and Gregory had arrived back in England, Amy told John about the relationship and the extent of their commitment to each other. He was, quite naturally, devastated, but he was also extremely strong. They put the children's well-being first and decided that until the situation was clearer, Amy would spend the week in London – to be nearer Gregory – returning to the family home at the weekends.

It wasn't the easiest of arrangements. Gregory was living in a friend's house and I was also sharing a flat, but we were managing. We were setting up our company and already attending meetings with financial advisors. I remember, one morning, we had a meeting with an accountant. Gregory arrived in this red sweater – I don't know why it seemed so important – but I knew something in him had changed fundamentally. We were so linked that any small deviation in either of us was immediately discerned by the other. Seven days later, he pulled out of the relationship.

He changed completely – and overnight. He went from being this man who adored me – this man who sat at my feet and eulogised about everything I said, everything I did . . . how I looked . . . what I meant to him – to this icy stranger. He took me out on my birthday. We sat down in the restaurant and after the wine had been poured, he looked at me coldly and said: 'You know I never loved you. You never got to my heart.' I remember staring at him in utter disbelief. I really thought he was joking. I thought it was some terrible bad joke and that any moment, he'd turn back into the Gregory I knew and all the warmth and passion would come back into his eyes. I reminded him of all our plans – the screenplay, the company, that we were going to marry. He said: 'Oh, you didn't really think I meant all that, did you?' I was in such a state of shock that I couldn't respond. I didn't cry. I didn't even plead. The following day, we cleared out the office in silence and I left.

All this had happened to Amy some months before she came to see me. During that time, she had been through all the emotions under the sun. The trauma of the rejection, of losing a man she loved deeply, and the suddenness and cruelty of his volte-face had numbed her emotionally. In effect, she was in the early stages of bereavement. Denial had been an important part of that stage: she believed in her heart that Gregory would 'come to his senses' once he had sorted him self out emotionally.

She believed that he had cut out of the relationship because of the severe conflict of emotions that he must have been experiencing – the guilt over his wife and the sense of being homeless and somehow rudderless clearly outweighing all that he had with Amy. She simply could not believe that any man could turn away from a relationship that was so rich on all levels; not only that, but later to diminish her to the extent that she was barely worth of 'the time of day'. What she was only to learn subsequently was the *degree* of his 'cut and run' tactics. Gregory had abandoned not just one or two women in his life but *countless* women – on one occasion breaking off his engagement with one girl to marry her sister. He nailed to the ground all the women who had ever loved him, first by criticizing them and increasingly stripping away their feminine assets, and eventually by leaving them. After the parting, Gregory and Amy had met once or twice to sort out some of the residue of the relationship, but he had been distant and all too ready to take any opportunity to denigrate her and their relationship. Finally, needing to complete with him in some way, she wrote to him. His curt and humiliating response now lay, crumpled, in my hands.

Amy was in the middle of some extremely powerful planetary transits throughout that time period. Saturn and Neptune in Capricorn were squaring her radical Venus, Jupiter was squaring her Sun, and Uranus squaring Mercury, while Pluto was trining her Mars–Saturn conjunction. Leaving aside Jupiter and Uranus, which had clearly contributed to an expansion of her personal and professional horizons, the Saturn–Neptune contact to Venus was entirely synchronous with a love affair of glorious Neptunian proportions that came with a heavy Saturnian backlash.

Amy's natal chart does not present an easy pattern for relationships. Mars, the ruler of her seventh house of relationships, is conjunct Saturn, and Venus, the chart ruler and a symbol of love, affection and all things romantic and feminine, is also squaring Saturn. This suggests that Amy is likely to encounter rejection and frustration in matters of the heart and that she has an ingrained expectation of hardship and suffering linked to love – and, indeed, an accompanying deep-seated lack of self-worth. Nevertheless, Amy has known as much happiness in love as she has sadness. And she is by no means the archetypal victim figure. Her marriage to John had been happy and fulfilling for some years before financial pressures and personality differences forged an ever deepening chasm between them.

Her career had always been a priority for Amy and she had achieved a modicum of success in both film and theatre. However, it was at the time that she met Gregory that her burgeoning interest in writing and production was beginning to take over from her work as an actress. Thus the loss of Gregory was two-fold: she not only lost a lover, but a valued and inspirational colleague.

Amy's description of Gregory's behaviour gave me every suspicion that he might well fall into the misogynist or commitment-phobic 'camp'; to clarify matters I asked her if she knew his birthday. But she had pre-empted my request and had brought Gregory's chart with her. Gregory was an amateur astrologer and had intrigued her by revealing through their horoscopes all manner of hidden dimensions to their relationship. Indeed, it was Gregory who had recommended that Amy consult a professional astrologer when they separated. He remarked that there was something about Amy that must have attracted this experience to her and that she ought to 'get in touch with her dark side'.

On first impressions, Gregory's chart seems innocuous enough. A Sun Gemini sensitized by Mars in Cancer and grounded by a Taurean Ascendant with Venus also in Taurus, Moon trine Venus reveals a natural charm and affinity with women and gives a gentle, artistic flavour to the chart. However, I was looking for someone who displayed all the characteristics of a man who was either terrified of getting in too deep into a relationship and/or someone who hated and feared women. As I discussed in Chapter 6, it is airy men who experience the most difficulty with the feeling area of life; because the mind is the busiest 'organ' in the body, the feelings often act in a semi-autonomous fashion. Gregory's Sun is in Gemini and his Sun-ruler, Mercury is conjunct volatile Uranus – an aspect entirely characteristic of the Uranian 'fight or flee' switch. A gifted man, intellectually, Gregory also had a genius for re-inventing the facts of a situation and was an accomplished U-turn artist. Geminis, of course, are known as the Jekyll and Hydes of the zodiac and Amy's description of the sudden and dramatic change in Gregory was entirely in keeping with this dual-edged sign – although, I hasten to add, not all Geminis are doomed to display such devastating personality changes as Gregory. But, given the 'right' childhood background, the astrological potential for misogynism or commitment-phobia was, indeed, present in Gregory's chart.

Gregory was one of five children and the result of a passionate and brief encounter between his mother and a Russian artist. Although he had been brought up as one of the family he had always felt 'different' from his brothers and sisters. Eventually, at the age of 18, he was told the truth of his origins; it was no coincidence that from this point he appeared to veer off course. He left university with an honours degree but from then on he could never seem to find a niche for his talents. He had tried marketing, politics, property and was, by the time Amy met him, a struggling, although talented, writer. His pattern in relationships was similar – he could never find the right woman. He had had two marriages (the first, around the time of his Saturn Return, lasted six months) and countless unsatisfactory affairs. It seemed that Gregory's fate was always to become entangled with women who drained him of his power; women who sapped his sexuality and made increasing and unreasonable demands on him.

Amy knew that Gregory's track record did not recommend him as a long-term proposition, but his honesty and understanding of the problem that underlay his 'restlessness' with women, and her ignorance of the extent of the damage he had inflicted on her predecessors, made her feel that their relationship, or rather she, could help him break his pattern. Gregory was aware that he experienced a sudden and alarming 'switch off' in a relationship. During the course of their relationship he wrote Amy a moving letter revealing what he knew he had done to Anne and how he despaired that he may do the same to her:

> This is not the first time I have behaved this way. It has been a constant pattern in my relationships. After an intoxicating opening, I rapidly raise the drawbridge and leave the maiden stranded. Countless times. So it is pointless of me to even think of complaining about a woman's sexuality when it is so obvious that it is mine that feels threatened beyond a certain degree of intimacy . . . So, I cannot pin my hopes on all that is us offering some sort of solution to what has to be admitted is a serious problem. I still carry the same dragon in my breast, and I know it will rage again. You, who would give me everything within your power, must not be my next victim.

It struck me immediately that here was a man expressing, quite graphically, his fear of the Beast within himself – a Beast that threatened his sexuality and a Beast that not only raised the drawbridge between himself and a maiden but ultimately destroyed her – not with fire – but who froze her to 'death' with an icy blast from his own feminine soul. The damage he inflicted on women was, to my mind, a reflection of the iced-over feminine in his psyche. Because the feminine was not wholly addressed within himself, 'she' couldn't help 'tame' the Beast and so this inner drama was played out relentlessly in his relationships. Effectively, this conflict had turned Gregory into an emotional psychopath – a man who was able to divorce himself emotionally from his cruel and callous behaviour, a man who lurched violently between two opposite poles of burning passion and icy dispassion. Like the psychopathic killer who feels no compassion for his victims, Gregory felt no pain, no remorse, no guilt, and certainly no compassion whatsoever, for the women he had loved and left. And like the archetypal psychopath – split within himself and divorced from reality – he was capable of delivering bare-faced lies in the face of unassailable evidence, because he genuinely believed whatever reality he chose to create.

Amy was to tell me that Gregory had been much abused as a child: his mother, in particular, had taken out much of her anger and frustration on him. She had gone abroad when Gregory was three, leaving him in England in the care of nuns who beat him. His birth itself had been traumatic: he was a large baby and his head had been damaged by forceps during the delivery. This wound took some months to heal and it seemed that this sense of being physically repulsive had become embedded in the unconscious. Despite his handsome appearance, deep inside Gregory believed no one could really love him because he was so ugly. With such a history, it is no surprise that he grew up with a deep insecurity about who he was and a deep animosity toward women, yet at the same time, a great need to be loved and nurtured by them. And women certainly loved this needy man – the only trouble was that the mature, sophisticated, sensitive and intellectual man they fell in love with had the emotional age of a boy of eight.

There is no Moon–Pluto theme in Gregory's chart to reinforce this history, nor is Pluto linked to the fourth or tenth house – the parental axis. In fact, an astrologer could be forgiven for giving Gregory a 'clean bill of health' where his early life is concerned: the Sun and Moon are beautifully aspected – a quintile between the two, the Sun trining Saturn–Neptune. Yet, his experience of early life is traumatic. Certainly Saturn's rulership of the tenth house – and this planet's conjunction to Neptune which in turn squares the Mercury–Uranus conjunction – suggests that mother has her problems, although with the Moon–Venus trine, I expect she cannot be 'all bad'. What is more to the point is Pluto's link to Gregory's relationships. Pluto rules the seventh house and this planet is conjunct the fifth house cusp and squaring the Ascendant–Descendant axis: in this way, whatever the underlying reasons for his problems with women in general and the feminine in particular, Gregory is seeking powerful and deep and meaningful encounters with women – hence his attraction for Plutonic–Scorpionic females. Unconsciously, he longs to tangle with his Dark Lady and in the process have her reveal the secrets of his creative soul. Yet, at the same time, he is terrified he will be annihilated by her. It is thus his own darkness that he projects on the women he loves – a reflection of his own hurt and vulnerability.

I saw Amy regularly for some weeks after our initial meeting – not in my capacity as an astrologer but as a therapist. She needed considerable help with the grieving process for, until she was further on psychologically, she could in no way address the problems within her marriage. We did some regression work in the hopes of discovering the nature of the karma between her and Gregory and, indeed, Anne and John, but the unconscious stubbornly refused to give up its secrets. What did emerge, however, was a longing in Amy to find a brother. Somewhere, deep within her psyche there is a sense of loss over a brother which I believe may hold the key to the difficulties and disappointments she experiences in relationships. The missing brother in the psyche urges her to seek out relationships with men who fall into the category of *Puer Eternus*, the eternal boy – a type personified by Gregory and, to a certain extent, her husband, John. In seeking out these men, she compensates for their Peter-Pan natures by taking over as the parent – a role that is deeply in conflict with her Mars–Saturn need to be dominated by a man. By bringing this brother image into consciousness, it may be that it will lose its fascination for her in outer life so that she can find more of a balance with the fatherly qualities of her animus. John was the proverbial tower of strength during this period: whatever anger roared in his heart was assuaged by Amy's utter decimation at what had happened to her. And through their joint pain and suffering, they grew closer. Gradually, John and I put together the pieces of her shattered heart and her wounded psyche.

The process, however, was belaboured by news of Gregory's subsequent behaviour. Anne, equally devastated by Gregory's treatment of her and in the process of divorcing him, shared her feelings with Amy and they became kindred spirits of sorts. It transpired that Gregory, unable to cope with the damage he had wreaked, re-invented his relationship with Amy to his wife and friends: she was now a woman of no importance – in fact, he'd only gone to South Africa to see what it looked like; it was just a coincidence that Amy happened to be there at the same time! He went on to further relationships with women whom he predictably left 'because they had a dark side'. Needless to say, Amy felt her sanity threatened – maybe, they had, indeed, been just two ships passing in the night.

The astrology, however, reveals the passionate nature of their relationship in no uncertain terms. In the composite chart, Pluto rises to the Ascendant conjunct Jupiter and squares a tenth house Sun: the power inherent in this combination, both sexually and professionally, could indeed, make them or break them. Amy's Moon in the Pluto-ruled sign of Scorpio 'sits' precisely on Gregory's Descendant – a

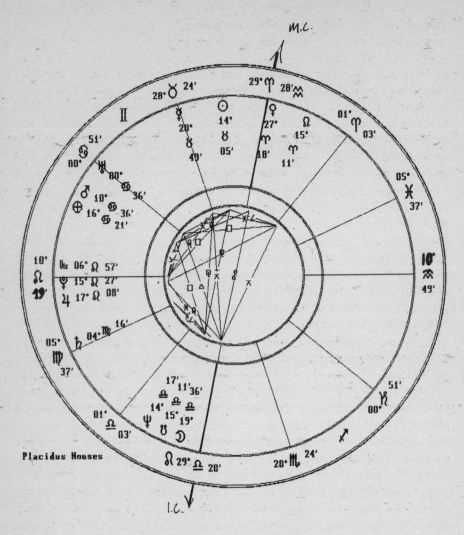

Figure 10: The Composite

contact that reveals she was the mirror image of Gregory's feminine soul – while her Pluto closely squares his Venus. Venus on the Midheaven of the composite, quintile Mars, shows that this was an encounter where love was paramount and that sexually they were in 'perfect harmony'. The Moon–Neptune conjunction in the third house was a clear indicator of the soul contact that they experienced, although this same aspect could have portended that their union was not to be consummated – a factor reinforced by Mars in the twelfth house in square to Neptune. There was, of course, a great deal of Neptune around during the period of their relationship, since this planet was also trining Gregory's Moon – the perfect moment to fall in love and to touch souls. The placing of Gregory's Saturn–Neptune conjunction on Amy's Ascendant is not an easy contact, especially since this also 'hooks' onto their Mercury–Uranus/Mars–Saturn combination: on the one hand, all Gregory's Saturn–Neptune doubts and fears (see Chapter 7, p.173) are triggered by Amy (while she also represents the medium through which they can be resolved) and, at the same time, she feels the full weight of his projected inner-dilemma. The odd quartet of Mercury–Uranus/Mars–Saturn worked well for them intellectually, although the potential for sadistic mind games cannot be ignored. But to my mind, the most significant factor of the importance of this relationship was the positioning of the vertex on the Ascendant in the composite chart. I consider this contact to indicate an extremely fated union – both the Prince and Princess of Wales and the Duke and Duchess of York have this in their composite charts. Also, Gregory's Sun in conjunction with Amy's North Node and the placing of his vertex precisely on her Ascendant reinforce this concept of an extremely fateful encounter, if not a divine one.

Pluto and Neptune emerge as leading actors on the stage of this relationship: on the one hand, Neptune provided them with the sense of soul contact and divine love, yet ultimately, this same planet was coincident with betrayal, loss and suffering. Amy might well have taken on the role of Senta to Gregory's Flying Dutchman – as it was, he boarded ship without accepting the gift she offered him. Yet they both suffered in their different ways and that suffering almost certainly enriched their souls. Pluto gave them tremendous magnetism for each other and allowed them to open new psychic avenues through their powerful and transformative sexual relationship; in this way, they were offered the opportunity to break out of past patterns and move onto a new level of relationship – both with themselves in an inner sense and in an outer relationship with each other.

Although, on the face of it, Amy's relationship with Gregory may have provided her with more hell than heaven, more despair than divinity, eventually she was able to perceive just how much she had gained from it. It was, in the way of Pluto, a hugely transformative affair. Her diary and his letters revealed the beauty they had found in each other and the numinous space they had been privileged to enter together. And such steps, once taken, lead forward and upward. In this way, Amy was able to comprehend that their love had not been wasted, nor despoiled, because once love is truly given its source is free to flood into other tributaries and other relationships. She came to understand that Gregory was a tormented man and that no women could fight the Beast that raged within his breast: it was a dragon he must, indeed, face alone and with the courage of the heart, not the dexterity of the mind. She also came to see that he was a man suffering not just from a Jekyll and Hyde split in his personality, and a division between Beauty and the Beast within, but a man whose personality was entirely divorced from his soul. When Gregory fell in love and soared into the expanded self, he was reunited with his soul. But as soon as the 'magic potion' had worn off, he was once again plunged into the dark despair and isolation of the small self. Because his emotional underpinning was so fragile, when it came to move on to form a deeper bond with Amy, he simply could not do it – all the old fears and anger for all women erupted. While he raged at her and blamed her for all the ills she had brought him, inwardly he wept for the loss of his soul: he could but hate the woman in whom he had found it for betraying him. But Amy had seen his beautiful soul and she did not forget it. And she had compassion for the man who was separated from it.

And because, ultimately, there was no anger left for him, but a love born of compassion, she was able to move on and meet John on an entirely new level of relationship. What had been born in Gregory was to be completed with John. They had much to resolve in their relationship, but they had been given a precious second chance, and it was not to be squandered.

In the year that I spent working with Amy, I came to see much of myself and Damon reflected in her relationship with Gregory. It was no mere coincidence that she walked into my life at a time I was struggling to come to terms with an uncannily similar experience. The mirror image enabled me to heal myself and to begin to understand the inner journey I was embarked upon – a journey, I believed, under the auspices of Persephone.

Pluto, together with Persephone, rules the transformative realm of the Underworld. As such, Pluto and Persephone represent the masculine and feminine dimensions of the psyche which both need to be addressed and integrated for an individual to become whole. Wholeness and completion have been themes we have met in this chapter through the symbolism of Beauty and the Beast and Tristan and Iseult, and we have also met the theme of surrender – and of surrendering power in particular. In The Wife of Bath's Tale, the importance of allowing the feminine to have sovereignty was revealed, because in acquiescing to her power – by neither ignoring her nor bludgeoning her into submission but allowing her equal status – she gives man what he most desires:

wholeness – not just wholeness as a fully related individual but a wholeness that connects man to his soul. The powerful creativity of Pluto, the power of the animus, can only destroy and brutalize unless it is married to the feminine. And when it is, transformation truly occurs. Elimination and regeneration, death and rebirth are Pluto's mighty themes, but without Persephone's participation and her spirit of relatedness and balance they form only part of the complete cycle of transformation.

To a certain extent, this can be explained by Mercury's role as the lower octave of Pluto (see Chapter 4). Mercury rules the mind, in the sense of logic, communication and mental dexterity, and as we well know through myth, he, alone of the gods, was allowed access both in and out of the Underworld. Pluto, thus, has dominion over the power of the mind to enlighten and transform. Through hypnosis, through opening the doorways of inner perception, huge shifts in consciousness can occur and so, in tandem, in outer life, new paths can emerge and the individual's life can be transformed. However, this is only half the picture; for transformation to be truly effected, the heart must be involved – and over that Persephone, Pluto's consort, has dominion: only through the *understanding of the heart* can an individual be totally transformed.

On the way to the wedding, whatever realizations we may make about the patterns that bind us and the inner images that prevent us from a divine union with an Other, they cannot be dissolved and transcended until we have reached that understanding through the heart. In the process of opening the heart, we may be awakened to love and the expanded self through Uranus, we may merge into the beloved and touch souls through Neptune, and we may be exalted through the transformative gateway of Plutonic sexual passion, but the ultimate destination of true union can only be found through the heart, and that always demands Persephone's journey. In Persephone we learn about surrender, because in the act of surrender we allow her transformative process to work through us. Her journey is not an easy one: in surrendering to her process we must have total trust in her; her route is dark and we must go naked and unarmed. But it is through pain that we develop compassion – the higher nature of passion – and it is through this pathway of initiation that we earn the right to give and receive the divine nature of love and find union with the divine in the Self.

Appendix

1) D.H. Lawrence, *Women in Love* (Penguin, 1960).
2) Linda Schierse Leonard, *On the Way to the Wedding* (Shambhala, 1986).
3) Bram Stoker, *Dracula* (New American Library, New York, 1965).
4) Programme notes for *Dracula* by Richard Gere for a production in San Francisco, California, Jan–Feb 1985 – as quoted by Linda Leonard in *On the Way to the Wedding*, op.cit.
5) Pluto's realm contained both the blissful Elysian Fields and the diabolical Tartarus.
6) Bebe Moore Campbell, *Successful Women, Angry Men* (Jove Books, 1989).
7) Ibid.
8) Ethel Spector Person, *Love and Fateful Encounters: The Power of Romantic Passion* (Bloomsbury, 1989).
9) Andrew Lang edition, *The Blue Fairy Book* (Dover Publications, New York, 1965).
10) Ibid.
11) *On the Way to the Wedding*, op.cit.
12) Ibid.
13) Ibid.
14) Ibid.
15) This and following Tristan and Iseult quotations all from Robert A. Johnson, *The Psychology of Romantic Love* (Arkana, 1983).
16) *Love and Fateful Encounters*, op.cit.
17) *On the Way to the Wedding*, op.cit.
18) Whitley Strieber, *Transformation: The Breakthrough* (Arrow, 1989).
19) Ibid.
20) *Love and Fateful Encounters*, op.cit.

Last Words

*I*N CHAPTER 2, IN MY DISCUSSION ON WHAT THE NEW AGE MIGHT MEAN, I mentioned that several philosophers, mystics and writers had put forward the idea that humanity was moving toward a more advanced and compassionate mutation of itself and that Pierre Teilhard de Chardin had gone as far as to suggest that we were headed towards a transhuman, essentially divine, state. In the chapter on Uranus I covered the issues of misogynism and commitment-phobia and later went on to explore the problems men are experiencing over women's increasing hold on power. Regarding the current wave of such phenomena as misogynism and commitment-phobia I proposed that men's behaviour might 'represent an evolutionary thrust – a bizarre transitional stage – toward a new kind of loving between men and women and a new kind of relationship – one that transcends the sexual antagonism of male and female and brings to an end the battle of the sexes'. In the final chapter, on Pluto, I emphasized the need for both sides of the psyche to be addressed and integrated so that as whole individuals we may relate wholly to an Other; and in this way, perhaps when a greater overall balance between the masculine and feminine sides of the psyche has been achieved, men and women, societies, races and nations will no longer be so polarized. Therapist and sensitive, Mary Aver, considers, in light of AIDS and the general depleting of our bodies' immune systems, that we may be moving towards an androgynous society and while this may be some centuries away, the symbolic seeds of this potential may be staring us in the face.

Mercury is an androgynous figure and, as a planet, considered neither masculine nor feminine. Mercury's link with the Underworld connects him to both Pluto and Persephone; thus, might it not be possible for this link to demonstrate that the higher octave potential of Pluto and Persephone is to transform our sexuality and the nature of our relationships? In the chapter on Persephone, I talked about her alter-ego, the goddess, Kundalini, whom Kripananda describes as 'the divine force of transformation'. I went on the add that kundalini is more than an archetypal theme but a divine energy alive within us all. It is this divine energy that resonates with the higher octave potential of Persephone. Dr Kenneth Ring suggests that kundalini is being raised in more and more individuals and that 'the final target of the kundalini-mediated evolutionary process' is to move us to the next stage of human development. As our consciousness expands to access the higher nature of Pluto and Persephone, many aspects of our being, including our sexuality, may, indeed, be transformed. Thus, it may be that these planets, together, point the way to an era when we shall transcend the lower 'animal' passions completely. Tantric sex – already within human grasp – is an altogether higher dimension of sexual intercourse between male and female and, as consciousness is raised, we may be open to something even more divine – something that obviates any kind of physical touch or penetration. Or, perhaps, we may simply move into such a higher psychic space that sex becomes redundant. We already have the technology to procreate without any human coupling whatsoever . . .

I must admit, at this stage of my evolution, I find the prospect of global celibacy daunting, if not seriously depressing. However, it may be that androgyny applies to the psyche rather than soma and that this raising of humanity's consciousness may dispel the conflicts that exist within us which are, in turn, projected out onto the 'world and his wife'.

Whatever lies ahead for mankind as a whole, we, as individuals, can begin the transformation within ourselves now. And it is not a matter of thinking about it or even allowing the archetypal themes covered in this book to wash over one's consciousness – we may begin to know ourselves better for such processes, but we will not be *transformed* by them. We can only truly change when we charge the heart with that duty. Loving and finding the divine in love may, or may not, involve the passion of the heart, but what it certainly involves is com-passion. And when we have compassion for ourselves, when we have compassion for our darkness, we have compassion for others. And from that well-spring divine encounters are all about us.

The End

Index

Adonis, 88-9
AIDS, 43, 71, 181
Amatron (entity), 41-2, 48
Amy and Gregory, 120, 201-12
anima animus projection, 156, 158,
    159, 160, 161, 162, 163, 165, 166,
    190, 196
Antichrist, 21-4
Aphrodite, 88-9
apocalypse, 17, 20, 23, 31
Aquarius, Age of, 36, 44, 53
Aquitaine, Dukes of, 28, 29
Armageddon, 17, 20, 24, 52, 62
Arthur, King, 38, 152
Astrological Ages, Great, 36
Australia, author's experiences in,
    77-9
awareness, higher state of, 46, 53

Baigent, Leigh and Lincoln, *The Holy*
    Blood and the Holy Grail, 28, 29, 30,
    31, 37, 38
beasts, 16, 17, 22, 23
Beau Idéal, 162-3
Beauty and the Beast, 187-92
Bible, 16, 22
bilocation, 46
bloodline of Jesus, royal, 28-31, 36-9
Brackley, Peter and Barbara, 77-8

Carter, Steven, 125, 127
catharsis, spiritual, 31
Cayce, Edgar, 24-5, 31

channelling movement, 41-2, 65-6, 83
Chiron, 61
Christos energy, 40, 46, 53
comet, 60, 61
commitment-phobia, 125-9, 138, 139,
    183, 184, 185, 206, 215
communication, 64, 65, 67, 70
consciousness
    expansion of, 42, 46, 47, 67
    global raising of, 23-4, 71, 90
    new dimension of, 48, 49-50, 51
    requirements of New Age, 50-5
    shift in, 41-3, 50
control, 120, 192-3
Cook, Florence, 133-4, 142-3
Cossey, Caroline, 169-75
Cronos, 117

Damon, relationship with, 78-9, 83,
    92, 95-6, 212
Dark Lady, 182
death, 49, 177-8, 199-200; *see also*
    Near Death Experience
delusion, 151
Demon Lover, 179, 182, 191
denial, 121, 204
Dracula, 179-81
drugs, use of, 67, 151

Earth movements, 24-7, 43
earthquakes, 16, 20, 22, 31, 43, 52
ego
    dissolution of the boundaries of,
    63-4, 66, 69, 166

About the Author

Penny Thornton's original ambition was to become a ballet dancer, and at the age of 19 she gained a place in the Royal Ballet Company. In her mid-20s, after leaving the ballet world and spending some time in films and television, she studied astrology with the Faculty of Astrological Studies, gaining their diploma in 1977. Since then she has become best known for her work in the area of synastry, the astrology of relationships, but after qualifying as a hypnotherapist in 1990, her interests have widened into the fields of psychology and mysticism. She has written three previous books: *Synastry* (1982), *Romancing the Stars* (1988), and *The Forces of Destiny* (1990). Primarily an astrologer with a strong esoteric bias, she nonetheless enjoys a reputation as a popular astrologer, writing a regular monthly column for *Prima* magazine, and appearing on television and radio. She is married and has three young sons.

The Forces of Destiny

Reincarnation, Karma and Astrology

The Forces of Destiny brings together three of the most fascinating mysteries of all time: fate, reincarnation and astrology. In this highly original and illuminating book, Penny Thornton compares mystical beliefs about death and rebirth with today's literature on the Near Death Experience and suggests that fate is not a blind uncontrollable force but a process meted out by the soul itself.

As a highly experienced and respected astrologer, Penny Thornton has come to believe that astrology is 'spiritually arid' without a framework of reincarnation and karma. Through practical experiments, she has opened up a new avenue for understanding the horoscope and offered a new therapeutic route for astrologers. In preparation of the book, she collaborated with psychotherapist Dr Michael Hopwood who hypnotically regressed twenty-two volunteers to 'previous lives'. Under hypnosis, the subjects were able to reflect on the meaning of these lives and release much of the 'angst' associated with them. By setting up the charts of those 'previous lives' and comparing them with the present life horoscope, Penny Thornton was able to shed light on the origin of a person's difficulties by tracing repeating planetary themes life after life. In short, this is a book that will not only fascinate anyone interested in reincarnation but entice astrologers to examine this missing dimension of their craft.

Romancing the Stars

Whatever your experience, why is it there never seems to be a simple formula for successful relationships when you need one? Yet for centuries astrology has accumulated a wealth of observations and insight on the way men and women relate to each other and can offer indispensable guidance through the jungle of human relationships.

At last, *Romancing the Stars* addresses the problem in a truly comprehensive and witty manner. Sign by sign, Penny Thornton analyses the mythology and the basic psychological, emotional, and sexual characteristics of both sexes. Partnerships are examined in detail, as is the interplay between each and every sign.

To complete the picture she has assembled 24 personality profiles – most based on exclusive interviews – to demonstrate how the lives and relationships of the rich and famous fit into the astrological scheme of things. These celebrities include:

★ Jeremy Irons   ★ Christopher Reeve   ★ David Bowie
★ Suzi Quatro   ★ Jilly Cooper   ★ Shirley Maclaine
★ Jeffrey Archer   ★ The Duke and   ★ The Prince of Wales
★ Uri Geller   Duchess of York

Penny Thornton's command of her subject and her ability to communicate with her readers add up to a winning formula which makes *Romancing the Stars* compulsive and highly entertaining reading for anyone who is interested in finding out more about themselves – and their partners.

'A witty and informative foray into the astrology of personal relationships – easily one of the best books of its kind ever to appear in print'.

– Horoscope (USA)

Synastry

Synastry is a complex but precise method of charting the interplay and development of human relationships through astrological analysis. In synastry, birth charts are compared in order to bring out the fundamental interactions between two people and stimulate greater understanding of how they relate to each other on all levels.

In this comprehensive introduction the basic principles of chart comparison are explained and are illustrated by in-depth case studies – including a detailed critical analysis and composite charts of the Prince and Princess of Wales.

'Clear, substantive and emanates from the heart . . . Sparkling prose is backed up by solid astrological principle . . . Suitable for all levels of astrologers, it is highly recommended.'

– The Astrological Journal

'An excellent addition to the library of any astrologer interested in learning to use astrology as a tool for increased awareness and growth.'
– Barbara Somerfield, Director, National Astrological Society, USA

'A work of considerable insight and value.'
– Australian Astrologer's Journal